Contents

Contents

Approaches and Methods in Language Teaching
Second Edition

Jack C. Richards

Southeast Asian Ministers of Education Organization
Regional Language Centre, Singapore

and

Theodore S. Rodgers

University of Hawaii
Manoa

CAMBRIDGE
UNIVERSITY PRESS

CAMBRIDGE UNIVERSITY PRESS
Cambridge, New York, Melbourne, Madrid, Cape Town, Singapore, São Paulo

Cambridge University Press
40 West 20th Street, New York, NY 10011–4211, USA

www.cambridge.org
Information on this title:www.cambridge.org/9780521803656

First published 1986
Second edition 2001
11th printing 2006

Printed in the United States of America

A catalogue record for this book is available from the British Library.

Library of Congress Cataloging in Publication data
Richards, Jack C.
Approaches and methods in language teaching / Jack C. Richards and Theodore S.
Rodgers. – 2nd ed.
p.   cm. – (Cambridge language teaching library)
Includes bibliographic references and index.
ISBN 0-52180365-9   ISBN 0-521-00843-3 (pbk.)
1. Language and languages – Study and teaching. I. Rodgers, Theodore S. (Theodore
Stephen). II. Title. III. Series.
P51.R467   2001
418'.0071–dc21   00–048624

ISBN-13 978-0-521-80365-6 hardback
ISBN-10 0-521-80365-9 hardback

ISBN-13 978-0-521-00843-3 paperback
ISBN-10 0-521-00843-3 paperback

Preface

This is a revised and reorganized version of the first edition, originally published in 1986. More than half of the contents of this new edition has been specially written for this edition. Since the first edition was published, it has become one of the most widely referred to books on teaching methods. Since then, however, a great deal has happened in language teaching. In planning this new edition, we have therefore made a number of substantial changes.

We have divided the book into three main parts:

Part I deals with major trends in twentieth-century language teaching. The chapters in this section are substantially the same as those in the first edition but include an updated list of references.

Part II deals with alternative approaches and methods. This section describes approaches and methods that have attracted support at different times and in different places throughout the last 30 or so years, but have generally not been widely accepted or, in some cases, have not maintained substantial followings. The chapters on Total Physical Response, the Silent Way, Community Language Learning, and Suggestopedia are shorter versions of chapters from the first edition. Additional and more recent references have been added to these chapters. Because these methods are no longer widely used, a shorter treatment seemed appropriate. Readers requiring fuller discussion of these methods should consult the first edition. New chapters on Whole Language, Multiple Intelligences, Neurolinguistic Programming, the lexical approach, and Competency-Based Language Teaching complete Part II. Although these latter approaches share some features with communicative approaches in Part III, we feel that they are sufficiently distinct to be grouped with the other approaches discussed in Part II.

Part III deals with current communicative approaches. It includes two chapters from the first edition – Communicative Language Teaching and the Natural Approach – and new chapters on Cooperative Language Learning, Content-Based Instruction, Task-Based Language Teaching, and the post-methods era. New material has been added to the final sections of the chapter on Communicative Language Teaching, and additional references have been added to this chapter and to the one on the Natural Approach.

The history of language teaching has been characterized by a search for more effective ways of teaching second or foreign languages. For more than a hundred years, debate and discussion within the teaching profession have often centered on issues such as the role of grammar in the language curriculum, the development of accuracy and fluency in teaching, the choice of syllabus frameworks in course design, the role of vocabulary in language learning, teaching productive and receptive skills, learning theories and their application in teaching, memorization and learning, motivating learners, effective learning strategies, techniques for teaching the four skills, and the role of materials and technology. Although much has been done to clarify these and other important questions in language teaching, the teaching profession is continually exploring new options for addressing these and other basic issues and the effectiveness of different instructional strategies and methods in the classroom.

The teaching of any subject matter is usually based on an analysis of the nature of the subject itself and the application of teaching and learning principles drawn from research and theory in educational psychology. The result is generally referred to as a teaching method or approach, by which we refer to a set of core teaching and learning principles together with a body of classroom practices that are derived from them. The same is true in language teaching, and the field of teaching methods has been a very active one in language teaching since the 1900s. New approaches and methods proliferated throughout the twentieth century. Some achieved wide levels of acceptance and popularity at different times but were then were replaced by methods based on newer or more appealing ideas and theories. Examples of this kind include the Direct Method, Audiolingualism, and the Situational Approach. Some, such as Communicative Language Teaching, were adopted almost universally and achieved the status of methodological orthodoxy. At the same time, alternatives to mainstream approaches have always found some level of support within language teaching, though often this has not led to wider acceptance or use. Methods in this category include those from the 1970s such as the Silent Way, Counseling-Learning, Suggestopedia, and Total Physical Response, as well as more recent alternative methods and approaches such as Multiple Intelligences, Neurolinguistic Programming, and the Lexical Approach.

Approaches and Methods in Language Teaching seeks to provide a comprehensive and comprehensible account of major and minor trends in language teaching methods from the beginning of the twentieth century to the present. To highlight the similarities and differences between approaches and methods, the same descriptive framework is used throughout. This model is presented in Chapter 2 and is used in subsequent chapters. It describes approaches and methods according to their underlying theories of language and language learning; the learning objectives; the syllabus model used; the roles of teachers, learners, and materials within the method or approach; and the classroom procedures and techniques that the method uses. Where a method or approach has extensive and acknowledged links to a particular tradition in second or foreign language teaching, this historical background is treated in the first section of each chapter. In other cases we have attempted to establish links between the method or approach and more general linguistic, psychological, or educational traditions.

Within each chapter, our aim has been to present an objective and comprehensive picture of a particular approach or method. We have avoided personal evaluation, preferring to let the method speak for itself and allow readers to make their own appraisals. The book is not intended to popularize or promote particular approaches or methods, nor is it an attempt to train teachers in the use of the methods described. Rather, it is designed to give the teacher or teacher trainee a straightforward introduction to commonly and less commonly used methods, and a set of criteria by which to critically read, observe, analyze, and question approaches and methods.

We have included several references to articles that are available on or through the Internet through the ERIC databases and ERIC Digests. In order to see abstracts of the ERIC references cited or to order copies of the full articles in hard copy or microfiche or to read the complete texts of the ERIC Digests, consult the ERIC Web site(s) and follow the search procedures listed there.

Jack C. Richards
Theodore S. Rodgers

1 *Major trends in twentieth-century language teaching*

Language teaching came into its own as a profession in the twentieth century. The whole foundation of contemporary language teaching was developed during the early part of the twentieth century, as applied linguists and others sought to develop principles and procedures for the design of teaching methods and materials, drawing on the developing fields of linguistics and psychology to support a succession of proposals for what were thought to be more effective and theoretically sound teaching methods. Language teaching in the twentieth century was characterized by frequent change and innovation and by the development of sometimes competing language teaching ideologies. Much of the impetus for change in approaches to language teaching came about from changes in teaching methods. The method concept in teaching – the notion of a systematic set of teaching practices based on a particular theory of language and language learning – is a powerful one, and the quest for better methods was a preoccupation of many teachers and applied linguists throughout the twentieth century. Common to each method is the belief that the teaching practices it supports provide a more effective and theoretically sound basis for teaching than the methods that preceded it. The chapters in Part I examine the developments that led to the first major paradigm in modern language teaching – the adoption of grammar-based teaching methods that came to be known as the structural approach or Situational Language Teaching in the United Kingdom, and Audiolingualism in the United States. In Chapter 1 we outline the historical precedents to language teaching in the first part of the twentieth century. In Chapter 2 we introduce a model or framework for the description of methods, one that identifies three levels of organization underlying approaches and methods that we refer to as Approach, Design, and Procedure. In Chapter 3 we describe one of the most important British language teaching proposals of the twentieth century, the Oral Approach or Situational Language Teaching, a method that continues to be widely used today in textbooks and teaching materials, though in somewhat modified form. In Chapter 4 we describe the method known as Audiolingualism, an American teaching method that has similarly left a lasting and continuing legacy in terms of commonly used teaching procedures.

1 A brief history of language teaching

This chapter, in briefly reviewing the history of language teaching methods, provides a background for discussion of contemporary methods and suggests the issues we will refer to in analyzing these methods. From this historical perspective we are also able to see that the concerns that have prompted modern method innovations were similar to those that have always been at the center of discussions on how to teach foreign languages. Changes in language teaching methods throughout history have reflected recognition of changes in the kind of proficiency learners need, such as a move toward oral proficiency rather than reading comprehension as the goal of language study; they have also reflected changes in theories of the nature of language and of language learning. Kelly (1969) and Howatt (1984) have demonstrated that many current issues in language teaching are not particularly new. Today's controversies reflect contemporary responses to questions that have been asked often throughout the history of language teaching.

It has been estimated that some 60 percent of today's world population is multilingual. From both a contemporary and a historical perspective, bilingualism or multilingualism is the norm rather than the exception. It is fair, then, to say that throughout history foreign language learning has always been an important practical concern. Whereas today English is the world's most widely studied foreign language, 500 years ago it was Latin, for it was the dominant language of education, commerce, religion, and government in the Western world. In the sixteenth century, however, French, Italian, and English gained in importance as a result of political changes in Europe, and Latin gradually became displaced as a language of spoken and written communication.

As the status of Latin diminished from that of a living language to that of an "occasional" subject in the school curriculum, the study of Latin took on a different function. The study of classical Latin (the Latin in which the classical works of Virgil, Ovid, and Cicero were written) and an analysis of its grammar and rhetoric became the model for foreign language study from the seventeenth to the nineteenth centuries. Children entering "grammar school" in the sixteenth, seventeenth, and eighteenth centuries in England were initially given a rigorous introduction to Latin grammar, which was taught through rote learning of grammar rules, study of declensions and conjugations, translation, and practice in

3

writing sample sentences, sometimes with the use of parallel bilingual texts and dialogue (Kelly 1969; Howatt 1984). Once basic proficiency was established, students were introduced to the advanced study of grammar and rhetoric. School learning must have been a deadening experience for children, for lapses in knowledge were often met with brutal punishment. There were occasional attempts to promote alternative approaches to education; Roger Ascham and Montaigne in the sixteenth century and Comenius and John Locke in the seventeenth century, for example, had made specific proposals for curriculum reform and for changes in the way Latin was taught (Kelly 1969; Howatt 1984), but since Latin (and, to a lesser extent, Greek) had for so long been regarded as the classical and therefore most ideal form of language, it was not surprising that ideas about the role of language study in the curriculum reflected the long-established status of Latin.

The decline of Latin also brought with it a new justification for teaching Latin. Latin was said to develop intellectual abilities, and the study of Latin grammar became an end in itself.

When once the Latin tongue had ceased to be a normal vehicle for communication, and was replaced as such by the vernacular languages, then it most speedily became a 'mental gymnastic', the supremely 'dead' language, a disciplined and systematic study of which was held to be indispensable as a basis for all forms of higher education. (V. Mallison, cited in Titone 1968: 26)

As "modern" languages began to enter the curriculum of European schools in the eighteenth century, they were taught using the same basic procedures that were used for teaching Latin. Textbooks consisted of statements of abstract grammar rules, lists of vocabulary, and sentences for translation. Speaking the foreign language was not the goal, and oral practice was limited to students reading aloud the sentences they had translated. These sentences were constructed to illustrate the grammatical system of the language and consequently bore no relation to the language of real communication. Students labored over translating sentences such as the following:

The philosopher pulled the lower jaw of the hen.
My sons have bought the mirrors of the Duke.
The cat of my aunt is more treacherous than the dog of your uncle.

(Titone 1968: 28)

By the nineteenth century, this approach based on the study of Latin had become the standard way of studying foreign languages in schools. A typical textbook in the mid-nineteenth century thus consisted of chapters or lessons organized around grammar points. Each grammar point was listed, rules on its use were explained, and it was illustrated by sample sentences.

Nineteenth-century textbook compilers were mainly determined to codify the foreign language into frozen rules of morphology and syntax to be explained and eventually memorized. Oral work was reduced to an absolute minimum, while a handful of written exercises, constructed at random, came as a sort of appendix to the rules. Of the many books published during this period, those by Seidenstücker and Plötz were perhaps the most typical. . . . [Seidenstücker] reduced the material to disconnected sentences to illustrate specific rules. He divided his text carefully into two parts, one giving the rules and necessary paradigms, the other giving French sentences for translation into German and German sentences for translation into French. The immediate aim was for the student to apply the given rules by means of appropriate exercises. . . . In [Plötz's] textbooks, divided into the two parts described above, the sole form of instruction was mechanical translation. Typical sentences were: 'Thou hast a book. The house is beautiful. He has a kind dog. We have a bread [*sic*]. The door is black. He has a book and a dog. The horse of the father was kind.' (Titone 1968: 27)

This approach to foreign language teaching became known as the Grammar-Translation Method.

The Grammar-Translation Method

As the names of some of its leading exponents suggest (Johann Seidenstücker, Karl Plötz, H. S. Ollendorf, and Johann Meidinger), Grammar Translation was the offspring of German scholarship, the object of which, according to one of its less charitable critics, was "to know everything about something rather than the thing itself" (W. H. D. Rouse, quoted in Kelly 1969: 53). Grammar Translation was in fact first known in the United States as the Prussian Method. (A book by B. Sears, an American classics teacher, published in 1845 was titled *The Ciceronian or the Prussian Method of Teaching the Elements of the Latin Language* [Kelly 1969].) The principal characteristics of the Grammar-Translation Method were these:

1. The goal of foreign language study is to learn a language in order to read its literature or in order to benefit from the mental discipline and intellectual development that result from foreign language study. Grammar Translation is a way of studying a language that approaches the language first through detailed analysis of its grammar rules, followed by application of this knowledge to the task of translating sentences and texts into and out of the target language. It hence views language learning as consisting of little more than memorizing rules and facts in order to understand and manipulate the morphology and syntax of the foreign language. "The first language is maintained as the reference system in the acquisition of the second language" (Stern 1983: 455).

2. Reading and writing are the major focus; little or no systematic attention is paid to speaking or listening.
3. Vocabulary selection is based solely on the reading texts used, and words are taught through bilingual word lists, dictionary study, and memorization. In a typical Grammar-Translation text, the grammar rules are presented and illustrated, a list of vocabulary items is presented with their translation equivalents, and translation exercises are prescribed.
4. The sentence is the basic unit of teaching and language practice. Much of the lesson is devoted to translating sentences into and out of the target language, and it is this focus on the sentence that is a distinctive feature of the method. Earlier approaches to foreign language study used grammar as an aid to the study of texts in a foreign language. But this was thought to be too difficult for students in secondary schools, and the focus on the sentence was an attempt to make language learning easier (see Howatt 1984: 131).
5. Accuracy is emphasized. Students are expected to attain high standards in translation, because of "the high priority attached to meticulous standards of accuracy which, as well as having an intrinsic moral value, was a prerequisite for passing the increasing number of formal written examinations that grew up during the century" (Howatt 1984: 132).
6. Grammar is taught deductively – that is, by presentation and study of grammar rules, which are then practiced through translation exercises. In most Grammar-Translation texts, a syllabus was followed for the sequencing of grammar points throughout a text, and there was an attempt to teach grammar in an organized and systematic way.
7. The student's native language is the medium of instruction. It is used to explain new items and to enable comparisons to be made between the foreign language and the student's native language.

Grammar Translation dominated European and foreign language teaching from the 1840s to the 1940s, and in modified form it continues to be widely used in some parts of the world today. At its best, as Howatt (1984) points out, it was not necessarily the horror that its critics depicted it as. Its worst excesses were introduced by those who wanted to demonstrate that the study of French or German was no less rigorous than the study of classical languages. This resulted in the type of Grammar-Translation courses remembered with distaste by thousands of school learners, for whom foreign language learning meant a tedious experience of memorizing endless lists of unusable grammar rules and vocabulary and attempting to produce perfect translations of stilted or literary prose. Although the Grammar-Translation Method often creates frustration for students, it makes few demands on teachers. It is still used in situations where understanding literary texts is the primary focus of foreign language study and there is little need for a speaking knowledge of the language. Contemporary texts for the teaching of foreign languages at the college level often reflect Grammar-Translation principles. These texts are frequently the products of people trained in literature rather than in language teaching or applied linguistics. Consequently, though it may be true to say that the Grammar-Translation Method is still widely practiced, it has no advocates. It is a method for which there is no theory. There is no literature that offers a rationale or justification for it or that attempts to relate it to issues in linguistics, psychology, or educational theory.

In the mid- and late nineteenth century, opposition to the Grammar-Translation Method gradually developed in several European countries. This Reform Movement, as it was referred to, laid the foundations for the development of new ways of teaching languages and raised controversies that have continued to the present day.

Language teaching innovations in the nineteenth century

Toward the mid-nineteenth century several factors contributed to a questioning and rejection of the Grammar-Translation Method. Increased opportunities for communication among Europeans created a demand for oral proficiency in foreign languages. Initially this created a market for conversation books and phrase books intended for private study, but language teaching specialists also turned their attention to the way modern languages were being taught in secondary schools. Increasingly, the public education system was seen to be failing in its responsibilities. In Germany, England, France, and other parts of Europe, new approaches to language teaching were developed by individual language teaching specialists, each with a specific method for reforming the teaching of modern languages. Some of these specialists, such as C. Marcel, T. Prendergast, and F. Gouin, did not manage to achieve any lasting impact, though their ideas are of historical interest.

The Frenchman C. Marcel (1793–1896) referred to child language learning as a model for language teaching, emphasized the importance of meaning in learning, proposed that reading be taught before other skills, and tried to locate language teaching within a broader educational framework. The Englishman T. Prendergast (1806–1886) was one of the first to record the observation that children use contextual and situational cues to interpret utterances and that they use memorized phrases and "routines" in speaking. He proposed the first "structural syllabus," advocating that learners be taught the most basic structural patterns occurring in the language. In this way he was anticipating an issue that was to be taken up in the 1920s and 1930s, as we shall see in Chapter 3. The Frenchman F. Gouin (1831–1896) is perhaps the best known of these mid-nineteenth century reformers. Gouin developed an approach to teaching a foreign language based on his observations of children's use of language. He believed that language learning was facilitated through using language to accomplish events consisting of a sequence of related actions. His method used situations and themes as ways of organizing and presenting oral language – the famous Gouin "series," which includes sequences of sentences related to such activities as chopping wood and opening the door. Gouin established schools to teach according to his method, and it was quite popular for a time. In the first lesson of a foreign language, the following series would be learned:

I walk toward the door.	I walk.
I draw near to the door.	I draw near.
I draw nearer to the door.	I draw nearer.
I get to the door.	I get to.
I stop at the door.	I stop.
I stretch out my arm.	I stretch out.
I take hold of the handle.	I take hold.
I turn the handle.	I turn.
I open the door.	I open.
I pull the door.	I pull.
The door moves.	moves
The door turns on its hinges	turns
The door turns and turns.	turns
I open the door wide.	I open.
I let go of the handle.	I let go.

(Titone 1968: 35)

Gouin's emphasis on the need to present new teaching items in a context that makes their meaning clear, and the use of gestures and actions to convey the meanings of utterances, are practices that later became part of such approaches and methods as Situational Language Teaching (Chapter 3) and Total Physical Response (Chapter 5).

The work of individual language specialists like these reflects the changing climate of the times in which they worked. Educators recognized the need for speaking proficiency rather than reading comprehension, grammar, or literary appreciation as the goal for foreign language programs; there was an interest in how children learn languages, which prompted attempts to develop teaching principles from observation of (or, more typically, reflections about) child language learning. But the ideas and methods of Marcel, Prendergast, Gouin, and other innovators were developed outside the context of established circles of education and hence lacked the means for wider dissemination, acceptance, and implementation. They were writing at a time when there was not sufficient organizational structure in the language teaching profession (i.e., in the form of professional associations, journals, and conferences) to enable new ideas to develop into an educational movement. This began to change toward the end of the nineteenth century, however, when a more concerted effort arose in which the interests of reform-minded language teachers and linguists coincided. Teachers and linguists began to write about the need for new approaches to language teaching, and through their pamphlets, books, speeches, and articles, the foundation for more widespread pedagogical reforms was laid. This effort became known as the Reform Movement in language teaching.

The Reform Movement

Language teaching specialists such as Marcel, Prendergast, and Gouin had done much to promote alternative approaches to language teaching, but their ideas failed to receive widespread support or attention. From the 1880s, however, practical-minded linguists such as Henry Sweet in England, Wilhelm Viëtor in Germany, and Paul Passy in France began to provide the intellectual leadership needed to give reformist ideas greater credibility and acceptance. The discipline of linguistics was revitalized. Phonetics – the scientific analysis and description of the sound systems of languages – was established, giving new insights into speech processes. Linguists emphasized that speech, rather than the written word, was the primary form of language. The International Phonetic Association was founded in 1886, and its International Phonetic Alphabet (IPA) was designed to enable the sounds of any language to be accurately transcribed. One of the earliest goals of the association was to improve the teaching of modern languages. It advocated

1. the study of the spoken language
2. phonetic training in order to establish good pronunciation habits
3. the use of conversation texts and dialogues to introduce conversational phrases and idioms
4. an inductive approach to the teaching of grammar
5. teaching new meanings through establishing associations within the target language rather than by establishing associations with the native language

Linguists too became interested in the controversies that emerged about the best way to teach foreign languages, and ideas were fiercely discussed and defended in books, articles, and pamphlets. Henry Sweet (1845–1912) argued that sound methodological principles should be based on a scientific analysis of language and a study of psychology. In his book *The Practical Study of Languages* (1899), he set forth principles for the development of teaching method. These included

1. careful selection of what is to be taught
2. imposing limits on what is to be taught
3. arranging what is to be taught in terms of the four skills of listening, speaking, reading, and writing
4. grading materials from simple to complex

In Germany, the prominent scholar Wilhelm Viëtor (1850–1918) used linguistic theory to justify his views on language teaching. He argued that training in phonetics would enable teachers to pronounce the language accurately. Speech patterns, rather than grammar, were the fundamental elements of language. In 1882 he published his views in an influential pamphlet, *Language Teaching Must Start Afresh,* in which he strongly criticized the inadequacies of Grammar Translation and stressed the value of training teachers in the new science of phonetics.

Viëtor, Sweet, and other reformers in the late nineteenth century shared many beliefs about the principles on which a new approach to teaching foreign languages should be based, although they often differed considerably in the specific procedures they advocated for teaching a language. In general the reformers believed that

1. the spoken language is primary and that this should be reflected in an oral-based methodology
2. the findings of phonetics should be applied to teaching and to teacher training
3. learners should hear the language first, before seeing it in written form
4. words should be presented in sentences, and sentences should be practiced in meaningful contexts and not be taught as isolated, disconnected elements
5. the rules of grammar should be taught only after the students have practiced the grammar points in context – that is, grammar should be taught inductively
6. translation should be avoided, although the native language could be used in order to explain new words or to check comprehension

These principles provided the theoretical foundations for a principled approach to language teaching, one based on a scientific approach to the study of language and of language learning. They reflect the beginnings of the discipline of applied linguistics – that branch of language study concerned with the scientific study of second and foreign language teaching and learning. The writings of such scholars as Sweet, Viëtor, and Passy provided suggestions on how these applied linguistic principles could best be put into practice. None of these proposals assumed the status of a method, however, in the sense of a widely recognized and uniformly implemented design for teaching a language. But parallel to the ideas put forward by members of the Reform Movement was an interest in developing principles for language teaching out of naturalistic principles of language learning, such as are seen in first language acquisition. This led to what have been termed *natural methods* and ultimately led to the development of what came to be known as the Direct Method.

The Direct Method

Gouin had been one of the first of the nineteenth-century reformers to attempt to build a methodology around observation of child language learning. Other reformers toward the end of the century likewise turned their attention to naturalistic principles of language learning, and for this reason they are sometimes referred to as advocates of a "natural" method. In fact, at various times throughout the history of language teaching, attempts have been made to make second language learning more like first language learning. In the sixteenth century, for example, Montaigne described how he was entrusted to a guardian who addressed him exclusively in Latin for the first years of his life, since Montaigne's father wanted his son to speak Latin well. Among those who tried to apply natural principles to language classes in the nineteenth century was L. Sauveur (1826–1907), who used intensive oral interaction in the target language, employing questions as a way of presenting and eliciting language. He opened a language school in Boston in the late 1860s, and his method soon became referred to as the Natural Method.

Sauveur and other believers in the Natural Method argued that a foreign language could be taught without translation or the use of the learner's native language if meaning was conveyed directly through demonstration and action. The German scholar F. Franke wrote on the psychological principles of direct association between forms and meanings in the target language (1884) and provided a theoretical justification for a monolingual approach to teaching. According to Franke, a language could best be taught by using it actively in the classroom. Rather than using analytical procedures that focus on explanation of grammar rules in classroom teaching, teachers must encourage direct and spontaneous use of the foreign language in the classroom. Learners would then be able to induce rules of grammar. The teacher replaced the textbook in the early stages of learning. Speaking began with systematic attention to pronunciation. Known words could be used to teach new vocabulary, using mime, demonstration, and pictures.

These natural language learning principles provided the foundation for what came to be known as the Direct Method, which refers to the most widely known of the natural methods. Enthusiastic supporters of the

11

Direct Method introduced it in France and Germany (it was officially approved in both countries at the turn of the century), and it became widely known in the United States through its use by Sauveur and Maximilian Berlitz in successful commercial language schools. (Berlitz, in fact, never used the term; he referred to the method used in his schools as the Berlitz Method.) In practice it stood for the following principles and procedures:

1. Classroom instruction was conducted exclusively in the target language.
2. Only everyday vocabulary and sentences were taught.
3. Oral communication skills were built up in a carefully graded progression organized around question-and-answer exchanges between teachers and students in small, intensive classes.
4. Grammar was taught inductively.
5. New teaching points were introduced orally.
6. Concrete vocabulary was taught through demonstration, objects, and pictures; abstract vocabulary was taught by association of ideas.
7. Both speech and listening comprehension were taught.
8. Correct pronunciation and grammar were emphasized.

These principles are seen in the following guidelines for teaching oral language, which are still followed in contemporary Berlitz schools:

Never translate: demonstrate
Never explain: act
Never make a speech: ask questions
Never imitate mistakes: correct
Never speak with single words: use sentences
Never speak too much: make students speak much
Never use the book: use your lesson plan
Never jump around: follow your plan
Never go too fast: keep the pace of the student
Never speak too slowly: speak normally
Never speak too quickly: speak naturally
Never speak too loudly: speak naturally
Never be impatient: take it easy

(cited in Titone 1968: 100–101)

The Direct Method was quite successful in private language schools, such as those of the Berlitz chain, where paying clients had high motivation and the use of native-speaking teachers was the norm. But despite pressure from proponents of the method, it was difficult to implement in public secondary school education. It overemphasized and distorted the similarities between naturalistic first language learning and classroom foreign language learning and failed to consider the practical realities of the classroom. In addition, it lacked a rigorous basis in applied linguistic theory, and for this reason it was often criticized by the more academically based proponents of the Reform Movement. The Direct Method represented the product of enlightened amateurism. It was perceived to have several drawbacks. It required teachers who were native speakers or who had nativelike fluency in the foreign language. It was largely dependent on the teacher's skill, rather than on a textbook, and not all teachers were proficient enough in the foreign language to adhere to the principles of the method. Critics pointed out that strict adherence to Direct Method principles was often counterproductive, since teachers were required to go to great lengths to avoid using the native language, when sometimes a simple, brief explanation in the student's native language would have been a more efficient route to comprehension.

The Harvard psychologist Roger Brown has documented similar problems with strict Direct Method techniques. He described his frustration in observing a teacher performing verbal gymnastics in an attempt to convey the meaning of Japanese words, when translation would have been a much more efficient technique (Brown 1973: 5).

By the 1920s, use of the Direct Method in noncommercial schools in Europe had consequently declined. In France and Germany it was gradually modified into versions that combined some Direct Method techniques with more controlled grammar-based activities. The European popularity of the Direct Method in the early part of the twentieth century caused foreign language specialists in the United States to attempt to have it implemented in American schools and colleges, although they decided to move with caution. A study begun in 1923 on the state of foreign language teaching concluded that no single method could guarantee successful results. The goal of trying to teach conversation skills was considered impractical in view of the restricted time available for foreign language teaching in schools, the limited skills of teachers, and the perceived irrelevance of conversation skills in a foreign language for the average American college student. The study – published as the Coleman Report – argued that a more reasonable goal for a foreign language course would be a reading knowledge of a foreign language, achieved through the gradual introduction of words and grammatical structures in simple reading texts. The main result of this recommendation was that reading became the goal of most foreign language programs in the United States (Coleman 1929). The emphasis on reading continued to characterize foreign language teaching in the United States until World War II.

Although the Direct Method enjoyed popularity in Europe, not everyone embraced it enthusiastically. The British applied linguist Henry Sweet recognized its limitations. It offered innovations at the level of teaching procedures but lacked a thorough methodological basis. Its main focus was on the exclusive use of the target language in the classroom, but it failed to address many issues that Sweet thought more basic. Sweet and other applied linguists argued for the development of sound methodological principles that could serve as the basis for teaching techniques. In the 1920s and 1930s, applied linguists systematized the principles proposed earlier by the Reform Movement and so laid the foundations for what developed into the British approach to teaching English as a foreign language. Subsequent developments led to Audiolingualism (see Chapter 4) in the United States and the Oral Approach or Situational Language Teaching (see Chapter 3) in Britain.

What became of the concept of *method* as foreign language teaching emerged as a significant educational issue in the nineteenth and twentieth centuries? We have seen from this historical survey some of the questions that prompted innovations and new directions in language teaching in the past:

1. What should the goals of language teaching be? Should a language course try to teach conversational proficiency, reading, translation, or some other skill?
2. What is the basic nature of language, and how will this affect the teaching method?
3. What are the principles for the selection of language content in language teaching?
4. What principles of organization, sequencing, and presentation best facilitate learning?
5. What should the role of the native language be?
6. What processes do learners use in mastering a language, and can these be incorporated into a method?
7. What teaching techniques and activities work best and under what circumstances?

Particular teaching approaches and methods differ in the way they have addressed these issues from the late nineteenth century to the present, as we shall see throughout this book. The Direct Method can be regarded as the first language teaching method to have caught the attention of teachers and language teaching specialists, and it offered a methodology that appeared to move language teaching into a new era. It marked the beginning of the "methods era."

The methods era

One of the lasting legacies of the Direct Method was the notion of "method" itself. The controversy over the Direct Method was the first of many debates over how second and foreign languages should be taught. The history of language teaching throughout much of the twentieth century saw the rise and fall of a variety of language teaching approaches and methods, the major examples of which are described in this book. Common to most of them are the following assumptions:

- An approach or method refers to a theoretically consistent set of teaching procedures that define best practice in language teaching.
- Particular approaches and methods, if followed precisely, will lead to more effective levels of language learning than alternative ways of teaching.
- The quality of language teaching will improve if teachers use the best available approaches and methods.

The different teaching approaches and methods that have emerged in the last 60 or so years, while often having very different characteristics in terms of goals, assumptions about how a second language is learned, and preferred teaching techniques, have in common the belief that if language learning is to be improved, it will come about through changes and improvements in teaching methodology. This notion has been reinforced by professional organizations that endorse particular teaching approaches and methods, by academics who support some and reject others, by publishers who produce and sell textbooks based on the latest teaching approaches and methods, and by teachers who are constantly looking for the "best" method of teaching a language. Lange comments:

Foreign language teacher development . . . has a basic orientation to methods of teaching. Unfortunately, the latest bandwagon "methodologies" come into prominence without much study or understanding, particularly those that appear easiest to immediately apply in the classroom or those that are supported by a particular "guru". Although concern for method is certainly not a new issue, the current attraction to "method" stems from the late 1950s, when foreign language teachers were falsely led to believe that there was a method to remedy the "language teaching and learning problems." (1990: 253)

The most active period in the history of approaches and methods was from the 1950s to the 1980s. The 1950s and 1960s saw the emergence of the Audiolingual Method and the Situational Method, which were both superseded by the Communicative Approach. During the same period, other methods attracted smaller but equally enthusiastic followers, including the Silent Way, the Natural Approach, and Total Physical Response. In the 1990s, Content-Based Instruction and Task-Based Language Teaching emerged as new approaches to language teaching as did movements such as Competency-Based Instruction that focus on the outcomes of learning rather than methods of teaching. Other approaches, such as Cooperative Learning, Whole Language Approach, and Multiple Intelligences, originally developed in general education, have been extended to second language settings. These approaches and methods are discussed in Parts II and III of this book. By the 1990s, however, many applied linguists and language teachers moved away from a belief that newer and better approaches and methods are the solution to problems in language teaching. Alternative ways of understanding the nature of language teaching have emerged that are sometimes viewed as characterizing the "post-methods era." These are discussed in the final chapter of this book.

Approaches and methods in teacher preparation programs

Despite the changing status of approaches and methods in language teaching, the study of past and present teaching methods continues to form a significant component of teacher preparation programs. The reasons for this are the following:

– The study of approaches and methods provides teachers with a view of how the field of language teaching has evolved.
– Approaches and methods can be studied not as prescriptions for how to teach but as a source of well-used practices, which teachers can adapt or implement based on their own needs.
– Experience in using different teaching approaches and methods can provide teachers with basic teaching skills that they can later add to or supplement as they develop teaching experience.

This is the orientation we adopt toward the teaching approaches and methods described in this book. In order to understand the fundamental nature of methods in language teaching, however, it is necessary to conceptualize the notion of approach and method more systematically. This is the aim of the next chapter, in which we present a model for the description, analysis, and comparison of methods. This model will be used as a framework for our subsequent discussions and analyses of particular language teaching methods and philosophies.

Bibliography and further reading

Brown, R. 1973. *A First Language*. Cambridge: Harvard University Press.
Brown, H. D. 1993. *Principles of Language Learning and Teaching*. (3rd ed.). Englewood Cliffs, N.J.: Prentice Hall.
Coleman, A. 1929. *The Teaching of Modern Foreign Languages in the United States*. New York: Macmillan.
Darian, K. C. 1971. *Generative Grammar, Structural Linguistics, and Language Teaching*. Rowley, Mass.: Newbury House.
Franke, F. 1884. *Die Praktische Spracherlernung auf Grund der Psychologie und der Physiologie der Sprache Dargestellt*. Leipzig: O. R. Reisland.
Howatt, A. P. R. 1984. *A History of English Language Teaching*. Oxford: Oxford University Press.

Howatt, T. 1997. Talking shop: Transformation and change in ELT. *ELT Journal* 5(3): 263–268.

Kelly, L. 1969. *25 Centuries of Language Teaching.* Rowley, Mass.: Newbury House.

Lange, D. 1990. A blueprint for a teacher development program. In J. C. Richards and D. Nunan (eds.), *Second Language Teacher Education.* New York: Cambridge University Press. 245–268.

Larsen-Freeman, D. 1998. Expanding roles of learners and teachers in learner-centered instruction. In W. Renandya and G. Jacobs (eds.), *Learners and Language Learning.* Singapore: SEAMEO Regional Language Center.

Mackey, W. F. 1965. *Language Teaching Analysis.* London: Longman.

Marcella, F. 1998. The historical development of ESL materials in the United States. ERIC Document ED425653.

Richards, Jack C. 1985. The secret life of methods. In Jack C. Richards, *The Context of Language Teaching.* New York: Cambridge University Press.

Stern, H. H. 1983. *Fundamental Concepts of Language Teaching.* Oxford: Oxford University Press.

Sweet, H. 1899. *The Practical Study of Languages.* Reprinted London: Oxford University Press.

Titone, R. 1968. *Teaching Foreign Languages: An Historical Sketch.* Washington, D.C.: Georgetown University Press.

2 The nature of approaches and methods in language teaching

We saw in the preceding chapter that the changing rationale for foreign language study and the classroom techniques and procedures used to teach languages have reflected responses to a variety of historical issues and circumstances. Tradition was for many years the guiding principle. The Grammar-Translation Method reflected a time-honored and scholarly view of language and language study. At times, the practical realities of the classroom determined both goals and procedures, as with the determination of reading as the goal in American schools and colleges in the late 1920s. At other times, theories derived from linguistics, psychology, or a mixture of both were used to develop a both philosophical and practical basis for language teaching, as with the various reformist proposals of the nineteenth century. As the study of teaching methods and procedures in language teaching assumed a more central role within applied linguistics from the 1940s on, various attempts have been made to conceptualize the nature of methods and to explore more systematically the relationship between theory and practice within a method. In this chapter we will clarify the relationship between approach and method and present a model for the description, analysis, and comparison of methods.

Approach and method

When linguists and language specialists sought to improve the quality of language teaching in the late nineteenth century, they often did so by referring to general principles and theories concerning how languages are learned, how knowledge of language is represented and organized in memory, or how language itself is structured. The early applied linguists, such as Henry Sweet (1845–1912), Otto Jespersen (1860–1943), and Harold Palmer (1877–1949) (see Chapter 3), elaborated principles and theoretically accountable approaches to the design of language teaching programs, courses, and materials, though many of the specific practical details were left to be worked out by others. They sought a rational answer to questions such as those regarding principles for the selection and sequencing of vocabulary and grammar, though none of these applied linguists saw in any existing method the ideal embodiment of their ideas.

18

In describing methods, the difference between a philosophy of language teaching at the level of theory and principles, and a set of derived procedures for teaching a language, is central. In an attempt to clarify this difference, a scheme was proposed by the American applied linguist Edward Anthony in 1963. He identified three levels of conceptualization and organization, which he termed *approach, method,* and *technique*:

The arrangement is hierarchical. The organizational key is that techniques carry out a method which is consistent with an approach. . . .

. . . An approach is a set of correlative assumptions dealing with the nature of language teaching and learning. An approach is axiomatic. It describes the nature of the subject matter to be taught. . . .

. . . Method is an overall plan for the orderly presentation of language material, no part of which contradicts, and all of which is based upon, the selected approach. An approach is axiomatic, a method is procedural.

Within one approach, there can be many methods . . .

. . . A technique is implementational – that which actually takes place in a classroom. It is a particular trick, stratagem, or contrivance used to accomplish an immediate objective. Techniques must be consistent with a method, and therefore in harmony with an approach as well. (Anthony 1963: 63–67)

According to Anthony's model, approach is the level at which assumptions and beliefs about language and language learning are specified; method is the level at which theory is put into practice and at which choices are made about the particular skills to be taught, the content to be taught, and the order in which the content will be presented; technique is the level at which classroom procedures are described.

Anthony's model serves as a useful way of distinguishing between different degrees of abstraction and specificity found in different language teaching proposals. Thus we can see that the proposals of the Reform Movement were at the level of approach and that the Direct Method is one method derived from this approach. The so-called Reading Method, which evolved as a result of the Coleman Report (see Chapter 1), should really be described in the plural – reading methods – since a number of different ways of implementing a reading approach have been developed.

A number of other ways of conceptualizing approaches and methods in language teaching have been proposed. Mackey, in his book *Language Teaching Analysis* (1965), elaborated perhaps the most well known model of the 1960s, one that focuses primarily on the levels of method and technique. Mackey's model of language teaching analysis concentrates on the dimensions of selection, gradation, presentation, and repetition underlying a method. In fact, despite the title of Mackey's book, his concern is primarily with the analysis of textbooks and their underlying principles of organization. His model fails to address the level of approach, nor does it deal with the actual classroom behaviors of teachers

19

and learners, except as these are represented in textbooks. Hence it cannot really serve as a basis for comprehensive analysis of either approaches or methods.

Although Anthony's original proposal has the advantage of simplicity and comprehensiveness and serves as a useful way of distinguishing the relationship between underlying theoretical principles and the practices derived from them, it fails to give sufficient attention to the nature of a method itself. Nothing is said about the roles of teachers and learners assumed in a method, for example, nor about the role of instructional materials or the form they are expected to take. It fails to account for how an approach may be realized in a method, or for how method and technique are related. In order to provide a more comprehensive model for the discussion and analysis of approaches and methods, we have revised and extended the original Anthony model. The primary areas needing further clarification are, using Anthony's terms, method and technique. We see approach and method treated at the level of *design,* that level in which objectives, syllabus, and content are determined, and in which the roles of teachers, learners, and instructional materials are specified. The implementation phase (the level of technique in Anthony's model) we refer to by the slightly more comprehensive term *procedure.* Thus, a method is theoretically related to an approach, is organizationally determined by a design, and is practically realized in procedure. In the remainder of this chapter, we will elaborate on the relationship between approach, design, and procedure, using this framework to compare particular methods and approaches in language teaching. In the remaining chapters of the book, we will use the model presented here as a basis for describing a number of widely used approaches and methods.

Approach

Following Anthony, *approach* refers to theories about the nature of language and language learning that serve as the source of practices and principles in language teaching. We will examine the linguistic and psycholinguistic aspects of approach in turn.

Theory of language

At least three different theoretical views of language and the nature of language proficiency explicitly or implicitly inform current approaches and methods in language teaching. The first, and the most traditional of the three, is the *structural view,* the view that language is a system of structurally related elements for the coding of meaning. The target of language learning is seen to be the mastery of elements of this system, which are generally defined in terms of phonological units (e.g., phonemes), grammatical units (e.g., clauses, phrases, sentences), grammatical operations (e.g., adding, shifting, joining, or transforming elements), and lexical items (e.g., function words and structure words). As we see in Chapter 4, the Audiolingual Method embodies this particular view of language, as do such methods as Total Physical Response (Chapter 5) and the Silent Way (Chapter 6).

The second view of language is the *functional view,* the view that language is a vehicle for the expression of functional meaning. The communicative movement in language teaching subscribes to this view of language (see Chapter 14). This theory emphasizes the semantic and communicative dimension rather than merely the grammatical characteristics of language, and leads to a specification and organization of language teaching content by categories of meaning and function rather than by elements of structure and grammar. Wilkins's *Notional Syllabuses* (1976) is an attempt to spell out the implications of this view of language for syllabus design. A notional syllabus would include not only elements of grammar and lexis but also specify the topics, notions, and concepts the learner needs to communicate about. The English for Specific Purposes (ESP) movement likewise begins not from a structural theory of language but from a functional account of learner needs (Robinson 1980).

The third view of language can be called the *interactional view.* It sees language as a vehicle for the realization of interpersonal relations and for the performance of social transactions between individuals. Language is seen as a tool for the creation and maintenance of social relations. Areas of inquiry being drawn on in the development of interactional approaches to language teaching include interaction analysis, conversation analysis, and ethnomethodology. Interactional theories focus on the patterns of moves, acts, negotiation, and interaction found in conversational exchanges. Language teaching content, according to this view, may be specified and organized by patterns of exchange and interaction or may be left unspecified, to be shaped by the inclinations of learners as interactors.

"Interaction" has been central to theories of second language learning and pedagogy since the 1980s. Rivers (1987) defined the interactive perspective in language education: "Students achieve facility in *using* a language when their attention is focused on conveying and receiving authentic messages (that is, messages that contain information of interest to both speaker and listener in a situation of importance to both). This is *interaction*" (Rivers 1987: 4). The notion of interactivity has also been linked to the teaching of reading and writing as well as listening and speaking skills. Carrell, Devine, and Esky (1988) use the notion of "interactivity" to refer to the simultaneous use by effective readers of both top-down and bottom-up processing in reading comprehension. It is also used

21

to refer to the relationship between reader and writer who are viewed as engaged in a text-based conversation (Grabe in Carrell, Devine, and Esky 1988). Task-Based Language Teaching (Chapter 18) also draws on an interactional view of language, as to some extent do Whole Language (Chapter 9), Neurolinguistic Programming (Chapter 11), Cooperative Language Learning (Chapter 16), and Content-Based Instruction (Chapter 17). Despite this enthusiasm for "interactivity" as a defining notion in language teaching, a model of "Language as Interaction" has not been described in the same level of detail as those models that have been developed for structural and functional views of language theory.

Structural, functional, or interactional models of language (or variations on them) provide the axioms and theoretical framework that may motivate a particular teaching method, such as Audiolingualism. But in themselves they are incomplete and need to be complemented by theories of language learning. It is to this dimension that we now turn.

Theory of language learning

Although specific theories of the nature of language may provide the basis for a particular teaching method, other methods derive primarily from a theory of language learning. A learning theory underlying an approach or method responds to two questions: *(a)* What are the psycholinguistic and cognitive processes involved in language learning? and *(b)* What are the conditions that need to be met in order for these learning processes to be activated? Learning theories associated with a method at the level of approach may emphasize either one or both of these dimensions. Process-oriented theories build on learning processes, such as habit formation, induction, inferencing, hypothesis testing, and generalization. Condition-oriented theories emphasize the nature of the human and physical context in which language learning takes place.

Stephen D. Krashen's Monitor Model of second language development (1981) is an example of a learning theory on which a method (the Natural Approach) has been built (see Chapter 15). Monitor theory addresses both the process and the condition dimensions of learning. At the level of process, Krashen distinguishes between acquisition and learning. *Acquisition* refers to the natural assimilation of language rules through using language for communication. *Learning* refers to the formal study of language rules and is a conscious process. According to Krashen, however, learning is available only as a "monitor." The monitor is the repository of conscious grammatical knowledge about a language that is learned through formal instruction and that is called upon in the editing of utterances produced through the acquired system. Krashen's theory also addresses the conditions necessary for the process of "acquisition" to take place. Krashen describes these in terms of the type of "input" the learner receives. Input must be comprehensible, slightly above the learner's present level of competence, interesting or relevant, not grammatically sequenced, in sufficient quantity, and experienced in low-anxiety contexts.

Tracy D. Terrell's Natural Approach (1977) is an example of a method derived primarily from a learning theory rather than from a particular view of language. Although the Natural Approach is based on a learning theory that specifies both processes and conditions, the learning theory underlying such methods as Counseling-Learning and the Silent Way addresses primarily the conditions held to be necessary for learning to take place without specifying what the learning processes themselves are presumed to be (see Chapters 6 and 7).

Charles A. Curran in his writings on Counseling-Learning (1972), for example, focuses primarily on the conditions necessary for successful learning. He believes the atmosphere of the classroom is a crucial factor, and his method seeks to ameliorate the feelings of intimidation and insecurity that many learners experience. James Asher's Total Physical Response (Asher 1977) is likewise a method that derives primarily from learning theory rather than from a theory of the nature of language (see Chapter 5). Asher's learning theory addresses both the process and the condition aspects of learning. It is based on the belief that child language learning is based on motor activity, on coordinating language with action, and that this should form the basis of adult foreign language teaching. Orchestrating language production and comprehension with body movement and physical actions is thought to provide the conditions for success in language learning. Caleb Gattegno's Silent Way (1972, 1976) is likewise built around a theory of the conditions necessary for successful learning to be realized. Gattegno's writings address learners' needs to feel secure about learning and to assume conscious control of learning. Many of the techniques used in the method are designed to train learners to consciously use their intelligence to heighten learning potential.

There often appear to be natural affinities between certain theories of language and theories of language learning; however, one can imagine different pairings of language theory and learning theory that might work as well as those we observe. The linking of structuralism (a linguistic theory) to behaviorism (a learning theory) produced Audiolingualism. That particular link was not inevitable, however. Cognitive-code proponents (see Chapter 4), for example, have attempted to link a more sophisticated model of structuralism to a more mentalistic and less behavioristic brand of learning theory.

At the level of approach, we are hence concerned with theoretical principles. With respect to language theory, we are concerned with a model of language competence and an account of the basic features of linguistic organization and language use. With respect to learning theory, we are concerned with an account of the central processes of learning and an account of the conditions believed to promote successful language learning. These principles may or may not lead to "a" method. Teachers may, for example, develop their own teaching procedures, informed by a particular view of language and a particular theory of learning. They may constantly revise, vary, and modify teaching/learning procedures on the basis of the performance of the learners and their reactions to instructional practice. A group of teachers holding similar beliefs about language and language learning (i.e., sharing a similar approach) may each implement these principles in different ways. Approach does not specify procedure. Theory does not dictate a particular set of teaching techniques and activities. What links theory with practice (or approach with procedure) is what we have called design.

Design

In order for an approach to lead to a method, it is necessary to develop a design for an instructional system. *Design* is the level of method analysis in which we consider *(a)* what the objectives of a method are; *(b)* how language content is selected and organized within the method, that is, the syllabus model the method incorporates; *(c)* the types of learning tasks and teaching activities the method advocates; *(d)* the roles of learners; *(e)* the roles of teachers; and *(f)* the role of instructional materials.

Objectives

Different theories of language and language learning influence the focus of a method; that is, they determine what a method sets out to achieve. The specification of particular learning objectives, however, is a product of design, not of approach. Some methods focus primarily on oral skills and say that reading and writing skills are secondary and derive from transfer of oral skills. Some methods set out to teach general communication skills and give greater priority to the ability to express oneself meaningfully and to make oneself understood than to grammatical accuracy or perfect pronunciation. Others place a greater emphasis on accurate grammar and pronunciation from the very beginning. Some methods set out to teach the basic grammar and vocabulary of a language. Others may define their objectives less in linguistic terms than in terms of learning behaviors, that is, in terms of the processes or abilities the learner is expected to acquire as a result of instruction. Gattegno writes, for example, "Learning is not seen as the means of accumulating knowledge but as the means of becoming a more proficient learner in whatever one is engaged in" (1972: 89). This process-oriented objective may be offered in contrast to the linguistically oriented or product-oriented objectives of more traditional methods. The degree to which a method has process-oriented or product-oriented objectives may be revealed in how much emphasis is placed on vocabulary acquisition and grammatical proficiency and in how grammatical or pronunciation errors are treated in the method. Many methods that claim to be primarily process-oriented in fact show overriding concerns with grammatical and lexical attainment and with accurate grammar and pronunciation.

Content choice and organization: The syllabus

All methods of language teaching involve the use of the target language. All methods thus involve overt or covert decisions concerning the selection of language items (words, sentence patterns, tenses, constructions, functions, topics, etc.) that are to be used within a course or method. Decisions about the choice of language content relate to both subject matter and linguistic matter. In straightforward terms, one makes decisions about what to talk about (subject matter) and how to talk about it (linguistic matter). ESP courses, for example, are necessarily subject-matter focused. Structurally based methods, such as Situational Language Teaching and the Audiolingual Method, are necessarily linguistically focused. Methods typically differ in what they see as the relevant language and subject matter around which language teaching should be organized and the principles used in sequencing content within a course. Content issues involve the principles of selection (Mackey 1965) that ultimately shape the syllabus adopted in a course as well as the instructional materials that are used, together with the principles of gradation the method adopts. In grammar-based courses matters of sequencing and gradation are generally determined according to the difficulty of items or their frequency. In communicative or functionally oriented courses (e.g., in ESP programs) sequencing may be according to the learners' communicative needs.

Traditionally, the term *syllabus* has been used to refer to the form in which linguistic content is specified in a course or method. Inevitably, the term has been more closely associated with methods that are product-centered rather than those that are process-centered. Syllabuses and syllabus principles for Audiolingual, Structural-Situational, and notional-functional methods, as well as in ESP approaches to language program design, can be readily identified. The syllabus underlying the Situational and Audiolingual methods consists of a list of grammatical items and constructions, often together with an associated list of vocabulary items (Fries and Fries 1961; Alexander, Allen, Close, and O'Neill 1975). Notional-functional syllabuses specify the communicative content of a course in terms of functions, notions, topics, grammar, and vocabulary. Such syllabuses are usually determined in advance of teaching and for this reason have been referred to as "a priori syllabuses."

25

A number of taxonomies of syllabus types in language teaching have been proposed, for example, Yalden (1987), Long and Crookes (1992), and Brown (1995). Brown (1995: 7) lists seven basic syllabus types – Structural, Situational, Topical, Functional, Notional, Skills-based, and Task-based, and these can usually be linked to specific approaches or methods: Oral/Situational (Situational); Audiolingual (Structural), Communicative Language Teaching (Notional/Functional), Task-based Teaching (Task-based). However, for some of the approaches and methods discussed in this book we have had to infer syllabus assumptions since no explicit syllabus specification is given. This is particularly true where content organization rather than language organization or pedagogical issues determines syllabus design, as with Content-Based Instruction (Chapter 17).

The term *syllabus,* however, is less frequently used in process-based methods, in which considerations of language content are often secondary. Counseling-Learning, for example, has no language syllabus as such. Neither linguistic matter nor subject matter is specified in advance. Learners select content for themselves by choosing topics they want to talk about. These are then translated into the target language and used as the basis for interaction and language practice. To find out what linguistic content had in fact been generated and practiced during a course organized according to Counseling-Learning principles, it would be necessary to record the lessons and later determine what items of language had been covered. This would be an a posteriori approach to syllabus specification; that is, the syllabus would be determined from examining lesson protocols. With such methods as the Silent Way and Total Physical Response, an examination of lesson protocols, teacher's manuals, and texts derived from them reveals that the syllabuses underlying these methods are traditional lexico-grammatical syllabuses. In both there is a strong emphasis on grammar and grammatical accuracy.

Types of learning and teaching activities

The objectives of a method, whether defined primarily in terms of product or process, are attained through the instructional process, through the organized and directed interaction of teachers, learners, and materials in the classroom. Differences among methods at the level of approach manifest themselves in the choice of different kinds of learning and teaching activities in the classroom. Teaching activities that focus on grammatical accuracy may be quite different from those that focus on communicative skills. Activities designed to focus on the development of specific psycholinguistic processes in language acquisition will differ from those directed toward mastery of particular features of grammar. The activity types that a method advocates – the third component in the level of design in method analysis – often serve to distinguish methods. Audiolingualism, for example, uses dialogue and pattern practice extensively. The Silent Way employs problem-solving activities that involve the use of special charts and colored rods. Communicative language teaching theoreticians have advocated the use of tasks that involve an "information gap" and "information transfer"; that is, learners work on the same task, but each learner has different information needed to complete the task.

The notion of the "task" as a central activity type in language teaching has been considerably elaborated and refined since its emergence in early versions of Communicative Language Teaching. As well, tasks have become a central focus in both second language acquisition research and second language pedagogy. The history and some of the current interpretations of the nature of language teaching tasks are described in detail in Chapter 18 in relation to Task-Based Language Teaching.

Different philosophies at the level of approach may be reflected both in the use of different kinds of activities and in different uses for particular activity types. For example, interactive games are often used in audiolingual courses for motivation and to provide a change of pace from pattern-practice drills. In communicative language teaching, the same games may be used to introduce or provide practice for particular types of interactive exchanges. Differences in activity types in methods may also involve different arrangements and groupings of learners. A method that stresses oral chorus drilling will require different groupings of learners in the classroom from a method that uses problem-solving/information-exchange activities involving pair work. Activity types in methods thus include the primary categories of learning and teaching activity the method advocates, such as dialogue, responding to commands, group problem solving, information-exchange activities, improvisations, question and answer, or drills.

Because of the different assumptions they make about learning processes, syllabuses, and learning activities, methods also attribute different roles and functions to learners, teachers, and instructional materials within the instructional process. These constitute the next three components of design in method analysis.

Learner roles

The design of an instructional system will be considerably influenced by how learners are regarded. A method reflects explicit or implicit responses to questions concerning the learners' contribution to the learning process. This is seen in the types of activities learners carry out, the degree of control learners have over the content of learning, the patterns of learner groupings adopted, the degree to which learners influence the learning of others, and the view of the learner as processor, performer, initiator, problem solver.

Much of the criticism of Audiolingualism came from the recognition of the very limited roles available to learners in audiolingual methodology. Learners were seen as stimulus-response mechanisms whose learning was a direct result of repetitive practice. Newer methodologies customarily exhibit more concern for learner roles and for variation among learners. Johnson and Paulston (1976) spell out learner roles in an individualized approach to language learning in the following terms: *(a)* Learners plan their own learning program and thus ultimately assume responsibility for what they do in the classroom; *(b)* Learners monitor and evaluate their own progress; *(c)* Learners are members of a group and learn by interacting with others; *(d)* Learners tutor other learners; *(e)* Learners learn from the teacher, from other students, and from other teaching sources. Counseling-Learning views learners as having roles that change developmentally, and Curran (1976) uses an ontogenetic metaphor to suggest this development. He divides the developmental process into five stages, extending from total dependency on the teacher in stage 1 to total independence in stage 5. These learner stages Curran sees as parallel to the growth of a child from embryo to independent adulthood, passing through childhood and adolescence.

Teacher roles

Learner roles in an instructional system are closely linked to the teacher's status and function. Teacher roles are similarly related ultimately both to assumptions about language and language learning at the level of approach. Some methods are totally dependent on the teacher as a source of knowledge and direction; others see the teacher's role as catalyst, consultant, guide, and model for learning; still others try to "teacher-proof" the instructional system by limiting teacher initiative and by building instructional content and direction into texts or lesson plans. Teacher and learner roles define the type of interaction characteristic of classrooms in which a particular method is being used.

Teacher roles in methods are related to the following issues: *(a)* the types of functions teachers are expected to fulfill, whether that of practice director, counselor, or model, for example; *(b)* the degree of control the teacher has over how learning takes place; *(c)* the degree to which the teacher is responsible for determining the content of what is taught; and *(d)* the interactional patterns that develop between teachers and learners. Methods typically depend critically on teacher roles and their realizations. In the classical Audiolingual Method, the teacher is regarded as the primary source of language and of language learning. But less teacher-directed learning may still demand very specific and sometimes even more demanding roles for the teacher. The role of the teacher in the Silent Way, for example, depends on thorough training and methodological initiation. Only teachers who are thoroughly sure of their role and the concomitant learner's role will risk departure from the security of traditional textbook-oriented teaching.

For some methods, the role of the teacher has been specified in detail. Individualized approaches to learning define roles for the teacher that create specific patterns of interaction between teachers and learners in classrooms. These are designed to shift the responsibility for learning gradually from the teacher to the learner. Counseling-Learning sees the teacher's role as that of psychological counselor, the effectiveness of the teacher's role being a measure of counseling skills and attributes – warmth, sensitivity, and acceptance.

As these examples suggest, the potential role relationships of learner and teacher are many and varied. They may be asymmetrical relationships, such as those of conductor to orchestra member, therapist to patient, coach to player. Some contemporary methodologies have sought to establish more symmetrical kinds of learner–teacher relationships, such as friend to friend, colleague to colleague, teammate to teammate. The role of the teacher will ultimately reflect both the objectives of the method and the learning theory on which the method is predicated, since the success of a method may depend on the degree to which the teacher can provide the content or create the conditions for successful language learning.

The role of instructional materials

The last component within the level of design concerns the role of instructional materials within the instructional system. What is specified with respect to objectives, content (i.e., the syllabus), learning activities, and learner and teacher roles suggests the function for materials within the system. The syllabus defines linguistic content in terms of language elements – structures, topics, notions, functions – or, in some cases, of learning tasks (see Johnson 1982; Prabhu 1983). It also defines the goals for language learning in terms of speaking, listening, reading, or writing skills. The instructional materials in their turn further specify subject-matter content, even where no syllabus exists, and define or suggest the intensity of coverage for syllabus items, allocating the amount of time, attention, and detail particular syllabus items or tasks require. Instructional materials also define or imply the day-to-day learning objectives that collectively constitute the goals of the syllabus. Materials designed on the assumption that learning is initiated and monitored by the teacher must meet quite different requirements from those designed for student

29

self-instruction or for peer tutoring. Some methods require the instructional use of existing materials, found materials, and realia. Some assume teacher-proof materials that even poorly trained teachers with imperfect control of the target language can teach with. Some materials require specially trained teachers with near-native competence in the target language. Some are designed to replace the teacher, so that learning can take place independently. Some materials dictate various interactional patterns in the classroom; others inhibit classroom interaction; still others are noncommittal about interaction between teacher and learner and learner and learner.

The role of instructional materials within a method or instructional system will reflect decisions concerning the primary goal of materials (e.g., to present content, to practice content, to facilitate communication between learners, or to enable learners to practice content without the teacher's help), the form of materials (e.g., textbook, audiovisuals, computer software), the relation of materials to other sources of input (i.e., whether they serve as the major source of input or only as a minor component of it), and the abilities of teachers (e.g., their competence in the language or degree of training and experience).

A particular design for an instructional system may imply a particular set of roles for materials in support of the syllabus and the teachers and learners. For example, the role of instructional materials within a functional/communicative methodology might be specified in the following terms:

1. Materials will focus on the communicative abilities of interpretation, expression, and negotiation.
2. Materials will focus on understandable, relevant, and interesting exchanges of information, rather than on the presentation of grammatical form.
3. Materials will involve different kinds of texts and different media, which the learners can use to develop their competence through a variety of different activities and tasks.

By comparison, the role of instructional materials within an individualized instructional system might include the following specifications:

1. Materials will allow learners to progress at their own rates of learning.
2. Materials will allow for different styles of learning.
3. Materials will provide opportunities for independent study and use.
4. Materials will provide opportunities for self-evaluation and progress in learning.

The content of a method such as Counseling-Learning is assumed to be a product of the interests of the learners, since learners generate their own subject matter. In that sense it would appear that no linguistic content or materials are specified within the method. On the other hand, Counseling-Learning acknowledges the need for learner mastery of certain linguistic mechanics, such as vocabulary, grammar, and pronunciation. Counseling-Learning sees these issues as falling outside the teacher's central role as counselor. Thus, Counseling-Learning has proposed the use of teaching machines and other programmed materials to support the learning of some of the more mechanical aspects of language so as to free the teacher to function increasingly as a learning counselor.

Procedure

The last level of conceptualization and organization within a method is what we will refer to as *procedure*. This encompasses the actual moment-to-moment techniques, practices, and behaviors that operate in teaching a language according to a particular method. It is the level at which we describe how a method realizes its approach and design in classroom behavior. At the level of design we saw that a method will advocate the use of certain types of teaching activities as a consequence of its theoretical assumptions about language and learning. At the level of procedure, we are concerned with how these tasks and activities are integrated into lessons and used as the basis for teaching and learning. There are three dimensions to a method at the level of procedure: *(a)* the use of teaching activities (drills, dialogues, information-gap activities, etc.) to present new language and to clarify and demonstrate formal, communicative, or other aspects of the target language; *(b)* the ways in which particular teaching activities are used for practicing language; and *(c)* the procedures and techniques used in giving feedback to learners concerning the form or content of their utterances or sentences.

Essentially, then, procedure focuses on the way a method handles the presentation, practice, and feedback phases of teaching. Here, for example, is a description of the procedural aspects of a beginning Silent Way course based on Stevick (1980: 44–45):

1. The teacher points at meaningless symbols on a wall chart. The symbols represent the syllables of the spoken language. The students read the sounds aloud, first in chorus and then individually.
2. After the students can pronounce the sounds, the teacher moves to a second set of charts containing words frequently used in the language, including numbers. The teacher leads the students to pronounce long numbers.
3. The teacher uses colored rods together with charts and gestures to lead the students into producing the words and basic grammatical structures needed.

Of error treatment in the Silent Way Stevick notes:

31

When the students respond correctly to the teacher's initiative, she usually does not react with any overt confirmation that what they did was right. If a student's response is wrong, on the other hand, she indicates that the student needs to do further work on the word or phrase; if she thinks it necessary, she actually shows the student exactly where the additional work is to be done. (1980: 45)

Finocchiaro and Brumfit (1983) illustrate how the procedural phases of instruction are handled in what they call a notional-functional approach.

1. Presentation of a brief dialogue or several mini-dialogues.
2. Oral practice of each utterance in the dialogue.
3. Questions and answers based on the topic and situation in the dialogue.
4. Questions and answers related to the student's personal experience but centered on the theme of the dialogue.
5. Study of the basic communicative expressions used in the dialogue or one of the structures that exemplify the function.
6. Learner discovery of generalizations or rules underlying the functional expression of structure.
7. Oral recognition, interpretative procedures.
8. Oral production activities, proceeding from guided to freer communication.

We expect methods to be most obviously idiosyncratic at the level of procedure, though classroom observations often reveal that teachers do not necessarily follow the procedures a method prescribes.

The elements and subelements that constitute a method and that we have described under the rubrics of approach, design, and procedure are summarized in Figure 2.1.

Conclusion

The model presented in this chapter demonstrates that any language teaching method can be described in terms of the issues identified here at the levels of approach, design, and procedure. Very few methods are explicit with respect to all of these dimensions, however. In the remaining chapters of this book we will attempt to make each of these features of approach, design, and procedure explicit with reference to the major language teaching approaches and methods in use today. In so doing, we will often have to infer from what method developers have written in order to determine precisely what criteria are being used for teaching activities, what claims are being made about learning theory, what type of syllabus is being employed, and so on.

The model presented here is not intended to imply that methodological

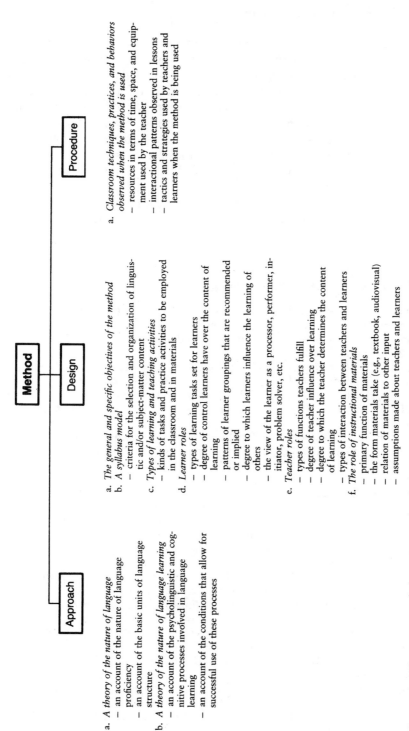

Method

Approach

a. *A theory of the nature of language*
  – an account of the nature of language proficiency
  – an account of the basic units of language structure
b. *A theory of the nature of language learning*
  – an account of the psycholinguistic and cognitive processes involved in language learning
  – an account of the conditions that allow for successful use of these processes

Design

a. *The general and specific objectives of the method*
b. *A syllabus model*
  – criteria for the selection and organization of linguistic and/or subject-matter content
c. *Types of learning and teaching activities*
  – kinds of tasks and practice activities to be employed in the classroom and in materials
d. *Learner roles*
  – types of learning tasks set for learners
  – degree of control learners have over the content of learning
  – patterns of learner groupings that are recommended or implied
  – degree to which learners influence the learning of others
  – the view of the learner as a processor, performer, initiator, problem solver, etc.
e. *Teacher roles*
  – types of functions teachers fulfill
  – degree of teacher influence over learning
  – degree to which the teacher determines the content of learning
  – types of interaction between teachers and learners
f. *The role of instructional materials*
  – primary function of materials
  – the form materials take (e.g., textbook, audiovisual)
  – relation of materials to other input
  – assumptions made about teachers and learners

Procedure

a. *Classroom techniques, practices, and behaviors observed when the method is used*
  – resources in terms of time, space, and equipment used by the teacher
  – interactional patterns observed in lessons
  – tactics and strategies used by teachers and learners when the method is being used

Figure 2.1 Summary of elements and subelements that constitute a method.

development proceeds neatly from approach, through design, to procedure. It is not clear whether such a developmental formula is possible, and our model certainly does not describe the typical case. Methods can develop out of any of the three categories. One can, for example, stumble on or invent a set of teaching procedures that appear to be successful and then later develop a design and a theoretical approach that explain or justify the procedures. Some methodologists would resist calling their proposals a method, although, if descriptions are possible at each of the levels described here, we would argue that what is advocated has, in fact, the status of a method. Let us now turn to the major approaches and teaching methods that are in use today and examine them according to how they reflect specific decisions at the levels of approach, design, and procedure.

Bibliography and further reading

Alexander, L. G., W. S. Allen, R. A. Close, and R. J. O'Neill. 1975. *English Grammatical Structure*. London: Longman.

Anthony, E. M. 1963. Approach, method and technique. *English Language Teaching* 17: 63–67.

Asher, J. 1977. *Learning Another Language through Actions: The Complete Teacher's Guidebook*. Los Gatos, Calif.: Sky Oakes Productions.

Bosco, F. J., and R. J. Di Pietro. 1970. Instructional strategies: Their psychological and linguistics bases. *International Review of Applied Linguistics* 8: 1–19.

Breen, M. P., and C. Candlin. 1980. The essentials of a communicative curriculum in language teaching. *Applied Linguistics* 1(2): 89–112.

Brown, J. 1995. *The Elements of the Language Curriculum*. Boston: Heinle & Heinle.

Carrell, P., A. Devine, and D. Esky. 1988. *Interactive Approaches to Second Language Reading*. Cambridge: Cambridge University Press.

Curran, C. A. 1972. *Counseling-Learning: A Whole-Person Model for Education*. New York: Grune and Stratton.

Curran, C. A. 1976. *Counseling-Learning in Second Languages*. Apple River, Ill.: Apple River Press.

Finocchiaro, M., and C. Brumfit. 1983. *The Functional-Notional Approach: From Theory to Practice*. New York: Oxford University Press.

Fries, C. C., and A. C. Fries. 1961. *Foundations for English Teaching*. Tokyo: Kenkyusha.

Gattegno, C. 1972. *Teaching Foreign Languages in Schools: The Silent Way*. (2nd ed.). New York: Educational Solutions.

Gattegno, C. 1976. *The Common Sense of Teaching Foreign Languages*. New York: Educational Solutions.

Holliday, A. 1994. *Appropriate Methodology*. Cambridge: Cambridge University Press.

Johnson, F., and C. B. Paulston. 1976. *Individualizing in the Language Classroom*. Cambridge, Mass.: Jacaranda.

Johnson, K. 1982. *Communicative Syllabus Design and Methodology.* Oxford: Pergamon.

Krashen, S. D. 1981. *Second Language Acquisition and Second Language Learning.* Oxford: Pergamon.

Long, M., and G. Crookes. 1992. Three approaches to task-based syllabus design. *TESOL Quarterly* 226(1) (spring): 27–56.

Mackey, W. F. 1965. *Language Teaching Analysis.* London: Longman.

Prabhu, N. 1983. Procedural syllabuses. Paper presented at the RELC Seminar. Singapore: Regional Language Centre.

Prabhu, N. 1990. There is no best method – why? *TESOL Quarterly* 24: 161–176.

Richards J. C. 1990. Beyond methods. In J. C. Richards, *The Language Teaching Matrix.* New York: Cambridge University Press.

Rivers, W. M. (ed.). 1987. *Interactive Language Teaching.* Cambridge: Cambridge University Press.

Robinson, P. 1980. *ESP (English for Specific Purposes).* Oxford: Pergamon.

Rodgers, T. 1990. After methods, what? In S. Aninan (ed.), *Language Teaching Methodology for the Nineties.* Singapore: SEAMEO Regional Language Centre.

Spolsky, B. 1998. *Conditions for Second Language Learning: Introduction to a General Theory.* Oxford: Oxford University Press.

Stevick, E. W. 1980. *Teaching Languages: A Way and Ways.* Rowley, Mass.: Newbury House.

Terrell, T. D. 1977. A natural approach to the acquisition and learning of a language. *Modern Language Journal* 61(7): 325–336.

Warschauer, M., and R. Kern (eds.). 1999. *Network-Based Language Teaching: Concepts and Practices.* New York: Cambridge University Press.

Wilkins, D. A. 1976. *Notional Syllabuses.* Oxford: Oxford University Press.

Yalden, J. 1987. *Principles of Course Design for Language Teaching.* Cambridge: Cambridge University Press.

3 The Oral Approach and Situational Language Teaching

Few language teachers today are familiar with the terms *Oral Approach* or *Situational Language Teaching,* which refer to an approach to language teaching developed by British applied linguists from the 1930s to the 1960s. Even though neither term is commonly used today, the impact of the Oral Approach has been long-lasting, and it has shaped the design of many widely used EFL/ESL textbooks and courses, including many still being used today. One of the most successful ESL courses published, *Streamline English* (Hartley and Viney 1978), reflected the classic principles of Situational Language Teaching, as did many other series that have been widely used (e.g., *Access to English,* Coles and Lord 1975; *Kernel Lessons Plus,* O'Neill 1973; and many of L. G. Alexander's widely used textbooks, e.g., Alexander 1967). Hubbard, Jones, Thornton, and Wheeler's comment in 1983 still holds true today: "This method is widely used at the time of writing and a very large number of textbooks are based on it" (Hubbard et al. 1983: 36). It is important, therefore, to understand the principles and practices of the Oral Approach and Situational Language Teaching.

Background

The origins of this approach began with the work of British applied linguists in the 1920s and 1930s. Beginning at this time, a number of outstanding applied linguists developed the basis for a principled approach to methodology in language teaching. Two of the leaders in this movement were Harold Palmer and A. S. Hornby, two of the most prominent figures in British twentieth-century language teaching. Both were familiar with the work of such linguists as Otto Jespersen and Daniel Jones, as well as with the Direct Method. They attempted to develop a more scientific foundation for an oral approach to teaching English than was evidenced in the Direct Method. The result was a systematic study of the principles and procedures that could be applied to the selection and organization of the content of a language course (Palmer 1917, 1921).

Vocabulary control

One of the first aspects of method design to receive attention was the role of vocabulary. In the 1920s and 1930s, several large-scale investigations of foreign language vocabulary were undertaken. The impetus for this research came from two quarters. First, there was a general consensus among language teaching specialists, such as Palmer, that vocabulary was one of the most important aspects of foreign language learning. A second influence was the increased emphasis on reading skills as the goal of foreign language study in some countries. This had been the recommendation of the Coleman Report (Chapter 1) and also the independent conclusion of another British language teaching specialist, Michael West, who had examined the role of English in India in the 1920s. Vocabulary was seen as an essential component of reading proficiency.

This led to the development of principles of vocabulary control, which were to have a major practical impact on the teaching of English in subsequent decades. Frequency counts showed that a core of two thousand or so words occurred frequently in written texts and that a knowledge of these words would greatly assist in reading a foreign language. Harold Palmer, Michael West, and other specialists produced a guide to the English vocabulary needed for teaching English as a foreign language, *The Interim Report on Vocabulary Selection* (Faucett, West, Palmer, and Thorndike 1936), based on frequency as well as other criteria. This was later revised by West and published in 1953 as *A General Service List of English Words,* which became a standard reference in developing teaching materials. These efforts to introduce a scientific and rational basis for choosing the vocabulary content of a language course represented the first attempts to establish principles of syllabus design in language teaching.

Grammar control

Parallel to the interest in developing rational principles for vocabulary selection was a focus on the grammatical content of a language course. Palmer had emphasized the problems of grammar for the foreign learner. Much of his work in Japan, where he directed the Institute for Research in English Teaching from 1922 until World War II, was directed toward developing classroom procedures suited to teaching basic grammatical patterns through an oral approach. His view of grammar was very different from the abstract model of grammar seen in the Grammar-Translation Method, however, which was based on the assumption that one universal logic formed the basis of all languages and that the teacher's responsibility was to show how each category of the universal grammar was to be expressed in the foreign language. Palmer viewed grammar as the underlying sentence patterns of the spoken language. Palmer, Hornby, and other British applied linguists analyzed English and classified its major grammatical structures into sentence patterns (later called " substitution tables"), which could be used to help internalize the rules of English sentence structure.

A classification of English sentence patterns was incorporated into the first dictionary for students of English as a foreign language, developed by Hornby, Gatenby, and Wakefield and published in 1953 as *The Advanced Learner's Dictionary of Current English*. A number of pedagogically motivated descriptions of English grammar were undertaken, including *A Grammar of Spoken English on a Strictly Phonetic Basis* (Palmer and Blandford 1939), *A Handbook of English Grammar* (Zandvoort 1945), and Hornby's *Guide to Patterns and Usage in English* (1954), which became a standard reference source of basic English sentence patterns for textbook writers. With the development of systematic approaches to the lexical and grammatical content of a language course and with the efforts of such specialists as Palmer, West, and Hornby in using these resources as part of a comprehensive methodological framework for the teaching of English as a foreign language, the foundations for the British approach in TEFL/TESL – the Oral Approach – were firmly established.

The Oral Approach and Situational Language Teaching

Palmer, Hornby, and other British applied linguists from the 1920s onward developed an approach to methodology that involved systematic principles of *selection* (the procedures by which lexical and grammatical content was chosen), *gradation* (principles by which the organization and sequencing of content were determined), and *presentation* (techniques used for presentation and practice of items in a course). Although Palmer, Hornby, and other English teaching specialists had differing views on the specific procedures to be used in teaching English, their general principles were referred to as the Oral Approach to language teaching. This was not to be confused with the Direct Method, which, although it used oral procedures, lacked a systematic basis in applied linguistic theory and practice.

An oral approach should not be confused with the obsolete Direct Method, which meant only that the learner was bewildered by a flow of ungraded speech, suffering all the difficulties he would have encountered in picking up the language in its normal environment and losing most of the compensating benefits of better contextualization in those circumstances. (Pattison 1964: 4)

The Oral Approach was the accepted British approach to English language teaching by the 1950s. It is described in the standard methodology textbooks of the period, such as French (1948–1950), Gurrey (1955), Frisby (1957), and Billows (1961). Its principles are seen in Hornby's famous *Oxford Progressive English Course for Adult Learners* (1954–1956) and in many other more recent textbooks. One of the most active proponents of the Oral Approach in the 1960s was the Australian George Pittman. Pittman and his colleagues were responsible for developing an influential set of teaching materials based on the Situational Approach, which were widely used in Australia, New Guinea, and the Pacific territories. Most Pacific territories continue to use the so-called Tate materials, developed by Pittman's colleague Gloria Tate. Pittman was also responsible for the situationally based materials developed by the Commonwealth Office of Education in Sydney, Australia, used in the English programs for immigrants in Australia. These were published for worldwide use in 1965 as the series *Situational English*. Materials by Alexander and other leading British textbook writers also reflected the principles of Situational Language Teaching as they had evolved over a 20-year period. The main characteristics of the approach were as follows:

1. Language teaching begins with the spoken language. Material is taught orally before it is presented in written form.
2. The target language is the language of the classroom.
3. New language points are introduced and practiced situationally.
4. Vocabulary selection procedures are followed to ensure that an essential general service vocabulary is covered.
5. Items of grammar are graded following the principle that simple forms should be taught before complex ones.
6. Reading and writing are introduced once a sufficient lexical and grammatical basis is established.

It was the third principle that became a key feature of the approach in the 1960s, and it was then that the term *situational* was used increasingly in referring to the Oral Approach. Hornby himself used the term *the Situational Approach* in the title of an influential series of articles published in *English Language Teaching* in 1950. Later, the terms *Structural-Situational Approach* and *Situational Language Teaching* came into common usage. To avoid further confusion, we will use the term *Situational Language Teaching* (SLT) to include the Structural-Situational and Oral approaches. How can Situational Language Teaching be characterized at the levels of approach, design, and procedure?

Approach

Theory of language

The theory of language underlying Situational Language Teaching can be characterized as a type of British "structuralism." Speech was regarded as the basis of language, and structure was viewed as being at the heart of speaking ability. Palmer, Hornby, and other British applied linguists had prepared pedagogical descriptions of the basic grammatical structures of English, and these were to be followed in developing methodology. "Word order, Structural Words, the few inflexions of English, and Content Words, will form the material of our teaching" (Frisby 1957: 134). In terms of language theory, there was little to distinguish such a view from that proposed by American linguists, such as Charles Fries. Indeed, Pittman drew heavily on Fries's theories of language in the 1960s, but American theory was largely unknown by British applied linguists in the 1950s. The British theoreticians, however, had a different focus to their version of structuralism – the notion of "situation." "Our principal classroom activity in the teaching of English structure will be the oral practice of structures. This oral practice of controlled sentence patterns should be given in situations designed to give the greatest amount of practice in English speech to the pupil" (Pittman 1963: 179).

The theory that knowledge of structures must be linked to situations in which they could be used gave Situational Language Teaching one of its distinctive features. This may have reflected the functional trend in British linguistics since the 1930s. Many British linguists had emphasized the close relationship between the structure of language and the context and situations in which language is used. British linguists, such as J. R. Firth and M. A. K. Halliday, developed powerful views of language in which meaning, context, and situation were given a prominent place: "The emphasis now is on the description of language activity as part of the whole complex of events which, together with the participants and relevant objects, make up actual situations" (Halliday, McIntosh, and Strevens 1964: 38). Thus, in contrast to American structuralist views on language (see Chapter 4), language was viewed as purposeful activity related to goals and situations in the real world. "The language which a person originates . . . is always expressed for a purpose" (Frisby 1957: 16).

Theory of learning

The theory of learning underlying Situational Language Teaching is a type of behaviorist habit-learning theory. It addresses primarily the processes rather than the conditions of learning. Frisby, for example, cites Palmer's views as authoritative:

As Palmer has pointed out, there are three processes in learning a language – receiving the knowledge or materials, fixing it in the memory by repetition, and using it in actual practice until it becomes a personal skill. (1957: 136)

French likewise saw language learning as habit formation:

The fundamental is correct speech habits. . . . The pupils should be able to put the words, without hesitation and almost without thought, into sentence patterns which are correct. Such speech habits can be cultivated by blind imitative drill. (1950, vol. 3: 9)

Like the Direct Method, Situational Language Teaching adopts an inductive approach to the teaching of grammar. The meaning of words or structures is not to be given through explanation in either the native language or the target language but is to be induced from the way the form is used in a situation. "If we give the meaning of a new word, either by translation into the home language or by an equivalent in the same language, as soon as we introduce it, we weaken the impression which the word makes on the mind" (Billows 1961: 28). Explanation is therefore discouraged, and the learner is expected to deduce the meaning of a particular structure or vocabulary item from the situation in which it is presented. Extending structures and vocabulary to new situations takes place by generalization. The learner is expected to apply the language learned in a classroom to situations outside the classroom. This is how child language learning is believed to take place, and the same processes are thought to occur in second and foreign language learning, according to practitioners of Situational Language Teaching.

Design

Objectives

The objectives of the Situational Language Teaching method are to teach a practical command of the four basic skills of language, goals it shares with most methods of language teaching. But the skills are approached through structure. Accuracy in both pronunciation and grammar is regarded as crucial, and errors are to be avoided at all costs. Automatic control of basic structures and sentence patterns is fundamental to reading and writing skills, and this is achieved through speech work. "Before our pupils read new structures and new vocabulary, we shall teach orally both the new structures and the new vocabulary" (Pittman 1963: 186). Writing likewise derives from speech.

Oral composition can be a very valuable exercise. . . .

Nevertheless, the skill with which this activity is handled depends largely on the control of the language suggested by the teacher and used by the children. . . . Only when the teacher is reasonably certain that learners can speak fairly correctly within the limits of their knowledge of sentence structure and vocabulary may he allow them free choice in sentence patterns and vocabulary. (Pittman 1963: 188)

The syllabus

Basic to the teaching of English in Situational Language Teaching is a structural syllabus and a word list. A structural syllabus is a list of the basic structures and sentence patterns of English, arranged according to their order of presentation. In Situational Language Teaching, structures are always taught within sentences, and vocabulary is chosen according to how well it enables sentence patterns to be taught. "Our early course will consist of a list of sentence patterns [statement patterns, question patterns, and request or command patterns] . . . will include as many structural words as possible, and sufficient content words to provide us with material upon which to base our language practice" (Frisby 1957: 134). Frisby gives an example of the typical structural syllabus around which situational teaching was based:

	Sentence pattern	*Vocabulary*
1st lesson	This is . . .	book, pencil, ruler,
	That is . . .	desk
2nd lesson	These are . . .	chair, picture, door,
	Those are . . .	window
3rd lesson	Is this . . . ? Yes it is.	watch, box, pen,
	Is that . . . ? Yes it is.	blackboard

(1957: 134)

The syllabus was not therefore a situational syllabus in the sense that this term is sometimes used (i.e., a list of situations and the language associated with them). Rather, situation refers to the manner of presenting and practicing sentence patterns, as we shall see later.

Types of learning and teaching activities

Situational Language Teaching employs a situational approach to presenting new sentence patterns and a drill-based manner of practicing them:

our method will . . . be situational. The situation will be controlled carefully to teach the new language material . . . in such a way that there can be no doubt in the learner's mind of the meaning of what he hears. . . . almost all the vocabulary and structures taught in the first four or five years and even

42

later can be placed in situations in which the meaning is quite clear. (Pittman 1963: 155–156)

By *situation* Pittman means the use of concrete objects, pictures, and realia, which together with actions and gestures can be used to demonstrate the meanings of new language items:

The form of new words and sentence patterns is demonstrated with examples and not through grammatical explanation or description. The meaning of new words and sentence patterns is not conveyed through translation. It is made clear visually (with objects, pictures, action and mime). Wherever possible model sentences are related and taken from a single situation. (Davies, Roberts, and Rossner 1975: 3)

The practice techniques employed generally consist of guided repetition and substitution activities, including chorus repetition, dictation, drills, and controlled oral-based reading and writing tasks. Other oral-practice techniques are sometimes used, including pair practice and group work.

Learner roles

In the initial stages of learning, the learner is required simply to listen and repeat what the teacher says and to respond to questions and commands. The learner has no control over the content of learning and is often regarded as likely to succumb to undesirable behaviors unless skillfully manipulated by the teacher. For example, the learner might lapse into faulty grammar or pronunciation, forget what has been taught, or fail to respond quickly enough; incorrect habits are to be avoided at all costs (see Pittman 1963). Later, more active participation is encouraged. This includes learners initiating responses and asking each other questions, although teacher-controlled introduction and practice of new language is stressed throughout (see Davies, Roberts, and Rossner 1975: 3–4).

Teacher roles

The teacher's function is threefold. In the presentation stage of the lesson, the teacher serves as a model, setting up situations in which the need for the target structure is created and then modeling the new structure for students to repeat. Then the teacher "becomes more like the skillful conductor of an orchestra, drawing the music out of the performers" (Byrne 1976: 2). The teacher is required to be a skillful manipulator, using questions, commands, and other cues to elicit correct sentences from the learners. Lessons are hence teacher-directed, and the teacher sets the pace.

During the practice phase of the lesson, students are given more of an opportunity to use the language in less controlled situations, but the teacher is ever on the lookout for grammatical and structural errors that can form the basis of subsequent lessons. Organizing review is a primary task for the teacher, according to Pittman (1963), who summarizes the teacher's responsibilities as dealing with

1. timing
2. oral practice, to support the textbook structures
3. revision [i.e., review]
4. adjustment to special needs of individuals
5. testing
6. developing language activities other than those arising from the textbook
(Pittman 1963: 177–178)

The teacher is essential to the success of the method, since the textbook is able only to describe activities for the teacher to carry out in class.

The role of instructional materials

Situational Language Teaching is dependent on both a textbook and visual aids. The textbook contains tightly organized lessons planned around different grammatical structures. Visual aids may be produced by the teacher or may be commercially produced; they consist of wall charts, flashcards, pictures, stick figures, and so on. The visual element together with a carefully graded grammatical syllabus is a crucial aspect of Situational Language Teaching, hence the importance of the textbook. In principle, however, the textbook should be used "only as a guide to the learning process. The teacher is expected to be the master of his textbook" (Pittman 1963: 176).

Procedure

Classroom procedures in Situational Language Teaching vary according to the level of the class, but procedures at any level aim to move from controlled to freer practice of structures and from oral use of sentence patterns to their automatic use in speech, reading, and writing. Pittman gives an example of a typical lesson plan:

The first part of the lesson will be stress and intonation practice. . . . The main body of the lesson should then follow. This might consist of the teaching of a structure. If so, the lesson would then consist of four parts:

1. pronunciation
2. revision (to prepare for new work if necessary)
3. presentation of new structure or vocabulary
4. oral practice (drilling)
5. reading of material on the new structure, or written exercises
(1963: 173)

Davies et al. give sample lesson plans for use with Situational Language Teaching. The structures being taught in the following lesson are "This is a . . ." and "That's a . . ."

Teacher:	(holding up a watch) Look. This is a watch. (2×) (pointing to a clock on wall or table) That's a clock. (2×) That's a clock. (2×) This is a watch. (putting down watch and moving across to touch the clock or pick it up) This is a clock. (2×) (pointing to watch) That's a watch. (2×) (picking up a pen) This is a pen. (2×) (drawing large pencil on blackboard and moving away) That's a pencil. (2×) Take your pens. All take your pens. (students all pick up their pens)
Teacher:	Listen. This is a pen. (3×) This. (3×)
Students:	This. (3×)
A student:	This. (6×)
Teacher:	This is a pen.
Students:	This is a pen. (3×)
Student:	(moving pen) This is a pen. (6×)
Teacher:	(pointing to blackboard) That's a pencil. (3×) That. (3×)
Students:	That. (3×)
A student.	That. (6×)
Teacher:	That's a pencil.
Students:	(all pointing at blackboard) That's a pencil. (3×)
Student:	(pointing at blackboard) That's a pencil. (6×)
Teacher:	Take your books. (taking a book himself) This is a book. (3×)
Students:	This is a book. (3×)
Teacher:	(placing notebook in a visible place) Tell me . . .
Student 1:	That's a notebook.

You can now begin taking objects out of your box, making sure they are as far as possible not new vocabulary items. Large objects may be placed in visible places at the front of the classroom. Smaller ones distributed to students.

(1975: 56)

These procedures illustrate the techniques used in presenting new language items in situations. Drills are likewise related to "situations." Pittman illustrates oral drilling on a pattern, using a box full of objects to create the situation. The pattern being practiced is "There's a NOUN + of + (noun) in the box." The teacher takes objects out of the box and the class repeats:

There's a tin of cigarettes in the box.
There's a packet of matches in the box.
There's a reel of cotton in the box.
There's a bottle of ink in the box.
There's a packet of pins in the box.

There's a pair of shoes in the box.
There's a jar of rice in the box.

(Pittman 1963: 168)

The teacher's kit, a collection of items and realia that can be used in situational language practice, is hence an essential part of the teacher's equipment.

Davies et al. likewise give detailed information about teaching procedures to be used with Situational Language Teaching. The sequence of activities they propose consists of the following:

1. Listening practice in which the teacher obtains his student's attention and repeats an example of the patterns or a word in isolation clearly, several times, probably saying it slowly at least once (where . . . is . . . the . . . pen?), separating the words.
2. Choral imitation in which students all together or in large groups repeat what the teacher has said. This works best if the teacher gives a clear instruction like "Repeat," or "Everybody" and hand signals to mark time and stress.
3. Individual imitation in which the teacher asks several individual students to repeat the model he has given in order to check their pronunciation.
4. Isolation, in which the teacher isolates sounds, words, or groups of words which cause trouble and goes through techniques 1–3 with them before replacing them in context.
5. Building up to a new model, in which the teacher gets students to ask and answer questions using patterns they already know in order to bring about the information necessary to introduce the new model.
6. Elicitation, in which the teacher, using mime, prompt words, gestures, etc., gets students to ask questions, make statements, or give new examples of the pattern.
7. Substitution drilling, in which the teacher uses cue words (words, pictures, numbers, names, etc.) to get individual students to mix the examples of the new patterns.
8. Question-answer drilling, in which the teacher gets one student to ask a question and another to answer until most students in the class have practiced asking and answering the new question form.
9. Correction, in which the teacher indicates by shaking his head, repeating the error, etc., that there is a mistake and invites the student or a different student to correct it. Where possible the teacher does not simply correct the mistake himself. He gets students to correct themselves so they will be encouraged to listen to each other carefully.

(Davies et al. 1975: 6–7)

Davies et al. then go on to discuss how follow-up reading and writing activities are to be carried out.

Conclusion

Procedures associated with Situational Language Teaching in the 1950s and 1960s were an extension and further development of well-established techniques advocated by proponents of the earlier Oral Approach in the British school of language teaching. The essential features of SLT are seen in the "P-P-P" lesson model that thousands of teachers who studied for the RSA/Cambridge Certificate in TEFL were required to master in the 1980s and early 1990s, with a lesson having three phases: Presentation (introduction of a new teaching item in context), Practice (controlled practice of the item), and Production (a freer practice phase) (Willis and Willis 1996). SLT provided the methodology of major methodology texts throughout the 1980s and beyond (e.g., Hubbard et al. 1983), and, as we noted, textbooks written according to the principles of Situational Language Teaching continue to be widely used in many parts of the world, particularly when materials are based on a grammatical syllabus. In the mid-1960s, however, the view of language, language learning, and language teaching underlying Situational Language Teaching was called into question. We discuss this reaction and how it led to Communicative Language Teaching in Chapter 14. But because the principles of Situational Language Teaching, with its strong emphasis on oral practice, grammar, and sentence patterns, conform to the intuitions of many language teachers and offer a practical methodology suited to countries where national EFL/ESL syllabuses continue to be grammatically based, it continues to be widely used, though not necessarily widely acknowledged.

Bibliography and further reading

Alexander, L. G. 1967. *New Concept English*. 4 vols. London: Longman.

Billows, F. L. 1961. *The Techniques of Language Teaching*. London: Longman.

Byrne, D. 1976. *Teaching Oral English*. London: Longman.

Coles, M., and B. Lord. 1975. *Access to English*. Oxford: Oxford University Press.

Commonwealth Office of Education. 1965. *Situational English*. London: Longman.

Davies, P., J. Roberts, and R. Rossner. 1975. *Situational Lesson Plans*. Mexico City: Macmillan.

Faucett, L., M. West, H. E. Palmer, and E. L. Thorndike. 1936. *The Interim Report on Vocabulary Selection for the Teaching of English as a Foreign Language*. London: P. S. King.

French, F. G. 1948–1950. *The Teaching of English Abroad*. 3 vols. Oxford: Oxford University Press.

Frisby, A. W. 1957. *Teaching English: Notes and Comments on Teaching English Overseas*. London: Longman.

Gatenby, E. V. 1944. *English as a Foreign Language*. London: Longman.

Gauntlett, J. O. 1957. *Teaching English as a Foreign Language*. London: Macmillan.

Gurrey, P. 1955. *Teaching English as a Foreign Language*. London: Longman.

Halliday, M. A. K., A. McIntosh, and P. Strevens. 1964. *The Linguistic Sciences and Language Teaching*. London: Longman.

Hartley, B., and P. Viney. 1978 (current edition 1999). *Streamline English*. Oxford: Oxford University Press.

Hodgson, F. M. 1955. *Learning Modern Languages*. London: Routledge and Kegan Paul.

Hornby, A. S. 1950. The situational approach in language teaching. A series of three articles in *English Language Teaching*. 4: 98–104, 121–128, 150–156.

Hornby, A. S. 1954. *A Guide to Patterns and Usage in English*. London: Oxford University Press.

Hornby, A. S. 1954–1956. *Oxford Progressive English Course for Adult Learners*. 3 vols. London: Oxford University Press.

Hornby, A. S., E. V. Gatenby, and H. Wakefield. 1953. *The Advanced Learner's Dictionary of Current English*. London: Oxford University Press.

Howatt, A. P. R. 1984. *A History of English Language Teaching*. Oxford: Oxford University Press.

Hubbard, P., H. Jones, B. Thornton, and R. Wheeler. 1983. *A Training Course for TEFL*. Oxford: Oxford University Press.

Jespersen, O. E. 1933. *Essentials of English Grammar*. London: Allen and Unwin.

Mennon, T. K. N., and M. S. Patel. 1957. *The Teaching of English as a Foreign Language*. Baroda, India: Acharya.

Morris, I. 1954. *The Art of Teaching English as a Living Language*. London: Macmillan.

O'Neill, R. 1973. *Kernel Lessons Plus*. London: Longman.

Palmer, H. E. 1917. *The Scientific Study and Teaching of Languages*. Reprinted: London: Oxford University Press, 1968.

Palmer, H. E. 1921. *Principles of Language Study*. New York: World Book Co.

Palmer, H. E. 1923. *The Oral Method of Teaching Languages*. Cambridge: Heffer.

Palmer, H. E. 1934. *Specimens of English Construction Patterns*. Tokyo: Department of Education.

Palmer, H. E. 1938. *Grammar of English Words*. London: Longman.

Palmer, H. E. 1940. *The Teaching of Oral English*. London: Longman.

Palmer, H. E., and F. G. Blandford. 1939. *A Grammar of Spoken English on a Strictly Phonetic Basis*. Cambridge: Heffer.

Pattison, B. 1952. *English Teaching in the World Today*. London: Evans.

Pattison, B. 1964. Modern methods of language teaching. *English Language Teaching* 19(1): 2–6.

Pittman, G. 1963. *Teaching Structural English*. Brisbane: Jacaranda.

Richards, J. C., B. Ho, and K. Giblin. 1996. Learning how to teach in the RSA Cert. In D. Freeman and J. Richards (eds.), *Teacher Learning in Language Teaching*. New York: Cambridge University Press. 242–259.

Situational English for Newcomers to Australia. Sydney: Longman.

West, M. (ed.). 1953a. *A General Service List of English Words*. London: Longman.

West, M. 1953b. *The Teaching of English: A Guide to the New Method Series.* London: Longman.

White, R. 1988. *The ELT Curriculum.* Oxford: Blackwell.

Willis, J., and D. Willis (eds.). 1996. *Challenge and Change in Language Teaching.* Oxford: Heinemann.

Zandvoort, R. W. 1945. *A Handbook of English Grammar.* Groningen: Wolters.

4 The Audiolingual Method

Background

The Coleman Report in 1929 recommended a reading-based approach to foreign language teaching for use in American schools and colleges (Chapter 1). This emphasized teaching the comprehension of texts. Teachers taught from books containing short reading passages in the foreign language, preceded by lists of vocabulary. Rapid silent reading was the goal, but in practice teachers often resorted to discussing the content of the passage in English. Those involved in the teaching of English as a second language in the United States between the two world wars used either a modified Direct Method approach, a reading-based approach, or a reading-oral approach (Darian 1972). Unlike the approach that was being developed by British applied linguists during the same period, there was little attempt to treat language content systematically. Sentence patterns and grammar were introduced at the whim of the textbook writer. There was no standardization of the vocabulary or grammar that was included. Neither was there a consensus on what grammar, sentence patterns, and vocabulary were most important for beginning, intermediate, or advanced learners.

But the entry of the United States into World War II had a significant effect on language teaching in America. To supply the U.S. government with personnel who were fluent in German, French, Italian, Chinese, Japanese, Malay, and other languages, and who could work as interpreters, code-room assistants, and translators, it was necessary to set up a special language training program. The government commissioned American universities to develop foreign language programs for military personnel. Thus the Army Specialized Training Program (ASTP) was established in 1942. Fifty-five American universities were involved in the program by the beginning of 1943.

The objective of the army programs was for students to attain conversational proficiency in a variety of foreign languages. Since this was not the goal of conventional foreign language courses in the United States, new approaches were necessary. Linguists, such as Leonard Bloomfield at Yale, had already developed training programs as part of their linguistic research that were designed to give linguists and anthropologists mastery of American Indian languages and other languages they were studying.

50

Textbooks did not exist for such languages. The technique Bloomfield and his colleagues used was sometimes known as the "informant method," since it used a native speaker of the language – the informant – who served as a source of phrases and vocabulary and who provided sentences for imitation, and a linguist, who supervised the learning experience. The linguist did not necessarily know the language but was trained in eliciting the basic structure of the language from the informant. Thus the students and the linguist were able to take part in guided conversation with the informant, and together they gradually learned how to speak the language, as well as to understand much of its basic grammar. Students in such courses studied 10 hours a day, 6 days a week. There were generally 15 hours of drill with native speakers and 20 to 30 hours of private study spread over two to three 6-week sessions. This was the system adopted by the army, and in small classes of mature and highly motivated students, excellent results were often achieved.

The Army Specialized Training Program lasted only about two years but attracted considerable attention in the popular press and in the academic community. For the next 10 years the "Army Method" and its suitability for use in regular language programs were discussed. But the linguists who developed the ASTP were not interested primarily in language teaching. The "methodology" of the Army Method, like the Direct Method, derived from the intensity of contact with the target language rather than from any well-developed methodological basis. It was a program innovative mainly in terms of the procedures used and the intensity of teaching rather than in terms of its underlying theory. However, it did convince a number of prominent linguists of the value of an intensive, oral-based approach to the learning of a foreign language.

Linguists and applied linguists during this period were becoming increasingly involved in the teaching of English as a foreign language. America had now emerged as a major international power. There was a growing demand for foreign expertise in the teaching of English. Thousands of foreign students entered the United States to study in universities, and many of these students required training in English before they could begin their studies. These factors led to the emergence of the American approach to ESL, which by the mid-1950s had become Audiolingualism.

In 1939, the University of Michigan developed the first English Language Institute in the United States; it specialized in the training of teachers of English as a foreign language and in teaching English as a second or foreign language. Charles Fries, director of the institute, was trained in structural linguistics, and he applied the principles of structural linguistics to language teaching. Fries and his colleagues rejected approaches such as those of the Direct Method, in which learners are exposed to the language, use it, and gradually absorb its grammatical patterns. For Fries, grammar, or "structure," was the starting point. The structure of the language was identified with its basic sentence patterns and grammatical structures. The language was taught by systematic attention to pronunciation and by intensive oral drilling of its basic sentence patterns. Pattern practice was a basic classroom technique. "It is these basic patterns that constitute the learner's task. They require drill, drill, and more drill, and only enough vocabulary to make such drills possible" (Hockett 1959).

Michigan was not the only university involved in developing courses and materials for teaching English. A number of other similar programs were established, some of the earliest being at Georgetown University and American University, Washington, D.C., and at the University of Texas, Austin. U.S. linguists were becoming increasingly active, both within the United States and abroad, in supervising programs for the teaching of English (Moulton 1961). In 1950, the American Council of Learned Societies, under contract to the U.S. State Department, was commissioned to develop textbooks for teaching English to speakers of a wide number of foreign languages. The format the linguists involved in this project followed was known as the "general form": A lesson began with work on pronunciation, morphology, and grammar, followed by drills and exercises. The guidelines were published as *Structural Notes and Corpus: A Basis for the Preparation of Materials to Teach English as a Foreign Language* (American Council of Learned Societies 1952). This became an influential document and together with the "general form" was used as a guide to developing English courses for speakers of ten different languages (the famous *Spoken Language* series), published between 1953 and 1956 (Moulton 1961).

In many ways the methodology used by U.S. linguists and language teaching experts during this period sounded similar to the British Oral Approach, although the two traditions developed independently. The American approach differed, however, in its strong alliance with American structural linguistics and its applied linguistic applications, particularly contrastive analysis. Fries set forth his principles in *Teaching and Learning English as a Foreign Language* (1945), in which the problems of learning a foreign language were attributed to the conflict of different structural systems (i.e., differences between the grammatical and phonological patterns of the native language and the target language). Contrastive analysis of the two languages would allow potential problems of interference to be predicted and addressed through carefully prepared teaching materials. Thus was born a major industry in American applied linguistics – systematic comparisons of English with other languages, with a view toward solving the fundamental problems of foreign language learning.

The approach developed by linguists at Michigan and other universities became known variously as the Oral Approach, the Aural-Oral Approach, and the Structural Approach. It advocated aural training first, then pronunciation training, followed by speaking, reading, and writing. Language was identified with speech, and speech was approached through structure. This approach influenced the way languages were taught in the United States throughout the 1950s. As an approach to the teaching of English as a foreign language the new orthodoxy was promoted through the University of Michigan's journal *Language Learning*. This was a period when expertise in linguistics was regarded as a necessary and sufficient foundation for expertise in language teaching. Not surprisingly, the classroom materials produced by Fries and linguists at Yale, Cornell, and elsewhere evidenced considerable linguistic analysis but very little pedagogy. They were widely used, however, and the applied linguistic principles on which they were based were thought to incorporate the most advanced scientific approach to language teaching. If there was any learning theory underlying the Aural-Oral materials, it was a commonsense application of the idea that practice makes perfect. There is no explicit reference to then-current learning theory in Fries's work. It was the incorporation of the linguistic principles of the Aural-Oral approach with state-of-the-art psychological learning theory in the mid-1950s that led to the method that came to be known as Audiolingualism.

The emergence of the Audiolingual Method resulted from the increased attention given to foreign language teaching in the United States toward the end of the 1950s. The need for a radical change and rethinking of foreign language teaching methodology (most of which was still linked to the Reading Method) was prompted by the launching of the first Russian satellite in 1957. The U.S. government acknowledged the need for a more intensive effort to teach foreign languages in order to prevent Americans from becoming isolated from scientific advances made in other countries. The National Defense Education Act (1958), among other measures, provided funds for the study and analysis of modern languages, for the development of teaching materials, and for the training of teachers. Teachers were encouraged to attend summer institutes to improve their knowledge of foreign languages and to learn the principles of linguistics and the new linguistically based teaching methods. Language teaching specialists set about developing a method that was applicable to conditions in U.S. colleges and university classrooms. They drew on the earlier experience of the army programs and the Aural-Oral or Structural Approach developed by Fries and his colleagues, adding insights taken from behaviorist psychology. This combination of structural linguistic theory, contrastive analysis, aural-oral procedures, and behaviorist psychology led to the Audiolingual Method. Audiolingualism (the term was coined by Professor Nelson Brooks in 1964) claimed to have transformed language teaching from an art into a science, which would enable learners to achieve mastery of a foreign language effectively and efficiently. The method was widely adopted for teaching foreign languages in North American colleges and universities. It provided the methodological foundation for materials for the teaching of foreign languages at the college and university level in the United States and Canada, and its principles formed the basis of such widely used series as the *Lado English Series* (Lado 1977) and *English 900* (English Language Services 1964). Although the method began to fall from favor in the late 1960s for reasons we shall discuss later, Audiolingualism and materials based on audiolingual principles continue to be used today. Let us examine the features of the Audiolingual Method at the levels of approach, design, and procedure.

Approach

Theory of language

The theory of language underlying Audiolingualism was derived from a view proposed by American linguists in the 1950s – a view that came to be known as *structural linguistics*. Linguistics had emerged as a flourishing academic discipline in the 1950s, and the structural theory of language constituted its backbone. Structural linguistics had developed in part as a reaction to traditional grammar. Traditional approaches to the study of language had linked the study of language to philosophy and to a mentalist approach to grammar. Grammar was considered a branch of logic, and the grammatical categories of Indo-European languages were thought to represent ideal categories in languages. Many nineteenth-century language scholars had viewed modern European languages as corruptions of classical grammar, and languages from other parts of the world were viewed as primitive and underdeveloped.

The reaction against traditional grammar was prompted by the movement toward positivism and empiricism, which Darwin's *On the Origin of Species* had helped promote, and by an increased interest in non-European languages on the part of scholars. A more practical interest in language study emerged. As linguists discovered new sound types and new patterns of linguistic invention and organization, a new interest in phonetics, phonology, morphology, and syntax developed. By the 1930s, the scientific approach to the study of language was thought to consist of collecting examples of what speakers said and analyzing them according to different levels of structural organization rather than according to categories of Latin grammar. A sophisticated methodology for collecting and analyzing data developed, which involved transcribing spoken utterances in a language phonetically and later working out the phonemic, morphological (stems, prefixes, suffixes, etc.), and syntactic (phrases, clauses, sentence types) systems underlying the grammar of the language. Language was viewed as a system of structurally related elements for the encoding of meaning, the elements being phonemes, morphemes, words, structures, and sentence types. The term *structural* referred to these characteristics: *(a)* Elements in a language were thought of as being linearly produced in a rule-governed (structured) way; *(b)* Language samples could be exhaustively described at any structural level of description (phonetic, phonemic, morphological, etc.); *(c)* Linguistic levels were thought of as systems within systems – that is, as being pyramidally structured; phonemic systems led to morphemic systems, and these in turn led to the higher-level systems of phrases, clauses, and sentences. Learning a language, it was assumed, entails mastering the elements or building blocks of the language and learning the rules by which these elements are combined, from phoneme to morpheme to word to phrase to sentence. The phonological system defines those sound elements that contrast meaningfully with one another in the language (phonemes), their phonetic realizations in specific environments (allophones), and their permissible sequences (phonotactics). The phonological and grammatical systems of the language constitute the organization of language and by implication the units of production and comprehension. The grammatical system consists of a listing of grammatical elements and rules for their linear combination into words, phrases, and sentences. Rule-ordered processes involve addition, deletion, and transposition of elements.

An important tenet of structural linguistics was that the primary medium of language is oral: Speech is language. Since many languages do not have a written form and we learn to speak before we learn to read or write, it was argued that language is "primarily what is spoken and only secondarily what is written" (Brooks 1964). Therefore, it was assumed that speech had a priority in language teaching. This was contrary to popular views of the relationship of the spoken and written forms of language, since it had been widely assumed that language existed principally as symbols written on paper, and that spoken language was an imperfect realization of the pure written version.

This scientific approach to language analysis appeared to offer the foundations for a scientific approach to language teaching. In 1961, the American linguist William Moulton, in a report prepared for the 9th International Congress of Linguists, proclaimed the linguistic principles on which language teaching methodology should be based: "Language is speech, not writing. . . . A language is a set of habits. . . . Teach the language, not about the language. . . . A language is what its native speakers say, not what someone thinks they ought to say. . . . Languages are different" (quoted in Rivers 1964: 5). But a method cannot be based simply on a theory of language. It also needs to refer to the psychology of learning and to learning theory. It is to this aspect of Audiolingualism that we now turn.

Theory of learning

The language teaching theoreticians and methodologists who developed Audiolingualism not only had a convincing and powerful theory of language to draw upon but they were also working in a period when a prominent school of American psychology – known as behavioral psychology – claimed to have tapped the secrets of all human learning, including language learning. Behaviorism, like structural linguistics, is another antimentalist, empirically based approach to the study of human behavior. To the behaviorist, the human being is an organism capable of a wide repertoire of behaviors. The occurrence of these behaviors is dependent on three crucial elements in learning: a *stimulus,* which serves to elicit behavior; a *response* triggered by a stimulus; and *reinforcement,* which serves to mark the response as being appropriate (or inappropriate) and encourages the repetition (or suppression) of the response in the future (see Skinner 1957; Brown 1980). A representation of this can be seen in Figure 4.1.

Reinforcement is a vital element in the learning process, because it increases the likelihood that the behavior will occur again and eventually become a habit. To apply this theory to language learning is to identify the organism as the foreign language learner, the behavior as verbal behavior, the stimulus as what is taught or presented of the foreign language, the response as the learner's reaction to the stimulus, and the reinforcement as the extrinsic approval and praise of the teacher or fellow students or the intrinsic self-satisfaction of target language use. Language mastery is represented as acquiring a set of appropriate language stimulus-response chains.

The descriptive practices of structural linguists suggested a number of hypotheses about language learning, and hence about language teaching as well. For example, since linguists normally described languages beginning with the phonological level and finishing with the sentence level, it was assumed that this was also the appropriate sequence for learning and teaching. Since speech was now held to be primary and writing secondary, it was assumed that language teaching should focus on mastery of speech and that writing or even written prompts should be withheld until reasonably late in the language learning process. Since the structure is what is important and unique about a language, early practice should focus on mastery of phonological and grammatical structures rather than on mastery of vocabulary.

Out of these various influences emerged a number of learning principles, which became the psychological foundations of Audiolingualism

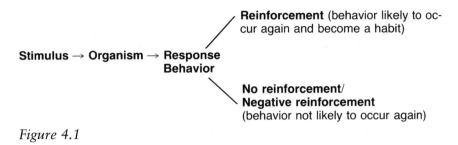

Figure 4.1

and came to shape its methodological practices. Among the more central are the following:

1. Foreign language learning is basically a process of mechanical habit formation. Good habits are formed by giving correct responses rather than by making mistakes. By memorizing dialogues and performing pattern drills the chances of producing mistakes are minimized. Language is verbal behavior – that is, the automatic production and comprehension of utterances – and can be learned by inducing the students to do likewise.
2. Language skills are learned more effectively if the items to be learned in the target language are presented in spoken form before they are seen in written form. Aural-oral training is needed to provide the foundation for the development of other language skills.
3. Analogy provides a better foundation for language learning than analysis. Analogy involves the processes of generalization and discrimination. Explanations of rules are therefore not given until students have practiced a pattern in a variety of contexts and are thought to have acquired a perception of the analogies involved. Drills can enable learners to form correct analogies. Hence the approach to the teaching of grammar is essentially inductive rather than deductive.
4. The meanings that the words of a language have for the native speaker can be learned only in a linguistic and cultural context and not in isolation. Teaching a language thus involves teaching aspects of the cultural system of the people who speak the language. (Rivers 1964: 19–22)

In advocating these principles, proponents of Audiolingualism were drawing on the theory of a well-developed school of American psychology – behaviorism. The prominent Harvard behaviorist B. F. Skinner had elaborated a theory of learning applicable to language learning in his influential book *Verbal Behavior* (1957), in which he stated, "We have no reason to assume . . . that verbal behavior differs in any fundamental respect from non-verbal behavior, or that any new principles must be invoked to account for it" (1957: 10). Armed with a powerful theory of the nature of language and of language learning, audiolingualists could now turn to the design of language teaching courses and materials.

Design

Audiolingualists demanded a complete reorientation of the foreign language curriculum. Like the nineteenth-century reformers, they advocated a return to speech-based instruction with the primary objective of oral proficiency, and dismissed the study of grammar or literature as the goal of foreign language teaching. "A radical transformation is called for, a new orientation of procedures is demanded, and a thorough house cleaning of methods, materials, texts and tests is unavoidable" (Brooks 1964: 50).

Objectives

Brooks distinguishes between short-range and long-range objectives of an audiolingual program. Short-range objectives include training in listening comprehension, accurate pronunciation, recognition of speech symbols as graphic signs on the printed page, and ability to reproduce these symbols in writing (Brooks 1964: 111). "These immediate objectives imply three others: first, control of the structures of sound, form, and order in the new language; second, acquaintance with vocabulary items that bring content into these structures; and third, meaning, in terms of the significance these verbal symbols have for those who speak the language natively" (Brooks 1964: 113). Long-range objectives "must be language as the native speaker uses it. . . . There must be some knowledge of a second language as it is possessed by a true bilingualist" (Brooks 1964: 107).

In practice this means that the focus in the early stages is on oral skills, with gradual links to other skills as learning develops. Oral proficiency is equated with accurate pronunciation and grammar and the ability to respond quickly and accurately in speech situations. The teaching of listening comprehension, pronunciation, grammar, and vocabulary are all related to development of oral fluency. Reading and writing skills may be taught, but they are dependent on prior oral skills. Language is primarily speech in audiolingual theory, but speaking skills are themselves dependent on the ability to accurately perceive and produce the major phonological features of the target language, fluency in the use of the key grammatical patterns in the language, and knowledge of sufficient vocabulary to use with these patterns.

The syllabus

Audiolingualism is a linguistic, or structure-based, approach to language teaching. The starting point is a linguistic syllabus, which contains the key items of phonology, morphology, and syntax of the language arranged according to their order of presentation. These may have been derived in part from a *contrastive analysis* of the differences between the native language and the target language, since these differences are thought to be the cause of the major difficulties the learner will encounter. In addition, a lexical syllabus of basic vocabulary items is usually specified in advance. In *Foundations for English Teaching* (Fries and Fries 1961), for example, a corpus of structural and lexical items graded into three levels is proposed, together with suggestions as to the situations that could be used to contextualize them.

The language skills are taught in the order of listening, speaking, reading, and writing. Listening is viewed largely as training in aural discrimination of basic sound patterns. The language may be presented entirely orally at first; written representations are usually withheld from learners in early stages.

The learner's activities must at first be confined to the audiolingual and gestural-visual bands of language behavior. . . .

Recognition and discrimination are followed by imitation, repetition and memorization. Only when he is thoroughly familiar with sounds, arrangements, and forms does he center his attention on enlarging his vocabulary. . . . Throughout he concentrates upon gaining accuracy before striving for fluency. (Brooks 1964: 50)

When reading and writing are introduced, students are taught to read and write what they have already learned to say orally. An attempt is made to minimize the possibilities for making mistakes in both speaking and writing by using a tightly structured approach to the presentation of new language items. At more advanced levels, more complex reading and writing tasks may be introduced.

Types of learning and teaching activities

Dialogues and drills form the basis of audiolingual classroom practices. Dialogues provide the means of contextualizing key structures and illustrate situations in which structures might be used as well as some cultural aspects of the target language. Dialogues are used for repetition and memorization. Correct pronunciation, stress, rhythm, and intonation are emphasized. After a dialogue has been presented and memorized, specific grammatical patterns in the dialogue are selected and become the focus of various kinds of drill and pattern-practice exercises.

The use of drills and pattern practice is a distinctive feature of the Audiolingual Method. Various kinds of drills are used. Brooks (1964: 156–61) includes the following:

1. *Repetition.* The student repeats an utterance aloud as soon as he has heard it. He does this without looking at a printed text. The utterance must be brief enough to be retained by the ear. Sound is as important as form and order.

    EXAMPLE
    This is the seventh month. –This is the seventh month.
    After a student has repeated an utterance, he may repeat it again and add a few words, then repeat that whole utterance and add more words.

    EXAMPLES
    I used to know him. –I used to know him.
    I used to know him *years ago.* –I used to know him *years ago when we were in school. . . .*

2. *Inflection.* One word in an utterance appears in another form when repeated.

    EXAMPLES
    I bought the *ticket.* –I bought the *tickets.*
    He bought the candy. –*She* bought the candy.
    I called the young *man.* –I called the young *men. . . .*

3. *Replacement.* One word in an utterance is replaced by another.

    EXAMPLES
    He bought *this house* cheap. –He bought *it* cheap.
    Helen left early. –*She* left early.
    They gave their *boss* a watch. –They gave *him* a watch. . . .

4. *Restatement.* The student rephrases an utterance and addresses it to someone else, according to instructions.

    EXAMPLES
    Tell him to wait for you. –Wait for me.
    Ask her how old she is. –How old are you?
    Ask John when he began. –John, when did you begin? . . .

5. *Completion.* The student hears an utterance that is complete except for one word, then repeats the utterance in completed form.

    EXAMPLES
    I'll go my way and you go. . . . –I'll go my way and you go *yours.*
    We all have . . . own troubles. –We all have *our* own troubles. . . .

6. *Transposition*. A change in word order is necessary when a word is added.

EXAMPLES
I'm hungry. (so). –So *am* I.
I'll never do it again. (neither). –Neither *will* I. . . .

7. *Expansion*. When a word is added it takes a certain place in the sequence.

EXAMPLES
I know him. (hardly). –I *hardly* know him.
I know him. (well). –I know him *well*. . . .

8. *Contraction*. A single word stands for a phrase or clause.

EXAMPLES
Put your hand *on the table*. –Put your hand *there*.
They believe *that the earth is flat*. –They believe *it*. . . .

9. *Transformation*. A sentence is transformed by being made negative or interrogative or through changes in tense, mood, voice, aspect, or modality.

EXAMPLES
He knows my address.
He doesn't know my address.
Does he know my address?
He used to know my address.
If he had known my address.

10. *Integration*. Two separate utterances are integrated into one.

EXAMPLES
They must be honest. This is important. –It is important that they be honest.
I know that man. He is looking for you. –I know the man who is looking for you. . . .

11. *Rejoinder*. The student makes an appropriate rejoinder to a given utterance. He is told in advance to respond in one of the following ways:

Be polite.
Answer the question.
Agree.
Agree emphatically.
Express surprise.
Express regret.
Disagree.

Disagree emphatically.
Question what is said.
Fail to understand.

BE POLITE.   EXAMPLES
Thank you. –You're welcome.
May I take one? –Certainly.

ANSWER THE QUESTION.   EXAMPLES
What is your name? –My name is Smith.
Where did it happen? –In the middle of the street.

AGREE.   EXAMPLES
He's following us. –I think you're right.
This is good coffee. –It's very good. . . .

12. *Restoration.* The student is given a sequence of words that have been culled from a sentence but still bear its basic meaning. He uses these words with a minimum of changes and additions to restore the sentence to its original form. He may be told whether the time is present, past, or future.

EXAMPLES
students/waiting/bus –The students are waiting for the bus.
boys/build/house/tree –The boys built a house in a tree. . . .

Learner roles

Learners are viewed as organisms that can be directed by skilled training techniques to produce correct responses. In accordance with behaviorist learning theory, teaching focuses on the external manifestations of learning rather than on the internal processes. Learners play a reactive role by responding to stimuli, and thus have little control over the content, pace, or style of learning. They are not encouraged to initiate interaction, because this may lead to mistakes. The fact that in the early stages learners do not always understand the meaning of what they are repeating is not perceived as a drawback, for by listening to the teacher, imitating accurately, and responding to and performing controlled tasks, they are learning a new form of verbal behavior.

Teacher roles

In Audiolingualism, as in Situational Language Teaching, the teacher's role is central and active; it is a teacher-dominated method. The teacher models the target language, controls the direction and pace of learning, and monitors and corrects the learners' performance. The teacher must keep the learners attentive by varying drills and tasks and choosing relevant situations to practice structures. Language learning is seen to result from active verbal interaction between the teacher and the learners. Failure to learn results only from the improper application of the method, for example, from the teacher not providing sufficient practice or from the learner not memorizing the essential patterns and structures; but the method itself is never to blame. Brooks argues that the teacher must be trained to do the following:

Introduce, sustain, and harmonize the learning of the four skills in this order: hearing, speaking, reading and writing.
Use – and not use – English in the language classroom.
Model the various types of language behavior that the student is to learn.
Teach spoken language in dialogue form.
Direct choral response by all or parts of the class.
Teach the use of structure through pattern practice.
Guide the student in choosing and learning vocabulary.
Show how words relate to meaning in the target language.
Get the individual student to talk.
Reward trials by the student in such a way that learning is reinforced.
Teach a short story and other literary forms.
Establish and maintain a cultural island.
Formalize on the first day the rules according to which the language class is to be conducted, and enforce them.

(Brooks 1964: 143)

The role of instructional materials

Instructional materials in the Audiolingual Method assist the teacher to develop language mastery in the learner. They are primarily teacher-oriented. A student textbook is often not used in the elementary phases of a course where students are primarily listening, repeating, and responding. At this stage in learning, exposure to the printed word may not be considered desirable, because it distracts attention from the aural input. The teacher, however, will have access to a teacher's book that contains the structured sequence of lessons to be followed and the dialogues, drills, and other practice activities. When textbooks and printed materials are introduced to the student, they provide the texts of dialogues and cues needed for drills and exercises.

Tape recorders and audiovisual equipment often have central roles in an audiolingual course. If the teacher is not a native speaker of the target language, the tape recorder provides accurate models for dialogues and drills. A language laboratory may also be considered essential. It provides the opportunity for further drill work and to receive controlled error-free practice of basic structures. It also adds variety by providing an alternative to classroom practice. A taped lesson may first present a dialogue for listening practice, allow for the student to repeat the sentences in the dialogue line by line, and provide follow-up fluency drills on grammar or pronunciation.

Procedure

Since Audiolingualism is primarily an oral approach to language teaching, it is not surprising that the process of teaching involves extensive oral instruction. The focus of instruction is on immediate and accurate speech; there is little provision for grammatical explanation or talking about the language. As far as possible, the target language is used as the medium of instruction, and translation or use of the native language is discouraged. Classes of ten or fewer are considered optimal, although larger classes are often the norm. Brooks lists the following procedures that the teacher should adopt in using the Audiolingual Method:

The modeling of all learnings by the teacher.

The subordination of the mother tongue to the second language by rendering English inactive while the new language is being learned.

The early and continued training of the ear and tongue without recourse to graphic symbols.

The learning of structure through the practice of patterns of sound, order, and form, rather than by explanation.

The gradual substitution of graphic symbols for sounds after sounds are thoroughly known.

The summarizing of the main principles of structure for the student's use when the structures are already familiar, especially when they differ from those of the mother tongue. . . .

The shortening of the time span between a performance and the pronouncement of its rightness or wrongness, without interrupting the response. This enhances the factor of reinforcement in learning.

The minimizing of vocabulary until all common structures have been learned.

The study of vocabulary only in context.

Sustained practice in the use of the language only in the molecular form of speaker-hearer-situation.

Practice in translation only as a literary exercise at an advanced level.

(Brooks 1964: 142)

In a typical audiolingual lesson, the following procedures would be observed:

1. Students first hear a model dialogue (either read by the teacher or on tape) containing the key structures that are the focus of the lesson. They repeat each line of the dialogue, individually and in chorus. The teacher pays attention to pronunciation, intonation, and fluency. Correction of mistakes of pronunciation or grammar is direct and immediate. The dialogue is memorized gradually, line by line. A line may be broken down into several phrases if necessary. The dialogue is read

aloud in chorus, one half saying one speaker's part and the other half responding. The students do not consult their book throughout this phase.

2. The dialogue is adapted to the students' interest or situation, through changing certain key words or phrases. This is acted out by the students.
3. Certain key structures from the dialogue are selected and used as the basis for pattern drills of different kinds. These are first practiced in chorus and then individually. Some grammatical explanation may be offered at this point, but this is kept to an absolute minimum.
4. The students may refer to their textbook, and follow-up reading, writing, or vocabulary activities based on the dialogue may be introduced. At the beginning level, writing is purely imitative and consists of little more than copying out sentences that have been practiced. As proficiency increases, students may write out variations of structural items they have practiced or write short compositions on given topics with the help of framing questions, which will guide their use of the language.
5. Follow-up activities may take place in the language laboratory, where further dialogue and drill work is carried out.

The decline of Audiolingualism

Audiolingualism reached its period of most widespread use in the 1960s and was applied both to the teaching of foreign languages in the United States and to the teaching of English as a second or foreign language. It led to such widely used courses as *English 900* and the *Lado English Series,* as well as to texts for teaching the major European languages. But then came criticism on two fronts. On the one hand, the theoretical foundations of Audiolingualism were attacked as being unsound in terms of both language theory and learning theory. On the other hand, practitioners found that the practical results fell short of expectations. Students were often found to be unable to transfer skills acquired through Audiolingualism to real communication outside the classroom, and many found the experience of studying through audiolingual procedures to be boring and unsatisfying.

The theoretical attack on audiolingual beliefs resulted from changes in American linguistic theory in the 1960s. The MIT linguist Noam Chomsky rejected the structuralist approach to language description as well as the behaviorist theory of language learning. "Language is not a habit structure. Ordinary linguistic behavior characteristically involves innovation, formation of new sentences and patterns in accordance with rules of great abstractness and intricacy" (Chomsky 1966: 153).

Chomsky's theory of transformational grammar proposed that the fundamental properties of language derive from innate aspects of the mind and from how humans process experience through language. His theories were to revolutionize American linguistics and focus the attention of linguists and psychologists on the mental properties people bring to bear on language use and language learning. Chomsky also proposed an alternative theory of language learning to that of the behaviorists. Behaviorism regarded language learning as similar in principle to any other kind of learning. It was subject to the same laws of stimulus and response, reinforcement and association. Chomsky argued that such a learning theory could not possibly serve as a model of how humans learn language, since much of human language use is not imitated behavior but is created anew from underlying knowledge of abstract rules. Sentences are not learned by imitation and repetition but "generated" from the learner's underlying "competence."

Suddenly the whole audiolingual paradigm was called into question: pattern practice, drilling, memorization. These might lead to language-like behaviors, but they were not resulting in competence. This created a crisis in American language teaching circles from which a full recovery has not yet been made. Temporary relief was offered in the form of a theory derived in part from Chomsky – cognitive code learning. In 1966, John B. Carroll, a psychologist who had taken a close interest in foreign language teaching, wrote:

The audio-lingual habit theory which is so prevalent in American foreign language teaching was, perhaps fifteen years ago, in step with the state of psychological thinking of that time, but it is no longer abreast of recent developments. It is ripe for major revision, particularly in the direction of joining it with some of the better elements of the cognitive-code learning theory. (Carroll 1966a: 105)

This referred to a view of learning that allowed for a conscious focus on grammar and that acknowledged the role of abstract mental processes in learning rather than defining learning simply in terms of habit formation. Practice activities should involve meaningful learning and language use. Learners should be encouraged to use their innate and creative abilities to derive and make explicit the underlying grammatical rules of the language. For a time in the early 1970s there was a considerable interest in the implication of the cognitive-code theory for language teaching (e.g., see Jakobovits 1970; Lugton 1971). But no clear-cut methodological guidelines emerged, nor did any particular method incorporating this view of learning. The term *cognitive code* is still sometimes invoked to refer to any conscious attempt to organize materials around a grammatical syllabus while allowing for meaningful practice and use of language. The lack of an alternative to Audiolingualism led in the 1970s and 1980s to a period of adaptation, innovation, experimentation, and some confusion. Several alternative method proposals appeared in the 1970s that made no claims to any links with mainstream language teaching and second language acquisition research. These included Total Physical Response, the Silent Way, and Counseling-Learning. These methods attracted some interest at first but have not continued to attract significant levels of acceptance. Other proposals since then have reflected developments in general education and other fields outside the second language teaching community, such as Whole Language, Multiple Intelligences, Neurolinguistic Programming, Competency-Based Language Teaching, and Cooperative Language Learning. Mainstream language teaching since the 1980s, however, has generally drawn on contemporary theories of language and second language acquisition as a basis for teaching proposals. The Lexical Approach, Communicative Language Teaching, the Natural Approach, Content-Based Teaching, and Task-Based Teaching are representative of this last group. The concern for grammatical accuracy that was a focus of Audiolingualism has not disappeared, however, and continues to provide a challenge for contemporary applied linguistics (see Doughty and Williams 1998).

Conclusion

Audiolingualism holds that language learning is like other forms of learning. Since language is a formal, rule-governed system, it can be formally organized to maximize teaching and learning efficiency. Audiolingualism thus stresses the mechanistic aspects of language learning and language use.

There are many similarities between Situational Language Teaching and Audiolingualism. The order in which the language skills are introduced, and the focus on accuracy through drill and practice in the basic structures and sentence patterns of the target language, might suggest that these methods drew from each other. In fact, however, Situational Language Teaching was a development of the earlier Direct Method (see Chapter 1) and does not have the strong ties to linguistics and behavioral psychology that characterize Audiolingualism. The similarities of the two methods reflect similar views about the nature of language and of language learning, though these views were in fact developed from quite different traditions.

Bibliography and further reading

Allen, V. F. 1965. *On Teaching English to Speakers of Other Languages.* Champaign, Ill.: National Council of Teachers of English.

American Council of Learned Societies. 1952. *Structural Notes and Corpus: A Basis for the Preparation of Materials to Teach English as a Foreign Language.* Washington, D.C.: American Council of Learned Societies.

Bloch, B., and G. Trager. 1942. *Outline of Linguistic Analysis.* Baltimore: Linguistic Society of America.

Bloomfield, L. 1933. *Language.* New York: Holt.

Brooks, N. 1964. *Language and Language Learning: Theory and Practice.* 2nd ed. New York: Harcourt Brace.

Brown, H.D. 1980. *Principles of Language Learning and Teaching.* Englewood Cliffs, N.J.: Prentice Hall.

Carroll, J. B. 1953. *The Study of Language: A Surveyor of Linguistics and Related Disciplines in America.* Cambridge: Harvard University Press.

Carroll, J. B. 1966a. The contributions of psychological theory and educational research to the teaching of foreign languages. In A. Valdman (ed.), *Trends in Language Teaching.* New York: McGraw-Hill. 93–106.

Carroll, J. B. 1966b. Research in foreign language teaching: The last five years. In R. G. Mead Jr. (ed.), *Language Teaching: Broader Contexts.* Northeast Conference Reports on the Teaching of Foreign Languages: Reports of the Working Committees. New York: MLA Materials Center. 12–42.

Chastain, K. 1969. The audio-lingual habit theory versus the cognitive code learning theory: Some theoretical considerations. *International Review of Applied Linguistics* 7: 79–106.

Chastain, K. 1971. *The Development of Modern Language Skills: Theory to Practice.* Chicago: Rand McNally.

Chomsky, N. 1957. *Syntactic Structures.* The Hague: Mouton.

Chomsky, N. 1959. A review of B. F. Skinner's *Verbal Behavior. Language* 35(1): 26–58.

Chomsky, N. 1965. *Aspects of the Theory of Syntax.* Cambridge: MIT Press.

Chomsky, N. 1966. Linguistic theory. Reprinted in J. P. B. Allen and P. Van Buren (eds.), *Chomsky: Selected Readings.* London: Oxford University Press. 152–159.

Darian, S. G. 1972. *English as a Foreign Language: History, Development, and Methods of Teaching.* Norman: University of Oklahoma Press.

Doughty, C., and J. Williams (eds.). 1998. *Focus on Form in Classroom Second Language Acquisitions.* Cambridge: Cambridge University Press.

English Language Services. 1964. *English 900.* New York: Collier Macmillan.

Fries, C. C. 1945. *Teaching and Learning English as a Foreign Language.* Ann Arbor: University of Michigan Press.

Fries, C. C., and A. C. Fries. 1961. *Foundations for English Teaching.* Tokyo: Kenkyusha.

Gagne, R. M. 1962. Military training and principles of learning. *American Psychologist* 17(2): 83–91.

Hilgard, E. R. 1975. *Theories of Learning.* 2nd ed. New York: Appleton-Century-Crofts.

Hockett, C. F. 1958. *A Course in Modern Linguistics.* New York: Macmillan.

Hockett, C. F. 1959. The objectives and process of language teaching. Reprinted in D. Byrne (ed.), *English Teaching Extracts.* London: Longman, 1969.

Hughes, J. P. 1968. *Linguistics and Language Teaching.* New York: Random House.

Jakobovits, L. A. 1970. *Foreign Language Learning: A Psycholinguistic Analysis of the Issues.* Rowley, Mass.: Newbury House.

Lado, R. 1957. *Linguistics across Cultures: Applied Linguistics for Language Teachers.* Ann Arbor: University of Michigan Press.

Lado, R. 1961. *Language Testing.* London: Longman.

Lado, R. 1977. *Lado English Series.* 7 vols. New York: Regents.

Lugton, R. (ed.). 1971. *Toward a Cognitive Approach to Second Language Acquisition.* Philadelphia: Center for Curriculum Development.

Matthew, R. J. 1947. *Language and Area Studies in the Armed Services: Their Future and Significance.* Washington, D.C.: American Council on Education.

Modern Language Association. 1962. *Reports of Surveys and Studies in the Teaching of Modern Foreign Languages.* New York: Modern Language Teaching Association.

Moulton, W. G. 1961. Linguistics and language teaching in the United States: 1940–1960. In C. Mohrmann, A. Sommerfelt, and J. Whatmough (eds.), *Trends in European and American Linguistics, 1930–1960.* Utrecht: Spectrum. 82–109.

Moulton, W. G. 1963. What is structural drill? *International Journal of American Linguistics* 29(2, pt. 3): 3–15.

Moulton, W. 1966. *A Linguistic Guide to Language Learning.* New York: Modern Language Association.

Parker, W. 1962. *The National Interest and Foreign Languages.* Washington, D.C.: Department of State.

Rivers, W. M. 1964. *The Psychologist and the Foreign Language Teacher.* Chicago: University of Chicago Press.

Rivers, W. M. 1981. *Teaching Foreign Language Skills.* Chicago: University of Chicago Press.

Skinner, B. F. 1957. *Verbal Behavior.* New York: Appleton-Century-Crofts.

Smith, H. L. 1956. *Linguistics Science and the Teaching of English.* Cambridge: Harvard University Press.

Stack, E. 1969. *The Language Laboratory and Modern Language Teaching.* New York: Oxford University Press.

Stern, H. H. 1983. *Fundamental Concepts of Language Teaching.* Oxford: Oxford University Press.

Tarvin, W., and Al Arishi. A. 1990. Literature in EFL: Communicative alternatives to audiolingual assumptions. *Journal of Readings* 34(1): 30–36.

United States Office of Education. 1963. *The Language Development Program.* Washington, D.C.: U.S. Government Printing Office.

Zimmerman, C. B. 1997. Historical trends in second language vocabulary instruction. In J. Coady and T. Huckin (eds.), *Second Language Vocabulary Acquisition.* Cambridge: Cambridge University Press.

II *Alternative approaches and methods*

The period from the 1970s through the 1980s witnessed a major paradigm shift in language teaching. The quest for alternatives to grammar-based approaches and methods led in several different directions. Mainstream language teaching embraced the growing interest in communicative approaches to language teaching. The communicative movement sought to move the focus away from grammar as the core component of language, to a different view of language, of language learning, of teachers, and of learners, one that focused on language as communication and on making the classroom an environment for authentic communication. This "communicative movement" and related approaches are discussed in Part III. However, other directions for language teaching also appeared during this period, and these are the focus of Part II.

Whereas Audiolingualism and Situational Language Teaching were mainstream teaching methods developed by linguists and applied linguists, the approaches and methods described in this section were either developed outside of mainstream language teaching or represent an application in language teaching of educational principles developed elsewhere. The former case is represented by such innovative methods of the 1970s as Total Physical Reponse, Silent Way, Counseling Learning, Suggestopedia, and more recently Neurolinguistic Programming and Multiple Intelligences. Rather than starting from a theory of language and drawing on research and theory in applied linguistics, these methods are developed around particular theories of learners and learning, sometimes the theories of a single theorizer or educator. These methods are consequently relatively underdeveloped in the domain of language theory, and the learning principles they reflect are generally different from theories found in second language acquisition textbooks. One exception is the Lexical Approach, which is based on an alternative syllabus model to that found in grammar-based methodologies, one that gives priority to vocabulary and lexical phrases as the building blocks of communicative competence. A different case is represented by Whole Language and Competency-Based Instruction. These are movements that emerged within mainstream education and have later been applied and extended to second and foreign language teaching.

Alternative approaches and methods of the 1970s and 1980s have had a somewhat varied history. Although Total Physical Response, Silent

71

Way, Counseling-Learning, and Suggestopedia did not succeed in attracting the support of mainstream language teaching, each can be seen as stressing important dimensions of the teaching–learning process. They can be seen as offering particular insights that have attracted the attention and/or allegiance of some teachers and educators, but they have each seen their popularity rise and wane since the 1970s. Today, in most places, they are of little more than historical interest. The fate of others, such as the Lexical Approach, Whole Language, Neurolinguistic Programming, and Multiple Intelligences, has yet to be fully determined. Because of the limited influence of most of the approaches and methods described here and because many of them have a relatively slight literature, we have generally provided less detailed description than for the approaches and methods described in Parts I and III. Competency-Based Instruction, however, has a different status, since it is used as the framework for the design of national curricula in English as well as other subjects in some countries.

5 Total Physical Response

Background

Total Physical Response (TPR) is a language teaching method built around the coordination of speech and action; it attempts to teach language through physical (motor) activity. Developed by James Asher, a professor of psychology at San Jose State University, California, it draws on several traditions, including developmental psychology, learning theory, and humanistic pedagogy, as well as on language teaching procedures proposed by Harold and Dorothy Palmer in 1925. In a developmental sense, Asher sees successful adult second language learning as a parallel process to child first language acquisition. He claims that speech directed to young children consists primarily of commands, which children respond to physically before they begin to produce verbal responses. Asher feels that adults should recapitulate the processes by which children acquire their native language.

Asher shares with the school of humanistic psychology a concern for the role of affective (emotional) factors in language learning. A method that is undemanding in terms of linguistic production and that involves gamelike movements reduces learner stress, he believes, and creates a positive mood in the learner, which facilitates learning.

Approach: Theory of language and learning

TPR reflects a grammar-based view of language. Asher states that "most of the grammatical structure of the target language and hundreds of vocabulary items can be learned from the skillful use of the imperative by the instructor" (1977: 4). He views the verb, and particularly the verb in the imperative, as the central linguistic motif around which language use and learning are organized.

Asher sees a stimulus-response view as providing the learning theory underlying language teaching pedagogy. TPR can also be linked to the "trace theory" of memory in psychology (e.g., Katona 1940), which holds that the more often or the more intensively a memory connection is traced, the stronger the memory association will be and the more likely it will be recalled. Retracing can be done verbally (e.g., by rote repetition)

73

and/or in association with motor activity. Combined tracing activities, such as verbal rehearsal accompanied by motor activity, hence increase the possibility of successful recall.

In addition, Asher has elaborated an account of what he feels facilitates or inhibits foreign language learning. For this dimension of his learning theory he draws on three rather influential learning hypotheses:

1. There exists a specific innate bio-program for language learning, which defines an optimal path for first and second language development.
2. Brain lateralization defines different learning functions in the left- and right-brain hemispheres.
3. Stress (an affective filter) intervenes between the act of learning and what is to be learned; the lower the stress, the greater the learning.

Let us consider how Asher views each of these in turn.

The bio-program

Asher's Total Physical Response is a "Natural Method" (see Chapter 1), inasmuch as Asher sees first and second language learning as parallel processes. Asher sees three processes as central:

1. Children develop listening competence before they develop the ability to speak. At the early stages of first language acquisition, they can understand complex utterances that they cannot spontaneously produce or imitate.
2. Children's ability in listening comprehension is acquired because children are required to respond physically to spoken language in the form of parental commands.
3. Once a foundation in listening comprehension has been established, speech evolves naturally and effortlessly out of it.

Parallel to the processes of first language learning, the foreign language learner should first internalize a "cognitive map" of the target language through listening exercises. Listening should be accompanied by physical movement. Speech and other productive skills should come later. Asher bases these assumptions on his belief in the existence in the human brain of a bio-program for language, which defines an optimal order for first and second language learning.

A reasonable hypothesis is that the brain and nervous system are biologically programmed to acquire language . . . in a particular sequence and in a particular mode. The sequence is listening before speaking and the mode is to synchronize language with the individual's body. (Asher 1977: 4)

Brain lateralization

Asher sees Total Physical Response as directed to right-brain learning, whereas most second language teaching methods are directed to left-brain learning. Drawing on work by Jean Piaget, Asher holds that the child language learner acquires language through motor movement – a right-hemisphere activity. Right-hemisphere activities must occur before the left hemisphere can process language for production.

Similarly, the adult should proceed to language mastery through right-hemisphere motor activities, while the left hemisphere watches and learns. When a sufficient amount of right-hemisphere learning has taken place, the left hemisphere will be triggered to produce language and to initiate other, more abstract language processes.

Reduction of stress

An important condition for successful language learning is the absence of stress. First language acquisition takes place in a stress-free environment, according to Asher, whereas the adult language learning environment often causes considerable stress and anxiety. The key to stress-free learning is to tap into the natural bio-program for language development and thus to recapture the relaxed and pleasurable experiences that accompany first language learning. By focusing on meaning interpreted through movement, rather than on language forms studied in the abstract, the learner is said to be liberated from self-conscious and stressful situations and is able to devote full energy to learning.

Design: Objectives, syllabus, learning activities, roles of learners, teachers, and materials

The general objectives of Total Physical Response are to teach oral proficiency at a beginning level. Comprehension is a means to an end, and the ultimate aim is to teach basic speaking skills. A TPR course aims to produce learners who are capable of an uninhibited communication that is intelligible to a native speaker. Specific instructional objectives are not elaborated, for these will depend on the particular needs of the learners. Whatever goals are set, however, must be attainable through the use of action-based drills in the imperative form.

The type of syllabus Asher uses can be inferred from an analysis of the exercise types employed in TPR classes. This analysis reveals the use of a sentence-based syllabus, with grammatical and lexical criteria being primary in selecting teaching items. Unlike methods that operate from a grammar-based or structural view of the core elements of language, Total

Physical Response requires initial attention to meaning rather than to the form of items. Grammar is thus taught inductively.

Asher also suggests that a fixed number of items be introduced at a time, to facilitate ease of differentiation and assimilation. "In an hour, it is possible for students to assimilate 12 to 36 new lexical items depending upon the size of the group and the stage of training" (Asher 1977: 42). A course designed around Total Physical Response principles, however, would not be expected to follow a TPR syllabus exclusively.

Imperative drills are the major classroom activity in Total Physical Response. They are typically used to elicit physical actions and activity on the part of the learners. Conversational dialogues are delayed until after about 120 hours of instruction. Other class activities include role plays and slide presentations. Role plays center on everyday situations, such as at the restaurant, supermarket, or gas station.

Learners in Total Physical Response have the primary roles of listener and performer. They listen attentively and respond physically to commands given by the teacher. Learners are also expected to recognize and respond to novel combinations of previously taught items. They are required to produce novel combinations of their own. Learners monitor and evaluate their own progress. They are encouraged to speak when they feel ready to speak – that is, when a sufficient basis in the language has been internalized. The teacher plays an active and direct role in Total Physical Response. It is the teacher who decides what to teach, who models and presents the new materials, and who selects supporting materials for classroom use. Asher recommends detailed lesson plans: "It is wise to write out the exact utterances you will be using and especially the novel commands because the action is so fast-moving there is usually not time for you to create spontaneously" (1977: 47).

Asher stresses, however, that the teacher's role is not so much to teach as to provide opportunities for learning. The teacher has the responsibility of providing the best kind of exposure to language so that the learner can internalize the basic rules of the target language. Thus the teacher controls the language input the learners receive, providing the raw material for the "cognitive map" that the learners will construct in their own minds. The teacher should also allow speaking abilities to develop in learners at the learners' own natural pace.

In giving feedback to learners, the teacher should follow the example of parents giving feedback to their children. At first, parents correct very little, but as the child grows older, parents are said to tolerate fewer mistakes in speech. Similarly, teachers should refrain from too much correction in the early stages and should not interrupt to correct errors, since this will inhibit learners. As time goes on, however, more teacher intervention is expected, as the learners' speech becomes "fine-tuned."

There is generally no basic text in a Total Physical Response course.

Materials and realia play an increasing role, however, in later learning stages. For absolute beginners, lessons may not require the use of materials, since the teacher's voice, actions, and gestures may be a sufficient basis for classroom activities. Later, the teacher may use common classroom objects, such as books, pens, cups, furniture. As the course develops, the teacher will need to make or collect supporting materials to support teaching points. These may include pictures, realia, slides, and word charts. Asher has developed TPR student kits that focus on specific situations, such as the home, the supermarket, the beach. Students may use the kits to construct scenes (e.g., "Put the stove in the kitchen").

Procedure

Asher (1977) provides a lesson-by-lesson account of a course taught according to TPR principles, which serves as a source of information on the procedures used in the TPR classroom. The course was for adult immigrants and consisted of 159 hours of classroom instruction. The sixth class in the course proceeded in the following way:

Review. This was a fast-moving warm-up in which individual students were moved with commands such as:

Pablo, drive your car around Miako and honk your horn.
Jeffe, throw the red flower to Maria.
Maria, scream.
Rita, pick up the knife and spoon and put them in the cup.
Eduardo, take a drink of water and give the cup to Elaine.

New commands. These verbs were introduced.

wash	your hands.
	your face.
	your hair.
look for	a towel.
	the soap.
	a comb.
hold	the book.
	the cup.
	the soap.
comb	your hair.
	Maria's hair.
	Shirou's hair.
brush	your teeth.
	your pants.
	the table.

Other items introduced were:

Rectangle	Draw a rectangle on the chalkboard.

	Pick up a rectangle from the table and give it to me.
	Put the rectangle next to the square.
Triangle	Pick up the triangle from the table and give it to me.
	Catch the triangle and put it next to the rectangle.
Quickly	Walk quickly to the door and hit it.
	Quickly, run to the table and touch the square.
	Sit down quickly and laugh.
Slowly	Walk slowly to the window and jump.
	Slowly, stand up.
	Slowly walk to me and hit me on the arm.
Toothpaste	Look for the toothpaste.
	Throw the toothpaste to Wing.
	Wing, unscrew the top of the toothpaste.
Toothbrush	Take out your toothbrush.
	Brush your teeth.
	Put your toothbrush in your book.
Teeth	Touch your teeth.
	Show your teeth to Dolores.
	Dolores, point to Eduardo's teeth.
Soap	Look for the soap.
	Give the soap to Elaine.
	Elaine, put the soap in Ramiro's ear.
Towel	Put the towel on Juan's arm.
	Juan, put the towel on your head and laugh.
	Maria, wipe your hands on the towel.

Next, the instructor asked simple questions which the student could answer with a gesture such as pointing. Examples would be:

Where is the towel? [Eduardo, point to the towel!]
Where is the toothbrush? [Miako, point to the toothbrush!]
Where is Dolores?

Role reversal. Students readily volunteered to utter commands that manipulated the behavior of the instructor and other students. . . .

Reading and writing. The instructor wrote on the chalkboard each new vocabulary item and a sentence to illustrate the item. Then she spoke each item and acted out the sentence. The students listened as she read the material. Some copied the information in their notebooks.

(Asher 1977: 54–56)

Conclusion

Total Physical Response enjoyed some popularity in the 1970s and 1980s because of its support by those who emphasize the role of comprehension in second language acquisition. Krashen (1981), for example, regards provision of comprehensible input and reduction of stress as keys to successful language acquisition, and he sees performing physical actions in the target language as a means of making input comprehensible and minimizing stress (see Chapter 15). Asher stressed that Total Physical Response should be used in association with other methods and techniques. Indeed, practitioners of TPR typically follow this recommendation, suggesting that for many teachers TPR represents a useful set of techniques and is compatible with other approaches to teaching. TPR practices therefore may be effective for reasons other than those proposed by Asher and do not necessarily demand commitment to the learning theories used to justify them.

Bibliography and further reading

Asher, J. 1965. The strategy of the total physical response: An application to learning Russian. *International Review of Applied Linguistics* 3: 291–300.

Asher, J. 1966. The learning strategy of the total physical response: A review. *Modern Language Journal* 50: 79–84.

Asher, J. 1969. The total physical response approach to second language learning. *Modern Language Journal* 53: 3–17.

Asher, J. 1972. Children's first language as a model of second language learning. *Modern Language Journal* 56: 133–139.

Asher, J. 1977. *Learning Another Language through Actions: The Complete Teacher's Guide Book.* Los Gatos, Calif.: Sky Oaks Productions. (2nd ed. 1982.)

Asher, J. 1981a. The extinction of second language learning in American schools: An intervention model. In H. Winitz (ed.), *The Comprehension Approach to Foreign Language Instruction.* Rowley, Mass.: Newbury House. 49–68.

Asher, J. 1981b. The fear of foreign languages. *Psychology Today* 15(8): 52–59.

Asher, J., J. A. Kusudo, and R. De La Torre. 1974. Learning a second language through commands: The second field test. *Modern Language Journal* 58: 24–32.

Asher, J., and B. S. Price. 1967. The learning strategy of the total physical response: Some age differences. *Child Development* 38: 1219–1227.

DeCecco, J. P. 1968. *The Psychology of Learning and Instruction: Educational Psychology.* Englewood Cliffs, N.J.: Prentice Hall.

Garcia, Ramiro. 1996. *Instructor's Notebook: How to Apply TPR for Best Results.* 4th ed. Los Gatos, Calif.: Sky Oakes Productions.

Hermanson, M. 1988. English as a Second Language tutor training guide. Portland, Oreg.: Portland Community College. ERIC Document ED318303.

Katona, G. 1940. *Organizing and Memorizing: Studies in the Psychology of Learning and Teaching.* New York: Columbia University Press.

Krashen, S. D. 1981. *Second Language Acquisition and Second Language Learning.* Oxford: Pergamon.

Kunihira, S., and J. Asher. 1965. The strategy of the total physical response: An application to learning Japanese. *International Review of Applied Linguistics* 3: 277–289.

Mangubhai, F. 1991. How does one learn a second language? Let me count the number of ways. ERIC Document ED358695.

Marlatt, E. 1995. Learning language through total physical response. *Perspectives in Education and Deafness* 13(4): 18–20.

Miller, G. A., E. Galanter, and K. H. Pribram. 1960. *Plans and the Structure of Behavior.* New York: Henry Holt.

Palmer, H., and D. Palmer. 1925. *English through Actions.* Reprint ed. London: Longman Green, 1959.

Seely, Contee. 1998. *TPR Is More Than Commands at All Levels.* Los Gatos, Calif.: Sky Oakes Productions.

Winitz, H. (ed.). 1981. *The Comprehension Approach to Foreign Language Instruction.* Rowley, Mass.: Newbury House.

Winitz, H., and J. Reeds. 1975. *Comprehension and Problem Solving as Strategies for Language Training.* The Hague: Mouton.

Yorio, C. 1980. Conventionalized language forms and the development of communicative competence. *TESOL Quarterly* 14(4): 433–442.

6 The Silent Way

Background

The Silent Way is the name of a method of language teaching devised by Caleb Gattegno. It is based on the premise that the teacher should be silent as much as possible in the classroom but the learner should be encouraged to produce as much language as possible. Elements of the Silent Way, particularly the use of color charts and the colored Cuisenaire rods, grew out of Gattegno's previous experience as an educational designer of reading and mathematics programs. The Silent Way shares a great deal with other learning theories and educational philosophies. Very broadly put, the learning hypotheses underlying Gattegno's work could be stated as follows:

1. Learning is facilitated if the learner discovers or creates rather than remembers and repeats what is to be learned.
2. Learning is facilitated by accompanying (mediating) physical objects.
3. Learning is facilitated by problem solving involving the material to be learned.

Let us consider each of these issues in turn.

1. The Silent Way belongs to a tradition that views learning as a problem-solving, creative, discovering activity, in which the learner is a principal actor rather than a bench-bound listener (Bruner 1966). Bruner discusses the benefits derived from "discovery learning" under four headings: *(a)* the increase in intellectual potency, *(b)* the shift from extrinsic to intrinsic rewards, *(c)* the learning of heuristics by discovering, and *(d)* the aid to conserving memory (Bruner 1966: 83). Gattegno claims similar benefits from learners taught via the Silent Way.
2. The rods and the color-coded pronunciation charts (called Fidel charts) provide physical foci for student learning and also create memorable images to facilitate student recall. In psychological terms, these visual devices serve as associative mediators for student learning and recall.
3. The Silent Way is also related to a set of premises that we have called "problem-solving approaches to learning." These premises are succinctly represented in the words of Benjamin Franklin:

Tell me and I forget,
teach me and I remember,
involve me and I learn.

Approach: Theory of language and learning

Gattegno takes an openly skeptical view of the role of linguistic theory in language teaching methodology. He feels that linguistic studies "may be a specialization, [that] carry with them a narrow opening of one's sensitivity and perhaps serve very little towards the broad end in mind" (Gattegno 1972: 84). Considerable discussion is devoted to the importance of grasping the "spirit" of the language, and not just its component forms. By the "spirit" of the language Gattegno is referring to the way each language is composed of phonological and suprasegmental elements that combine to give the language its unique sound system and melody. The learner must gain a "feel" for this aspect of the target language as soon as possible.

By looking at the material chosen and the sequence in which it is presented in a Silent Way classroom, it is clear that the Silent Way takes a structural approach to the organization of language to be taught. The sentence is the basic unit of teaching, and the teacher focuses on propositional meaning, rather than communicative value. Students are presented with the structural patterns of the target language and learn the grammar rules of the language through largely inductive processes.

Gattegno sees vocabulary as a central dimension of language learning and the choice of vocabulary as crucial. The most important vocabulary for the learner deals with the most functional and versatile words of the language, many of which may not have direct equivalents in the learner's native language. This "functional vocabulary" provides a key, says Gattegno, to comprehending the "spirit" of the language.

In elaborating a learning theory to support the principles of Silent Way, like many other method proponents Gattegno makes extensive use of his understanding of first language learning. He recommends, for example, that the learner needs to "return to the state of mind that characterizes a baby's learning – surrender" (Scott and Page 1982: 273).

Having referred to these processes, however, Gattegno states that the processes of learning a second language are "radically different" from those involved in learning a first language. The second language learner is unlike the first language learner and "cannot learn another language in the same way because of what he now knows" (Gattegno 1972: 11). The "natural" or "direct" approaches to acquiring a second language are thus misguided, says Gattegno, and a successful second language approach will "replace a 'natural' approach by one that is very 'artificial' and, for some purposes, strictly controlled" (1972: 12).

The "artificial approach" that Gattegno proposes is based on the principle that successful learning involves commitment of the self to language acquisition through the use of silent awareness and then active trial. Gattegno's repeated emphasis on the primacy of learning over teaching places a focus on the self of the learner, on the learner's priorities and commitments. The self, we are told, consists of two systems – a learning system and a retaining system. The learning system is activated only by way of intelligent awareness. "The learner must constantly test his powers to abstract, analyze, synthesize and integrate" (Scott and Page 1982: 273). Silence is considered the best vehicle for learning, because in silence students concentrate on the task to be accomplished and the potential means to its accomplishment. Repetition (as opposed to silence) "consumes time and encourages the scattered mind to remain scattered" (Gattegno 1976: 80). Silence, as avoidance of repetition, is thus an aid to alertness, concentration, and mental organization.

Awareness is educable. As one learns "in awareness," one's powers of awareness and one's capacity to learn become greater. The Silent Way thus claims to facilitate what psychologists call "learning to learn." Again, the process chain that develops awareness proceeds from attention, production, self-correction, and absorption. Silent Way learners acquire "inner criteria," which play a central role "in one's education throughout all of one's life" (Gattegno 1976: 29). These inner criteria allow learners to monitor and self-correct their own production. It is in the activity of self-correction through self-awareness that the Silent Way claims to differ most notably from other ways of language learning. It is this capacity for self-awareness that the Silent Way calls upon, a capacity said to be little appreciated or exercised by first language learners.

Design: Objectives, syllabus, learning activities, roles of learners, teachers, and materials

The general objective of the Silent Way is to give beginning-level students oral and aural facility in basic elements of the target language. The general goal set for language learning is near-native fluency in the target language, and correct pronunciation and mastery of the prosodic elements of the target language are emphasized. An immediate objective is to provide the learner with a basic practical knowledge of the grammar.

Gattegno discusses the following kinds of objectives as appropriate for a language course at an elementary level (Gattegno 1972: 81–83). Students should be able to

correctly and easily answer questions about themselves, their education, their
family, travel, and daily events;
speak with a good accent;
give either a written or an oral description of a picture, "including the existing
relationships that concern space, time and numbers";
answer general questions about the culture and the literature of the native
speakers of the target language;
perform adequately in the following areas: spelling, grammar (production
rather than explanation), reading comprehension, and writing.

The Silent Way adopts a basically structural syllabus, with lessons
planned around grammatical items and related vocabulary. Gattegno
does not, however, provide details as to the precise selection and arrangement of grammatical and lexical items to be covered. But language items
are introduced according to their grammatical complexity, their relationship to what has been taught previously, and the ease with which items
can be presented visually.

The following is a section of a Peace Corps Silent Way Syllabus for the
first 10 hours of instruction in Thai. It was used to teach American Peace
Corps volunteers being trained to teach in Thailand. At least 15 minutes
of every hour of instruction would be spent on pronunciation. A word
that is italicized can be substituted for by another word having the same
function.

Lesson	*Vocabulary*
1. Wood color *red*.	wood, red, green, yellow, brown, pink, white, orange, black, color
2. Using the numbers 1–10.	one, two, . . . ten
3. Wood color *red* two pieces.	
4. Take (pick up) wood color *red* two pieces.	take (pick up)
5. Take wood color *red* two pieces give *him*.	give, object pronouns
6. Wood *red* where? Wood *red* on table.	where, on, under, near, far, over, next to, here, there
7. Wood color red on table, *is it?* Yes, on. Not on.	Question-forming rules. Yes, No.
8. Wood color *red long.* Wood color green *longer.* Wood color orange *longest.*	adjectives of comparison
9. Wood color green *taller.* Wood color *red*, is it?	

10. Review. Students use struc-
    tures taught in new situa-
    tions, such as comparing the
    heights of students in the
    class.

(Joel Wiskin, personal communication)

Learning tasks and activities in the Silent Way have the function of encouraging and shaping student oral response without direct oral instruction from or unnecessary modeling by the teacher. Basic to the method are simple linguistic tasks in which the teacher models a word, phrase, or sentence and then elicits learner responses. Learners then go on to create their own utterances by putting together old and new information. Charts, rods, and other aids may be used to elicit learner responses. Teacher modeling is minimal, although much of the activity may be teacher-directed. Responses to commands, questions, and visual cues thus constitute the basis for classroom activities.

Learners are expected to develop independence, autonomy, and responsibility. Independent learners are those who are aware that they must depend on their own resources and realize that they can use "the knowledge of their own language to open up some things in a new language" or that they can "take their knowledge of the first few words in the new language and figure out additional words by using that knowledge" (Stevick 1980: 42). The absence of correction and repeated modeling from the teacher requires the students to develop "inner criteria" and to correct themselves. The absence of explanations requires learners to make generalizations, come to their own conclusions, and formulate whatever rules they themselves feel they need.

Learners have only themselves as individuals and the group to rely on, and so must learn to work cooperatively rather than competitively. They need to feel comfortable both correcting one another and being corrected by one another.

Teacher silence is, perhaps, the unique and, for many traditionally trained language teachers, the most demanding aspect of the Silent Way. Teachers are exhorted to resist their long-standing commitment to model, remodel, assist, and direct desired student responses. Stevick defines the Silent Way teacher's tasks as *(a)* to teach, *(b)* to test, and *(c)* to get out of the way (Stevick 1980: 56). Although this may not seem to constitute a radical alternative to standard teaching practice, the details of the steps the teacher is expected to follow are unique to the Silent Way. By "teaching" is meant the presentation of an item once, typically using nonverbal clues to get across meanings. Testing follows immediately and might better be termed elicitation and shaping of student production, which, again, is done in as silent a way as possible. Finally, the teacher silently monitors learners' interactions with each other and may even leave the room while learners struggle with their new linguistic tools.

The teacher uses gestures, charts, and manipulatives in order to elicit and shape student responses and so must be both facile and creative as a pantomimist and puppeteer. In sum, the Silent Way teacher, like the complete dramatist, writes the script, chooses the props, sets the mood, models the action, designates the players, and is critic for the performance.

Silent Way materials consist mainly of a set of colored rods, color-coded pronunciation and vocabulary wall charts, a pointer, and reading/writing exercises, all of which are used to illustrate the relationships between sound and meaning in the target language. The materials are designed for manipulation by the students as well as by the teacher, independently and cooperatively, in promoting language learning by direct association.

The pronunciation charts, called "Fidels," have been devised for a number of languages and contain symbols in the target language for all of the vowel and consonant sounds of the language. The symbols are color-coded according to pronunciation; thus, if a language possesses two different symbols for the same sound, they will be colored alike.

Just as the Fidel charts are used to visually illustrate pronunciation, the colored Cuisenaire rods are used to directly link words and structures with their meanings in the target language, thereby avoiding translation into the native language. The rods vary in length from 1 to 10 centimeters, and each length has a specific color. The rods may be used for naming colors, for size comparisons, to represent people, build floor plans, constitute a road map, and so on. Use of the rods is intended to promote inventiveness, creativity, and interest in forming communicative utterances on the part of the students, as they move from simple to more complex structures.

Procedure

A Silent Way lesson typically follows a standard format. The first part of the lesson focuses on pronunciation. Depending on student level, the class might work on sounds, phrases, even sentences designated on the Fidel chart. At the beginning stage, the teacher will model the appropriate sound after pointing to a symbol on the chart. Later, the teacher will silently point to individual symbols and combinations of utterances, and monitor student utterances. The teacher may say a word and have students guess what sequence of symbols compromised the word.

The pointer is used to indicate stress, phrasing, and intonation. Stress can be shown by touching certain symbols more forcibly than others when pointing out a word. Intonation and phrasing can be demonstrated by tapping on the chart to the rhythm of the utterance.

After practice with the sounds of the language, sentence patterns, structure, and vocabulary are practiced. The teacher models an utterance while creating a visual realization of it with the colored rods. After modeling the utterance, the teacher will have a student attempt to produce the utterance and will indicate its acceptability. If a response is incorrect, the teacher will attempt to reshape the utterance or have another student present the correct model. After a structure is introduced and understood, the teacher will create a situation in which the students can practice the structure through the manipulation of the rods. Variations on the structural theme will be elicited from the class using the rods and charts.

The sample lesson that follows illustrates a typical lesson format. The language being taught is Thai, for which this is the first lesson.

1. Teacher empties rods onto the table.
2. Teacher picks up two or three rods of different colors, and after each rod is picked up says: [mai].
3. Teacher holds up one rod of any color and indicates to a student that a response is required. Student says: [mai]. If response is incorrect, teacher elicits response from another student, who then models for the first student.
4. Teacher next picks up a red rod and says: [mai sii daeng].
5. Teacher picks up a green rod and says: [mai sii khiaw].
6. Teacher picks up either a red or green rod and elicits response from student. If response is incorrect, procedure in step 3 is followed (student modeling).
7. Teacher introduces two or three other colors in the same manner.
8. Teacher shows any of the rods whose forms were taught previously and elicits student response. Correction technique is through student modeling, or the teacher may help student isolate error and self-correct.
9. When mastery is achieved, teacher puts one red rod in plain view and says: [mai sii daeng nung an].
10. Teacher then puts two red rods in plain view and says: [mai sii daeng song an].
11. Teacher places two green rods in view and says: [mai sii khiaw song an].
12. Teacher holds up two rods of a different color and elicits student response.
13. Teacher introduces additional numbers, based on what the class can comfortably retain. Other colors might also be introduced.
14. Rods are put in a pile. Teacher indicates, through his or her own actions, that rods should be picked up, and the correct utterance

made. All the students in the group pick up rods and make utterances. Peer-group correction is encouraged.

15. Teacher then says: [kep mai sii daeng song an].
16. Teacher indicates that a student should give the teacher the rods called for. Teacher asks other students in the class to give him or her the rods that he or she asks for. This is all done in the target language through unambiguous actions on the part of the teacher.
17. Teacher now indicates that the students should give each other commands regarding the calling for of rods. Rods are put at the disposal of the class.
18. Experimentation is encouraged. Teacher speaks only to correct an incorrect utterance, if no peer-group correction is forthcoming.

(Joel Wiskin, personal communication)

Conclusion

Despite the philosophical and sometimes almost metaphysical quality of much of Gattegno's writings, the actual practices of the Silent Way are much less revolutionary than might be expected. Working from what is a rather traditional structural and lexical syllabus, the method exemplifies many of the features that characterize more traditional methods, such as Situational Language Teaching and Audiolingualism, with a strong focus on accurate repetition of sentences modeled initially by the teacher and a movement through guided elicitation exercises to freer communication. The innovations in Gattegno's method derive primarily from the manner in which classroom activities are organized, the indirect role the teacher is required to assume in directing and monitoring learner performance, the responsibility placed on learners to figure out and test their hypotheses about how the language works, and the materials used to elicit and practice language.

Bibliography and further reading

Arnold, F. 1981. *College English: A Silent-Way Approach*. Nara, Japan: Dawn Press.

Blair, R. W. (ed.). 1982. *Innovative Approaches to Language Teaching*. Rowley, Mass.: Newbury House.

Borasi, R., and B. Agor. 1990. What can mathematics educators learn from second language instruction? *Focus on Learning Problems in Mathematics*. 17(3/4): 1–27.

Bower, G. H., and D. Winzenz. 1970. Comparison of associative learning strategies. *Psychonomic Sciences* 20: 119–120.

Bruner, J. 1966. *On Knowing: Essays for the Left Hand*. New York: Atheneum.

Cheery, D. 1994. Learning with rods: One account. Master's thesis, School for International Training, Brattleboro, Vermont.

Craik, F. I. M. 1973. A levels of analysis view of memory. In P. Pliner, L. Krames, and T. Alloway (eds.), *Communication and Affect: Language and Thought.* New York: Academic Press.

Diller, K. C. 1978. *The Language Teaching Controversy.* Rowley, Mass.: Newbury House.

Gattegno, C. 1972. *Teaching Foreign Languages in Schools: The Silent Way.* 2nd ed. New York: Educational Solutions.

Gattegno, C. 1976. *The Common Sense of Teaching Foreign Languages.* New York: Educational Solutions.

Harbon, L. 1997. Constructivism in the language classroom. *Babel* 32(3): 12–15.

Lantolf, J. 1986. Silent Way in a university setting: An applied research report. *Canadian Modern Language Review* 43(1): 34–58.

Rossner, R. 1982. Talking shop: A conversation with Caleb Gattegno, inventor of the Silent Way. *ELT Journal* 36(4): 237–41.

Scott, R., and M. Page. 1982. The subordination of teaching to learning: A seminar conducted by Dr. Caleb Gattegno. *ELT Journal* 36(4): 273–274.

Selman, M. 1977. The Silent Way: Insights for ESL. *TESL Talk* 8: 33–6.

Stevick, E. W. 1976. *Memory, Meaning and Method: Some Psychological Perspectives on Language Learning.* Rowley, Mass.: Newbury House.

Stevick, E. W. 1980. *Teaching Languages: A Way and Ways.* Rowley, Mass.: Newbury House.

Stevick, E. W. 1990. *Humanism in Language Teaching.* Oxford: Oxford University Press.

Stevick, E. W. 1998. *Working with Teaching Methods: What's at Stake?* Boston, Mass.: Heinle & Heinle.

Thompson, G. J. 1980. The Silent Way: Interpretation and application. Master's thesis, University of Hawaii.

Varvel, T. 1979. The Silent Way: Panacea or pipedream? *TESOL Quarterly* 13(4): 483–494.

7 Community Language Learning

Background

Community Language Learning (CLL) is the name of a method developed by Charles A. Curran and his associates. Curran was a specialist in counseling and a professor of psychology at Loyola University, Chicago. His application of psychological counseling techniques to learning is known as Counseling-Learning. Community Language Learning represents the use of Counseling-Learning theory to teach languages. As the name indicates, CLL derives its primary insights, and indeed its organizing rationale, from Rogerian counseling (Rogers 1951). In lay terms, counseling is one person giving advice, assistance, and support to another who has a problem or is in some way in need. Community Language Learning draws on the counseling metaphor to redefine the roles of the teacher (the *counselor*) and learners (the *clients*) in the language classroom. The basic procedures of CLL can thus be seen as derived from the counselor–client relationship.

CLL techniques also belong to a larger set of foreign language teaching practices sometimes described as *humanistic techniques* (Moskowitz 1978). Moskowitz defines humanistic techniques as those that

blend what the student feels, thinks and knows with what he is learning in the target language. Rather than self-denial being the acceptable way of life, self-actualization and self-esteem are the ideals the exercises pursue. [The techniques] help build rapport, cohesiveness, and caring that far transcend what is already there . . . help students to be themselves, to accept themselves, and be proud of themselves . . . help foster a climate of caring and sharing in the foreign language class. (Moskowitz 1978: 2)

In sum, humanistic techniques engage the whole person, including the emotions and feelings (the affective realm) as well as linguistic knowledge and behavioral skills.

Another language teaching tradition with which Community Language Learning is linked is a set of practices used in certain kinds of bilingual education programs and referred to by Mackey (1972) as "language alternation." In language alternation, a message/lesson/class is presented first in the native language and then again in the second language. Students know the meaning and flow of an L2 message from their recall of the parallel meaning and flow of an L1 message. They begin to holistically piece together a view of the language out of these message sets. In CLL, a learner presents a message in L1 to the knower. The message is translated into L2 by the knower. The learner then repeats the message in L2, addressing it to another learner with whom he or she wishes to communicate. CLL learners are encouraged to attend to the "overhears" they experience between other learners and their knowers. The result of the "overhear" is that every member of the group can understand what any given learner is trying to communicate (La Forge 1983: 45).

Approach: Theory of language and learning

Curran himself wrote little about his theory of language. His student La Forge (1983) has attempted to be more explicit about this dimension of Community Language Learning theory. La Forge accepts that language theory must start, though not end, with criteria for sound features, the sentence, and abstract models of language (La Forge 1983:4). The foreign language learners' tasks are "to apprehend the sound system, assign fundamental meanings, and to construct a basic grammar of the foreign language." La Forge goes beyond this structuralist view of language, however, and elaborates an alternative theory of language, which is referred to as *Language as Social Process:*

communication is more than just a message being transmitted from a speaker to a listener. The speaker is at the same time both subject and object of his own message. . . . communication involves not just the unidirectional transfer of information to the other, but the very constitution of the speaking subject in relation to its other. . . . Communication is an exchange which is incomplete without a feedback reaction from the destinee of the message. (La Forge 1983: 3)

This social-process view of language is then elaborated in terms of six qualities or subprocesses. La Forge also elaborates on the interactional view of language underlying Community Language Learning (see Chapter 2): "Language is people; language is persons in contact; language is persons in response" (1983: 9). CLL interactions are of two distinct and fundamental kinds: interactions between learners and interactions between learners and knowers. Interactions between learners are unpredictable in content but typically are said to involve exchanges of affect. Learner exchanges deepen in intimacy as the class becomes a community of learners. The desire to be part of this growing intimacy pushes learners to keep pace with the learning of their peers.

Interaction between learners and knowers is initially dependent. The learner tells the knower what he or she wishes to say in the target language, and the knower tells the learner how to say it. In later stages, interactions between learner and knower are characterized as self-assertive (stage 2), resentful and indignant (stage 3), tolerant (stage 4), and independent (stage 5). These changes of interactive relationship are paralleled by five stages of language learning and five stages of affective conflicts (La Forge 1983: 50).

Curran's counseling experience led him to conclude that the techniques of counseling could be applied to learning in general (this became Counseling-Learning) and to language teaching in particular (Community Language Learning). The CLL view of learning is a holistic one, since "true" human learning is both cognitive and affective. This is termed *whole-person learning*. Such learning takes place in a communicative situation where teachers and learners are involved in "an interaction . . . in which both experience a sense of their own wholeness" (Curran 1972: 90). Within this, the development of the learner's relationship with the teacher is central. The process is divided into five stages and compared to the ontogenetic development of the child.

In the first, "birth" stage, feelings of security and belonging are established. In the second, as the learner's abilities improve, the learner, as child, begins to achieve a measure of independence from the parent. By the third, the learner "speaks independently" and may need to assert his or her own identity, often rejecting unasked-for advice. The fourth stage sees the learner as secure enough to take criticism, and by the last stage, the learner merely works on improving style and knowledge of linguistic appropriateness. By the end of the process, the child has become adult. The learner knows everything the teacher does and can become knower for a new learner. The process of learning a new language, then, is like being reborn and developing a new persona, with all the trials and challenges that are associated with birth and maturation.

Curran in many places discusses what he calls "consensual validation," or "convalidation," in which mutual warmth, understanding, and a positive evaluation of the other person's worth develop between the teacher and the learner. A relationship characterized by convalidation is considered essential to the learning process and is a key element of CLL classroom procedures. A group of ideas concerning the psychological requirements for successful learning are collected under the acronym SARD (Curran 1976: 6), which can be explained as follows:

S stands for security. Unless learners feel secure, they will find it difficult to enter into a successful learning experience.

A stands for attention and aggression. CLL recognizes that a loss of attention should be taken as an indication of the learner's lack of involvement in learning, the implication being that variety in the choice of learner tasks will increase attention and therefore promote learning. Aggression applies to the way in which a child, having learned something, seeks an opportunity to show his or her strength by taking over and demonstrating what has been learned, using the new knowledge as a tool for self-assertion.

R stands for retention and reflection. If the whole person is involved in the learning process, what is retained is internalized and becomes a part of the learner's new persona in the foreign language. Reflection is a consciously identified period of silence within the framework of the lesson for the student "to focus on the learning forces of the last hour, to assess his present stage of development, and to re-evaluate future goals" (La Forge 1983: 68).

D denotes discrimination. When learners "have retained a body of material, they are ready to sort it out and see how one thing relates to another" (La Forge 1983: 69). This discrimination process becomes more refined and ultimately "enables the students to use the language for purposes of communication outside the classroom" (La Forge 1983: 69).

These central aspects of Curran's learning philosophy address not the psycholinguistic and cognitive processes involved in second language acquisition, but rather the personal commitments that learners need to make before language acquisition processes can operate.

Design: Objectives, syllabus, learning activities, roles of learners, teachers, and materials

Since linguistic or communicative competence is specified only in social terms, explicit linguistic or communicative objectives are not defined in CLL. Most of what has been written about it describes its use in introductory conversation courses in a foreign language. CLL does not use a conventional language syllabus, which sets out in advance the grammar, vocabulary, and other language items to be taught and the order in which they will be covered. The progression is topic-based, with learners nominating things they wish to talk about and messages they wish to communicate to other learners. The teacher's responsibility is to provide a conveyance for these meanings in a way appropriate to the learners' proficiency level. In this sense, then, a CLL syllabus emerges from the interaction between the learner's expressed communicative intentions and the teacher's reformulations of these into suitable target-language utterances. Specific grammatical points, lexical patterns, and generalizations will sometimes be isolated by the teacher for more detailed study and analysis, and subsequent specification of these as a retrospective account of what the course covered could be a way of deriving a CLL language syllabus.

As with most methods, CLL combines innovative learning tasks and activities with conventional ones. They include:

1. *Translation.* Learners form a small circle. A learner whispers a message or meaning he or she wants to express, the teacher translates it

93

into (and may interpret it in) the target language, and the learner repeats the teacher's translation.

2. *Group work.* Learners may engage in various group tasks, such as small-group discussion of a topic, preparing a conversation, preparing a summary of a topic for presentation to another group, preparing a story that will be presented to the teacher and the rest of the class.
3. *Recording.* Students record conversations in the target language.
4. *Transcription.* Students transcribe utterances and conversations they have recorded for practice and analysis of linguistic forms.
5. *Analysis.* Students analyze and study transcriptions of target-language sentences in order to focus on particular lexical usage or on the application of particular grammar rules.
6. *Reflection and observation.* Learners reflect and report on their experience of the class, as a class or in groups. This usually consists of expressions of feelings – sense of one another, reactions to silence, concern for something to say, and so on.
7. *Listening.* Students listen to a monologue by the teacher involving elements they might have elicited or overheard in class interactions.
8. *Free conversation.* Students engage in free conversation with the teacher or with other learners. This might include discussion of what they learned as well as feelings they had about how they learned.

Learner roles in CLL are well defined. Learners become members of a community – their fellow learners and the teacher – and learn through interacting with the community. Learning is not viewed as an individual accomplishment but as something that is achieved collaboratively. Learners are expected to listen attentively to the knower, to freely provide meanings they wish to express, to repeat target utterances without hesitation, to support fellow members of the community, to report deep inner feelings and frustrations as well as joy and pleasure, and to become counselors of other learners. CLL learners are typically grouped in a circle of six to twelve learners, with the number of knowers varying from one per group to one per student.

Learner roles are keyed to the five stages of language learning outlined earlier. The view of the learner is an organic one, with each new role growing developmentally out of the one preceding. These role changes are not easily or automatically achieved. They are in fact seen as outcomes of affective crises:

When faced with a new cognitive task, the learner must solve an affective crisis. With the solution of the five affective crises, one for each CLL stage, the student progresses from a lower to a higher stage of development. (La Forge 1983: 44)

The teacher's role derives from the functions of the counselor in Rogerian psychological counseling. The counselor's role is to respond calmly and nonjudgmentally, in a supportive manner, and help the client try to understand his or her problems better by applying order and analysis to them. "One of the functions of the counseling response is to relate affect . . . to cognition. Understanding the language of 'feeling', the counselor replies in the language of cognition" (Curran 1976: 26). It was the model of teacher as counselor that Curran attempted to bring to language learning.

There is also room for actual counseling in Community Language Learning: "Personal learning conflicts . . . anger, anxiety and similar psychological disturbance – understood and responded to by the teacher's counseling sensitivity – are indicators of deep personal investment" (J. Rardin, in Curran 1976: 103).

More specific teacher roles are, like those of the students, keyed to the five developmental stages. In the early stages of learning, the teacher operates in a supportive role, providing target-language translations and a model for imitation on request of the clients. Later, interaction may be initiated by the students, and the teacher monitors learner utterances, providing assistance when requested. As learning progresses, students become increasingly capable of accepting criticism, and the teacher may intervene directly to correct deviant utterances, supply idioms, and advise on usage and fine points of grammar. The teacher's role is initially likened to that of a nurturing parent. The student gradually "grows" in ability, and the nature of the relationship changes so that the teacher's position becomes somewhat dependent on the learner. The knower derives a sense of self-worth through requests for the knower's assistance.

Since a CLL course evolves out of the interactions of the community, a textbook is not considered a necessary component. A textbook would impose a particular body of language content on the learners, thereby impeding their growth and interaction. Materials may be developed by the teacher as the course develops, although these generally consist of little more than summaries on the blackboard or overhead projector of some of the linguistic features of conversations generated by students. Conversations may also be transcribed and distributed for study and analysis, and learners may work in groups to produce their own materials, such as scripts for dialogues and mini-dramas.

Procedure

Because each Community Language Learning course is in a sense a unique experience, description of typical CLL procedures in a class period is problematic. Stevick (1980) distinguishes between "classical" CLL (based directly on the model proposed by Curran) and personal interpretations of it, such as those discussed by different advocates of CLL (e.g., La Forge 1983). The following description attempts to capture some typical activities in CLL classes.

Generally, the observer will see a circle of learners all facing one another. The learners are linked in some way to knowers or a single knower as teacher. The first class (and subsequent classes) may begin with a period of silence, in which learners try to determine what is supposed to happen in their language class. In later classes, learners may sit in silence while they decide what to talk about (La Forge 1983: 72). The observer may note that the awkwardness of silence becomes sufficiently agonizing for someone to volunteer to break the silence. The knower may use the volunteered comment as a way of introducing discussion of classroom contacts or as a stimulus for language interaction regarding how learners felt about the period of silence. The knower may encourage learners to address questions to one another or to the knower. These may be questions on any subject a learner is curious enough to inquire about. The questions and answers may be tape-recorded for later use, as a reminder and review of topics discussed and language used.

The teacher might then form the class into facing lines for 3-minute pair conversations. These are seen as equivalent to the brief wrestling sessions by which judo students practice. Following this the class might be re-formed into small groups in which a single topic, chosen by the class or the group, is discussed. The summary of the group discussion may be presented to another group, who in turn try to repeat or paraphrase the summary back to the original group.

In an intermediate or advanced class, a teacher may encourage groups to prepare a paper drama for presentation to the rest of the class. A paper drama group prepares a story that is told or shown to the counselor. The counselor provides or corrects target-language statements and suggests improvements to the story sequence. Students are then given materials with which they prepare large picture cards to accompany their story. After practicing the story dialogue and preparing the accompanying pictures, each group presents its paper drama to the rest of the class. The students accompany their story with music, puppets, and drums as well as with their pictures (La Forge 1983: 81–82).

Finally, the teacher asks learners to reflect on the language class, as a class or in groups. Reflection provides the basis for discussion of contracts (written or oral contracts that learners and teachers have agreed upon and that specify what they agree to accomplish within the course), personal interaction, feelings toward the knower and learner, and the sense of progress and frustration.

Dieter Stroinigg (in Stevick 1980: 185–186) presents a protocol of what a first day's CLL class covered, which is outlined here:

1. Informal greetings and self-introductions were made.
2. The teacher made a statement of the goals and guidelines for the course.
3. A conversation in the foreign language took place.
   a) A circle was formed so that everyone had visual contact with each other.
   b) One student initiated conversation with another student by giving a message in the L1 (English).
   c) The instructor, standing behind the student, whispered a close equivalent of the message in the L2 (German).
   d) The student then repeated the L2 message to its addressee and into the tape recorder as well.
   e) Each student had a chance to compose and record a few messages.
   f) The tape recorder was rewound and replayed at intervals.
   g) Each student repeated the meaning in English of what he or she had said in the L2 and helped to refresh the memory of others.
4. Students then participated in a reflection period, in which they were asked to express their feelings about the previous experience with total frankness.
5. From the materials just recorded the instructor chose sentences to write on the blackboard that highlighted elements of grammar, spelling, and peculiarities of capitalization in the L2.
6. Students were encouraged to ask questions about any of the items above.
7. Students were encouraged to copy sentences from the board with notes on meaning and usage. This became their "textbook" for home study.

Conclusion

Community Language Learning places unusual demands on language teachers. They must be highly proficient and sensitive to nuance in both L1 and L2. They must be familiar with and sympathetic to the role of counselors in psychological counseling. They must resist the pressure "to teach" in the traditional senses. The teacher must also be relatively non-directive and must be prepared to accept and even encourage the "adolescent" aggression of the learner as he or she strives for independence. The teacher must operate without conventional materials, depending on student topics to shape and motivate the class. Special training in Community Language Learning techniques is usually required.

Critics of Community Language Learning question the appropriateness of the counseling metaphor on which it is predicated. Questions also arise about whether teachers should attempt counseling without special training. Other concerns have been expressed regarding the lack of a syllabus, which makes objectives unclear and evaluation difficult to accomplish, and the focus on fluency rather than accuracy, which may lead to inadequate control of the grammatical system of the target language. Supporters of CLL, on the other hand, emphasize the positive benefits of a method that centers on the learner and stresses the humanistic side of language learning, and not merely its linguistic dimensions.

Bibliography and further reading

Brown, H. D. 1977. Some limitations of C-L/CLL models of second language teaching. *TESOL Quarterly* 11(4): 365–372.

Curran, C. A. 1972. *Counseling-Learning: A Whole-Person Model for Education.* New York: Grune and Stratton.

Curran, C. A. 1976. *Counseling-Learning in Second Languages.* Apple River, Ill.: Apple River Press.

La Forge, P. G. 1971. Community language learning: A pilot study. *Language Learning* 21(1): 45–61.

La Forge. P. G. 1975a. Community language learning: The Japanese case. In F. C. C. Peng (ed.), *Language in Japanese Society.* Tokyo: University of Tokyo Press. 215–246.

La Forge, P. G. 1975b. *Research Profiles with Community Language Learning.* Apple River, Ill.: Apple River Press.

La Forge, P. G. 1977. Uses of social silence in the interpersonal dynamics of Community Language Learning. *TESOL Quarterly* 11(4): 373–382.

La Forge, P. G. 1983. *Counseling and Culture in Second Language Acquisition.* Oxford: Pergamon.

Lim, K. B. 1968. The unified language project. *RELC Journal* 9(1): 19–27.

Mackey, W. F. 1972. *Bilingual Education in a Binational School.* Rowley, Mass.: Newbury House.

Moskowitz, G. 1978. *Caring and Sharing in the Foreign Language Class.* Rowley, Mass.: Newbury House.

Munby, J. 1978. *Communicative Syllabus Design.* Cambridge: Cambridge University Press.

Rardin, J. 1976. A Counseling-Learning model for second language learning. *TESOL Newsletter* 10(2): 21–22.

Rardin, J. 1977. The language teacher as facilitator. *TESOL Quarterly* 11(4): 383–38.

Rogers, C. R. 1951. *Client-Centered Therapy.* Boston: Houghton Mifflin.

Samimy, K. 1989. A comparative study of teaching Japanese in the audiolingual method and the counseling-learning approach. *Modern Language Journal* 73(2): 169–177.

Samimy, K., and J. Rardin. 1994. Adult language learners' affective reactions to community language learning: A descriptive study. *Foreign Language Annals* 27(3):379–90.

Shannon, J. 1994. Experimenting with a community language learning principle in an ESL second language writing class. ERIC Document ED373583.

Stevick, E. W. 1973. Review article: Charles A. Curran's Counseling-Learning: a whole person model for education. *Language Learning* 23(2): 259–271.

Stevick, E. W. 1976. *Memory, Meaning and Method: Some Psychological Perspectives on Language Learning.* Rowley, Mass.: Newbury House.

Stevick, E. W. 1980. *Teaching Languages: A Way and Ways.* Rowley, Mass.: Newbury House.

Taylor, B. P. 1979. Exploring Community Language Learning. In C. Yorio, K. Perkins, and J. Schachter (eds.), *On TESOL '79.* Washington, D.C.: TESOL. 80–84.

Tranel, D. D. 1968. Teaching Latin with the chromachord. *The Classical Journal* 63: 157–60.

8 Suggestopedia

Background

Suggestopedia, also known as Desuggestopedia, is a method developed by the Bulgarian psychiatrist-educator Georgi Lozanov. Suggestopedia is a specific set of learning recommendations derived from Suggestology, which Lozanov describes as a "science . . . concerned with the systematic study of the nonrational and/or nonconscious influences" that human beings are constantly responding to (Stevick 1976: 42). Suggestopedia tries to harness these influences and redirect them so as to optimize learning. The most conspicuous characteristics of Suggestopedia are the decoration, furniture, and arrangement of the classroom, the use of music, and the authoritative behavior of the teacher. The claims for suggestopedic learning are dramatic. "There is no sector of public life where suggestology would not be useful" (Lozanov 1978: 2). "Memorization in learning by the suggestopedic method seems to be accelerated 25 times over that in learning by conventional methods" (Lozanov 1978: 27).

Lozanov acknowledges ties in tradition to yoga and Soviet psychology. From raja-yoga Lozanov has borrowed and modified techniques for altering states of consciousness and concentration, and the use of rhythmic breathing. From Soviet psychology Lozanov has taken the notion that all students can be taught a given subject matter at the same level of skill. Lozanov claims that his method works equally well whether or not students spend time on outside study. He promises success through Suggestopedia to the academically gifted and the ungifted alike. (For an overview of the tenets of Soviet psychology and how these differ from those of Western psychology, see Bancroft 1978.)

A most conspicuous feature of Suggestopedia is the centrality of music and musical rhythm to learning. Suggestopedia thus has a kinship with other functional uses of music, particularly therapy. Gaston (1968) defines three functions of music in therapy: to facilitate the establishment and maintenance of personal relations; to bring about increased self-esteem through increased self-satisfaction in musical performance; and to use the unique potential of rhythm to energize and bring order. This last function seems to be the one that Lozanov calls upon in his use of music to relax learners as well as to structure, pace, and punctuate the presentation of linguistic material.

100

Approach: Theory of language and learning

Lozanov does not articulate a theory of language, nor does it seem that he is much concerned with any particular assumptions regarding language elements and their organization. The emphasis on memorization of vocabulary pairs – a target-language item and its native language translation – suggests a view of language in which lexis is central and in which lexical translation rather than contextualization is stressed. However, Lozanov does occasionally refer to the importance of experiencing language material in "whole meaningful texts" (Lozanov 1978: 268) and notes that the suggestopedic course directs "the student not to vocabulary memorization and acquiring habits of speech, but to acts of communication" (1978: 109).

In describing course work and text organization Lozanov refers most often to the language to be learned as "the material" (e.g., "The new material that is to be learned is read or recited by a well-trained teacher") (Lozanov 1978: 270). The sample protocol given for an Italian lesson (Lozanov 1978) does not suggest a theory of language markedly different from that which holds a language to be its vocabulary and the grammar rules for organizing vocabulary.

Suggestion is at the heart of the theory of learning underlying Suggestopedia. Lozonov distinguishes his theory of suggestion from the "narrow clinical concept of hypnosis as a kind of static, sleeplike, altered state of consciousness" (1978: 3). Lozanov further claims that what distinguishes his method from hypnosis and other forms of mind control is that these other forms lack "a desuggestive-suggestive sense" and "fail to create a constant set up access to reserves through concentrative psycho-relaxation" (1978: 267). There are six principal theoretical components through which desuggestion and suggestion operate and that set up access to reserves. We will describe these briefly following Bancroft (1972).

Authority

People remember best and are most influenced by information coming from an authoritative source. Lozanov appears to believe that scientific-sounding language, highly positive experimental data, and true-believer teachers constitute a ritual placebo system that is authoritatively appealing to most learners. Well-publicized accounts of learning success lend the method and the institution authority, and commitment to the method, self-confidence, personal distance, acting ability, and a highly positive attitude give an authoritative air to the teacher.

Infantilization

Authority is also used to suggest a teacher–student relation like that of parent to child. In the child's role the learner takes part in role playing, games, songs, and gymnastic exercises that help "the older student regain the self-confidence, spontaneity and receptivity of the child" (Bancroft 1972: 19).

Double-planedness

The learner learns not only from the effect of direct instruction but from the environment in which the instruction takes place. The bright decor of the classroom, the musical background, the shape of the chairs, and the personality of the teacher are considered as important in instruction as the form of the instructional material itself.

Intonation, rhythm, and concert pseudo-passiveness

Varying the tone and rhythm of presented material helps both to avoid boredom through monotony of repetition and to dramatize, emotionalize, and give meaning to linguistic material. In the first presentation of linguistic material, three phrases are read together, each with a different voice level and rhythm. In the second presentation, the linguistic material is given a proper dramatic reading, which helps learners visualize a context for the material and aids in memorization (Bancroft 1972: 19).

Both intonation and rhythm are coordinated with a musical background. The musical background helps to induce a relaxed attitude, which Lozanov refers to as concert pseudo-passiveness. This state is felt to be optimal for learning, in that anxieties and tension are relieved and power of concentration for new material is raised.

Design: Objectives, syllabus, learning activities, roles of learners, teachers, and materials

The objectives of Suggestopedia are to deliver advanced conversational proficiency quickly. It bases its learning claims on student mastery of prodigious lists of vocabulary pairs and, indeed, suggests to the students that it is appropriate that they set such goals for themselves. Lozanov emphasizes, however, that increased memory power is not an isolated skill but is a result of "positive, comprehensive stimulation of personality" (Lozanov 1978: 253).

A Suggestopedia course lasts 30 days and consists of ten units of study. Classes are held 4 hours a day, 6 days a week. The central focus of each unit is a dialogue consisting of 1,200 words or so, with an accompanying vocabulary list and grammatical commentary. The dialogues are graded by lexis and grammar.

There is a pattern of work within each unit and a pattern of work for the whole course. Unit study is organized around 3 days: day 1–half a day, day 2–full day, day 3–half a day. On the first day of work on a new unit the teacher discusses the general content (not structure) of the unit dialogue. The learners then receive the printed dialogue with a native language translation in a parallel column. The teacher answers any questions of interest or concern about the dialogue. The dialogue then is read a second and third time in ways to be discussed subsequently. This is the work for day 1. Days 2 and 3 are spent in primary and secondary elaboration of the text. Primary elaboration consists of imitation, question and answer, reading, and so on, of the dialogue and of working with the 150 new vocabulary items presented in the unit. The secondary elaboration involves encouraging students to make new combinations and productions based on the dialogues. A story or essay paralleling the dialogue is also read. The students engage in conversation and take small roles in response to the text read.

During the course there are two opportunities for generalization of material. In the middle of the course students are encouraged to practice the target language in a setting where it might be used, such as hotels or restaurants. The last day of the course is devoted to a performance in which every student participates. The students construct a play built on the material of the course. Rules and parts are planned, but students are expected to speak extempore rather than from memorized lines. Written tests are also given throughout the course, and these and the performance are reviewed on the final day of the course.

Learning activities used in the method include imitation, question and answer, and role play – which are not activities "that other language teachers would consider to be out of the ordinary" (Stevick 1976: 157). The type of activities that are more original to Suggestopedia are the listening activities, which concern the text and text vocabulary of each unit. These activities are typically part of the "pre-session phase," which takes place on the first day of a new unit. The students first look at and discuss a new text with the teacher. In the second reading, students relax comfortably in reclining chairs and listen to the teacher read the text in a certain way.

Learners' roles are carefully prescribed. The mental state of the learners is critical to success, which is why learners must forgo mind-altering substances and other distractions and immerse themselves in the procedures of the method. Learners must not try to figure out, manipulate, or study the material presented but must maintain a pseudo-passive state, in which the material rolls over and through them. Students are expected to tolerate and in fact encourage their own "infantilization." In part this is

103

accomplished by acknowledging the absolute authority of the teacher and in part by giving themselves over to activities and techniques designed to help them regain the self-confidence, spontaneity, and receptivity of the child. Such activities include role playing, games, songs, and gymnastic exercises (Bancroft 1972: 19).

Groups of learners are ideally socially homogeneous, twelve in number, and divided equally between men and women. Learners sit in a circle, which encourages face-to-face exchange and activity participation.

The primary role of the teacher is to create situations in which the learner is most suggestible and then to present linguisitic material in a way most likely to encourage positive reception and retention by the learner.

Lozanov lists several expected teacher behaviors that contribute to these presentations.

1. Show absolute confidence in the method.
2. Display fastidious conduct in manners and dress.
3. Organize properly and strictly observe the initial stages of the teaching process – this includes choice and play of music, as well as punctuality.
4. Maintain a solemn attitude toward the session.
5. Give tests and respond tactfully to poor papers (if any).
6. Stress global rather than analytical attitudes toward material.
7. Maintain a modest enthusiasm.

Materials consist of direct support materials, primarily text and tape, and indirect support materials, including classroom fixtures and music.

The text is organized around the ten units described earlier. The textbook should have emotional force, literary quality, and interesting characters. Language problems should be introduced in a way that does not worry or distract students from the content. "Traumatic themes and distasteful lexical material should be avoided" (Lozanov 1978: 278). Each unit should be governed by a single idea featuring a variety of subthemes, "the way it is in life" (p. 278).

Although not language materials per se, the learning environment plays such a central role in Suggestopedia that the important elements of the environment need to be briefly enumerated. The environment (the indirect support materials) comprises the appearance of the classroom (bright and cheery), the furniture (reclining chairs arranged in a circle), and the music (Baroque largo).

Procedure

As with other methods we have examined, there are variants both historical and individual in the actual conduct of Suggestopedia classes. Adaptations such as those we witnessed in Toronto by Jane Bancroft and her colleagues at Scarborough College, University of Toronto, showed a wide and diversified range of techniques unattested to in Lozanov's writings. We have tried here to characterize a class as described in the Suggestopedia literature while pointing out where the actual classes we have observed varied considerably from the description. Bancroft (1972) notes that the 4-hour language class has three distinct parts. The first part we might call an oral review section. Previously learned material is used as the basis for discussion by the teacher and twelve students in the class. All participants sit in a circle in their specially designed chairs, and the discussion proceeds like a seminar. This session may involve what are called micro-studies and macro-studies. In micro-studies specific attention is given to grammar, vocabulary, and precise questions and answers. A question from a micro-study might be, "What should one do in a hotel room if the bathroom taps are not working?" In the macro-studies, emphasis is on role playing and wider-ranging, innovative language constructions. "Describe to someone the Boyana church" (one of Bulgaria's most well known medieval churches) would be an example of a request for information from the macro-studies.

In the second part of the class new material is presented and discussed. This consists of looking over a new dialogue and its native language translation and discussing any issues of grammar, vocabulary, or content that the teacher feels important or that students are curious about. Bancroft notes that this section is typically conducted in the target language, although student questions or comments will be in whatever language the student feels he or she can handle. Students are led to view the experience of dealing with the new material as interesting and undemanding of any special effort or anxiety. The teacher's attitude and authority are considered critical to preparing students for success in the learning to come. The pattern of learning and use is noted (i.e., fixation, reproduction, and new creative production), so that students will know what is expected.

The third part – the séance or concert session – is the one by which Suggestopedia is best known. Since this constitutes the heart of the method, we will quote Lozanov as to how this session proceeds.

At the beginning of the session, all conversation stops for a minute or two, and the teacher listens to the music coming from a tape-recorder. He waits and listens to several passages in order to enter into the mood of the music and then begins to read or recite the new text, his voice modulated in harmony with the musical phrases. The students follow the text in their textbooks where each lesson is translated into the mother tongue. Between the first and second part of the concert, there are several minutes of solemn silence. In some cases, even longer pauses can be given to permit the students to stir a little. Before the beginning of the second part of the concert, there are again several minutes of silence and some phrases of the music are heard again before the teacher begins to read the text. Now the students close their textbooks and listen to the teacher's reading. At the end, the students silently leave the room. They are not told to do any homework on the lesson they have just had except for reading it cursorily once before going to bed and again before getting up in the morning. (Lozanov 1978: 272)

Conclusion

Suggestopedia received a rave review in *Parade* magazine of March 12, 1978. Suggestopedia also received a scathing review by a leading applied linguist (Scovel 1979). Having acknowledged that "there are techniques and procedures in Suggestopedy that may prove useful in a foreign language classroom," Scovel notes that Lozanov is unequivocally opposed to any eclectic use of the techniques outside of the full panoply of suggestopedic science. Of suggestopedic science Scovel comments, "If we have learnt anything at all in the seventies, it is that the art of language teaching will benefit very little from the pseudo-science of suggestology" (Scovel 1979: 265).

And yet, from Lozanov's point of view, this air of science (rather than its substance) is what gives Suggestopedia its authority in the eyes of students and prepares them to expect success. Lozanov makes no bones about the fact that Suggestopedia is introduced to students in the context of a "suggestive-desuggestive ritual placebo-system" (Lozanov 1978: 267), and that one of the tasks of the suggestopedic leader is to determine which current ritual placebo system carries most authority with students. Just as doctors tell patients that the placebo is a pill that will cure them, so teachers tell students that Suggestology is a science that will teach them. And Lozanov maintains that placebos do both cure and teach when the patient or pupil credits them with the power to do so. Perhaps, then, it is not productive to futher belabor the science/nonscience, data/double-talk issues and instead, as Bancroft and Stevick have done, try to identify and validate those techniques from Suggestopedia that appear effective and that harmonize with other successful techniques in the language teaching inventory.

Bibliography and further reading

Bancroft, W. J. 1972. The psychology of Suggestopedia or learning without stress. *The Educational Courier* (February): 16–19.

Bancroft, W. J. 1978. The Lozanov method and its American adaptions. *Modern Language Journal* 62(4): 167–175.

Bancroft, J. 1996. SALT for language acquisition. *Mosaic* 3(3): 16–20.

Blair, R. W. (ed.). 1982 *Innovative Approaches to Language Teaching*. Rowley, Mass.: Newbury House.

Brewer, C., and D. Campbell. 1991. *Rhythms of Learning: Creative Tools for Developing Lifelong Skills.* Tuscon, Ariz.: Zephyr Press.

Gaston, E. T. (ed.). 1968. *Music in Therapy.* New York: Macmillan.

Hammerly, H. 1982. *Synthesis in Second Language Teaching.* Vancouver, B.C.: Second Language Publications.

Hansen, G. H. 1998. Lozanov and the teaching text. In B. Tomlinson (ed.), *Materials Development in Language Teaching.* Cambridge: Cambridge University Press. 311–319.

Lozanov, G. 1978. *Suggestology and Outlines of Suggestopedy.* New York. Gordon and Breach.

Lozanov, G., and E. Gateva. 1988. *The Foreign Language Teacher's Suggestopedic Manual.* New York: Gordon and Breach.

Ostrander, S., L. Schroeder, and N. Ostrander. 1979. *Superlearning.* New York: Dell.

Scovel, T. 1979. Review of *Suggestology and Outlines of Suggestopedy. TESOL Quarterly* 13: 255–266.

Stevick, E. W. 1976. *Memory, Meaning and Method: Some Psychological Perspectives on Language Learning.* Rowley, Mass.: Newbury House.

Stevick, E. W. 1980. *Teaching Languages: A Way and Ways.* Rowley, Mass.: Newbury House.

Zence, R. 1995. Accelerated learning: madness with a method. *Training* 32(10): 93–96, 98–100.

9 Whole Language

Background

The term *Whole Language* was created in the 1980s by a group of U.S. educators concerned with the teaching of language arts, that is, reading and writing in the native language. The teaching of reading and writing in the first language (often termed the teaching of *literacy*) is a very active educational enterprise worldwide, and, like the field of second language teaching, has led to a number of different and at times competing approaches and methodologies. One widespread approach to both the teaching of reading and writing has focused on a "decoding" approach to language. By this is meant a focus on teaching the separate components of language such as grammar, vocabulary, and word recognition, and in particular the teaching of phonics. Phonics is based on the theory that reading involves identifying letters and turning them into sounds. Other reading theories approach reading through skills. The Whole Language movement is strongly opposed to these approaches to teaching reading and writing and argues that language should be taught as a "whole." "If language isn't kept whole, it isn't language anymore" (Rigg 1991: 522). Whole Language instruction is a theory of language instruction that was developed to help young children learn to read, and has also been extended to middle and secondary levels and to the teaching of ESL. "What began as a holistic way to teach reading has become a movement for change, key aspects of which are respect for each student as a member of a culture and as a creator of knowledge, and respect for each teacher as a professional" (Rigg 1991: 521).

The Whole Language Approach emphasizes learning to read and write naturally with a focus on real communication and reading and writing for pleasure. In the 1990s it became popular in the United States as a motivating and innovative way of teaching language arts skills to primary school children. In language teaching it shares a philosophical and instructional perspective with Communicative Language Teaching since it emphasizes the importance of meaning and meaning making in teaching and learning. It also relates to natural approaches to language learning (see Chapter 15) since it is designed to help children and adults learn a second language in the same way that children learn their first language.

Considerable discussion has been devoted to whether Whole Language is an approach, a method, a philosophy, or a belief. In a survey of sixty-four articles on Whole Language, Bergeron (1990) found Whole Language treated as an approach (34.4 percent of the articles), as a philosophy (23.4 percent), as a belief (14.1 percent), or as a method (6.3 percent). We see it as an approach based on key principles about language (language is whole) and learning (writing, reading, listening, and speaking should be integrated in learning). Each Whole Language teacher implements the theories of Whole Language as he or she interprets them and according to the kinds of classes and learners he or she is teaching.

Approach: theory of language and of learning

Whole language views language organization from what we have earlier called an interactional perspective. This perspective is most obviously a social one that views language as a vehicle for human communication and in which there is an interactional relationship between readers and writers. "Language use is always in a social context, and this applies to both oral and written language, to both first and second language use" (Rigg 1991: 523). Heavy emphasis in Whole Language is placed on "authenticity," on engagement with the authors of written texts, and also on conversation. For example, in mastering the sociolinguistic signals for "apologizing," "A whole language perspective requires an authentic, 'real' situation in which one truly needs to apologize to another" (Rigg 1991: 524).

Whole Language also views language psycholinguistically as a vehicle for internal "interaction," for egocentric speech, for thinking. "We use language to think: In order to discover what we know, we sometimes write, perhaps talk to a friend, or mutter to ourselves silently" (Rigg 1991: 323). A functional model of language is also referred to in many articles on Whole Language. Language is always seen as something that is used for meaningful purposes and to carry out authentic functions.

The learning theory underlying Whole Language is in the humanistic and constructivist schools. The descriptions of whole language classrooms recall terms familiar to humanistic approaches to education and to language learning: Whole Language is said to be authentic, personalized, self-directed, collaborative, pluralistic. Such characteristics are believed to focus learner attention and to motivate mastery. Constructivist learning theory holds that knowledge is socially constructed, rather than received or discovered. Thus, constructivist learners "create meaning," "learn by doing," and work collaboratively "in mixed groups on common projects." Rather than transmitting knowledge to students, teachers collaborate with them to create knowledge and understanding in their mutual social context. Rather than seeking to "cover the curriculum,"

109

learning focuses on the learners' experience, needs, interests, and aspirations.

Design: Objectives, syllabus, learning activities, roles of learners, teachers, and materials

The major principles underlying the design of Whole Language instruction are as follows:

- the use of authentic literature rather than artificial, specially prepared texts and exercises designed to practice individual reading skills
- a focus on real and natural events rather than on specially written stories that do not relate to the students' experience
- the reading of real texts of high interest, particularly literature
- reading for the sake of comprehension and for a real purpose
- writing for a real audience and not simply to practice writing skills
- writing as a process through which learners explore and discover meaning
- the use of student-produced texts rather than teacher-generated or other-generated texts
- integration of reading, writing, and other skills
- student-centered learning: students have choice over what they read and write, giving them power and understanding of their world
- reading and writing in partnership with other learners
- encouragement of risk taking and exploration and the acceptance of errors as signs of learning rather than of failure

The teacher is seen as a facilitator and an active participant in the learning community rather than an expert passing on knowledge. The teacher teaches students and not the subject matter and looks for the occurrence of teachable moments rather than following a preplanned lesson plan or script. The teacher creates a climate that will support collaborative learning. The teacher has the responsibility of negotiating a plan of work with the learners.

The learner is a collaborator, collaborating with fellow students, with the teacher, and with writers of texts. Students are also evaluators, evaluating their own and others' learning, with the help of the teacher. The learner is self-directed; his or her own learning experiences are used as resources for learning. Students are also selectors of learning materials and activities. "Choice is vital in a whole language class, because without the ability to select activities, materials, and conversational partners, the students cannot use language for their own purposes" (Rigg 1991: 526).

Whole Language instruction advocates the use of real-world materials rather than commercial texts. A piece of literature is an example of "real-world" materials in that its creation was not instructionally motivated but resulted from the author's wish to communicate with the reader. Other real-world materials are brought to class by the students in the form of newspapers, signs, handbills, storybooks, and printed materials from the workplace in the case of adults. Students also produce their own materials. Rather than purchase pedagogically prepared textbooks and "basal readers," schools make use of class sets of literature, both fictional and nonfictional.

Procedure

The issue of what instructional characteristics are specific to Whole Language is somewhat problematic. Bergeron (1990) found that Whole Language was described differently in each article of the sixty-four articles she surveyed (except those written by the same author). She found only four classroom features mentioned in more than 50 percent of the articles. These included:

– the use of literature
– the use of process writing
– encouragement of cooperative learning among students
– concern for students' attitude

Activities that are often used in Whole Language instruction are:

– individual and small group reading and writing
– ungraded dialogue journals
– writing portfolios
– writing conferences
– student-made books
– story writing

Many of these activities are also common in other instructional approaches, such as Communicative Language Teaching, Content-Based Teaching, and Task-Based Language Teaching. Perhaps the only feature of Whole Language that does not also appear centrally in discussions of communicative approaches to language teaching is the focus on literature, although this has obviously been of concern to other writers on ELT methodology. Suggestions for exploitation of literary resources in the Whole Language classroom will be familiar to language teachers with a similar interest in the use of literature in support of second language learning. What differs in Whole Language teaching is not the incidental use of such activities based on the topic of the lesson or an item in the syllabus but their use as part of an overall philosophy of teaching and learning that gives a new meaning and purpose to such activities.

111

The following is an example of the use of literary pieces in a Whole Language workshop and involves activities built around the use of "Parallel Texts." Two English translations of the same short story is an example of Parallel Texts. Study of the two translations highlights the range of linguistic choices open to the writer (and translator) in the contrast of linguistic choices made by the translators and the responses made to these choices by the students as readers. In pairs, one student acts as presenter/interpreter of one of the two short-story translations and a partner acts as presenter/interpreter of the other.

Parallel Texts: Opening sentences from two translations of a Korean short story.

1a. "Cranes" by Hwang Sun-Won (translated by Kevin O'Rourke)

"The village on the northern side of the 38th parallel frontier was ever so quiet and desolate beneath the high, clear autumn sky. White gourds leaned on white gourds as they swayed in the yard of an empty house."

1b. "The Crane" by Hwang Sun-Won (translated by Kim Se-young)

"The northern village at the border of the 38th Parallel was ever so snug under the bright high autumn sky. In the space between the two main rooms of the empty farm house a white empty gourd was lying against another white empty gourd."

Examples of student activities based on parallel texts:

1. Think of the village as described in 1a and 1b as two different villages. Which one would you choose to live in? Why?
2. Do the contrasting opening sentences set up any different expectations in the reader as to what kind of story will follow and what the tone of the story will be?
3. On a map of Korea, each partner should indicate where he/she thinks the village is located. Are the locations the same? If not, why not?
4. Write an opening sentence of a short story in which you briefly introduce the village of 1a as it might appear in winter rather than autumn.
5. Write two parallel text opening sentences in which you describe in different words a village you know. Ask a partner which village he/she prefers.
6. Discuss what different kinds of stories might follow on the basis of the opening sentences. Write an original first sentence of this story thinking of yourself as "translator" and drawing on both translations as your resources.

(Rodgers 1993)

Conclusions

The Whole Language movement is not a teaching method but an approach to learning that sees language as a whole entity. Each language teacher is free to implement the approach according to the needs of particular classes. Advantages claimed for Whole Language are that it focuses on experiences and activities that are relevant to learners' lives and needs, that it uses authentic materials, and that it can be used to facilitate the development of all aspects of a second language. Critics, however, see it as a rejection of the whole ESL approach in language teaching and one that seeks to apply native-language principles to ESL. Whole Language proposals are seen as anti-direct teaching, anti-skills, and anti-materials, assuming that authentic texts are sufficient to support second language learning and that skill development will follow without special attention (Aaron 1991). Many language teachers still have a strong commitment to specially developed materials to support instruction and some have argued that Whole Language promotes fluency at the expense of accuracy. On the other hand, supporters of Whole Language have developed a rich array of materials that can offer an integrated approach to ESL instruction and that can be adapted for use in a wide variety of contexts (e.g., Whiteson 1998). Whole Language activities may prove useful particularly for younger learners in ESL environments. Many of the activities for older learners in other environments are similar to those recommended in other instructional approaches (e.g., Communicative Language Teaching and Cooperative Learning), which can also serve as resources to support a Whole Language approach.

Bibliography and further reading

Aaron, P. 1991. Is there a hole in whole language? *Contemporary Education* 62 (winter): 127.

Adunyarittigun, D. 1996. Whole Language: A whole new world for ESL programs. ERIC Document ED386024.

Bergeron, B. S. 1990. What does the term Whole Language mean? *Journal of Reading Behavior* 22(4): 6–7.

Brockman, B. 1994. Whole language: A philosophy of literacy teaching for adults too! ERIC Document: ED376428.

Chitrapu, D. 1996. Whole Language: Adapting the approach for large classes. *Forum Magazine* 34(2): 28–29.

Freeman, D., and Y. Freeman. 1993. Whole Language: How does it support second language learners? ERIC Document: ED360875.

Goodman, K. 1986. *What's Whole in Whole Language?* Portsmouth, N.H.: Heinemann.

Hao, R. N. 1991. Whole Language: Some thoughts. *Kamehameha Journal of Education* (March): 16–18.

Heymsfeld, C. R. 1989. Filling the hole in Whole Language. *Educational Leadership* 46(6).

Krashen, S. 1998. Has whole language failed? ERIC Document: ED586010.

Lems, K. 1995. Whole Language and the ESL/EFL classroom. ERIC Document ED384210.

Patzelt, Karen E. 1993. Principles of Whole Language and implications for ESL learners. ERIC Document: ED400526.

Rigg, P. 1991. Whole Language in TESOL. *TESOL Quarterly* 25(3): 521–542.

Rodgers, T. S. 1993. Teacher training for Whole Language in ELT. Paper given at City University of Hong Kong Seminar on Teacher in Education in Language Teaching. April.

Shao, X. 1996. A bibliography of Whole Language materials. Biblio. Series 1993, No. 1. ERIC Document: ED393093.

Stahl, S. A. 1994. The effects of Whole Language instruction: An update and a reappraisal. ERIC Document: ED364830.

Whiteson, V. 1998. *Play's the Thing: A Whole Language Approach*. New York: St. Martin's Press.

10 Multiple Intelligences

Background

Multiple Intelligences (MI) refers to a learner-based philosophy that characterizes human intelligence as having multiple dimensions that must be acknowledged and developed in education. Traditional IQ or intelligence tests are based on a test called the Stanford-Binet, founded on the idea that intelligence is a single, unchanged, inborn capacity. However, traditional IQ tests, while still given to most schoolchildren, are increasingly being challenged by the MI movement. MI is based on the work of Howard Gardner of the Harvard Graduate School of Education (Gardner 1993). Gardner notes that traditional IQ tests measure only logic and language, yet the brain has other equally important types of intelligence. Gardner argues that all humans have these intelligences, but people differ in the strengths and combinations of intelligences. He believes that all of them can be enhanced through training and practice. MI thus belongs to a group of instructional perspectives that focus on differences between learners and the need to recognize learner differences in teaching. Learners are viewed as possessing individual learning styles, preferences, or intelligences. Pedagogy is most successful when these learner differences are acknowledged, analyzed for particular groups of learners, and accommodated in teaching. In both general education and language teaching, a focus on individual differences has been a recurring theme in the last 30 or so years, as seen in such movements or approaches as Individualized Instruction, Autonomous Learning, Learner Training, and Learner Strategies. The Multiple Intelligences model shares a number of commonalities with these earlier proposals.

Gardner (1993) proposed a view of natural human talents that is labeled the "Multiple Intelligences Model." This model is one of a variety of learning style models that have been proposed in general education and have subsequently been applied to language education (see, e.g., Christison 1998). Gardner claims that his view of intelligence(s) is culture-free and avoids the conceptual narrowness usually associated with traditional models of intelligence (e.g., the Intelligent Quotient [IQ] testing model). Gardner posits eight native "intelligences," which are described as follows:

1. *Linguistic:* the ability to use language in special and creative ways, which is something lawyers, writers, editors, and interpreters are strong in
2. *Logical/mathematical:* the ability to think rationally, often found with doctors, engineers, programmers, and scientists
3. *Spatial:* the ability to form mental models of the world, something architects, decorators, sculptors, and painters are good at
4. *Musical:* a good ear for music, as is strong in singers and composers
5. *Bodily/kinesthetic:* having a well-coordinated body, something found in athletes and craftspersons
6. *Interpersonal:* the ability to be able to work well with people, which is strong in salespeople, politicians, and teachers
7. *Intrapersonal:* the ability to understand oneself and apply one's talent successfully, which leads to happy and well-adjusted people in all areas of life
8. *Naturalist:* the ability to understand and organize the patterns of nature

The idea of Multiple Intelligences has attracted the interest of many educators as well as the general public. Schools that use MI theory encourage learning that goes beyond traditional books, pens, and pencils. Teachers and parents who recognize their learners'/children's particular gifts and talents can provide learning activities that build on those inherent gifts. As a result of strengthening such differences, individuals are free to be intelligent in their own ways.

Other "intelligences" have been proposed, such as Emotional Intelligence, Mechanical Intelligence, and Practical Intelligence, but Gardner defends his eight-dimensional model of intelligence by claiming that the particular intelligences he has nominated are verified by eight databased "signs." Detailed discussion of the signs is beyond the range of this chapter. However, signs include such clues as an intelligence having a distinct developmental and a distinct evolutionary history; that is, within individuals there is a similar sequence of development of an intelligence beginning in early childhood and continuing into maturity. This sequence will be universal for individuals but unique to each intelligence. Similarly, each intelligence is deeply embedded in evolutionary history. Human tool using, for example, has such an evidential evolutionary history and is an example, Gardner says, of bodily/kinesthetic intelligence.

Approach: Theory of language and language learning

MI theory was originally proposed by Gardner (1993) as a contribution to cognitive science. Fairly early on, it was interpreted by some general educators, such as Armstrong (1994), as a framework for rethinking school education. Some schools in the United States have indeed remade their educational programs around the MI model. Applications of MI in language teaching have been more recent, so it is not surprising that MI theory lacks some of the basic elements that might link it more directly to language education. One lack is a concrete view of how MI theory relates to any existing language and/or language learning theories, though attempts have been made to establish such links (e.g., Reid 1997; Christison 1998). It certainly is fair to say that MI proposals look at the language of an individual, including one or more second languages, not as an "added-on" and somewhat peripheral skill but as central to the whole life of the language learner and user. In this sense, language is held to be integrated with music, bodily activity, interpersonal relationships, and so on. Language is not seen as limited to a "linguistics" perspectives but encompasses all aspects of communication.

Language learning and use are obviously closely linked to what MI theorists label "Linguistic Intelligence." However, MI proponents believe there is more to language than what is usually subsumed under the rubric linguistics. There are aspects of language such as rhythm, tone, volume, and pitch that are more closely linked, say, to a theory of music than to a theory of linguistics. Other intelligences enrich the tapestry of communication we call "language." In addition, language has its ties to life through the senses. The senses provide the accompaniment and context for the linguistic message that give it meaning and purpose. A multisensory view of language is necessary, it seems, to construct an adequate theory of language as well as an effective design for language learning.

A widely accepted view of intelligence is that intelligence – however measured and in whatever circumstance – comprises a single factor, usually called the "g" factor. From this point of view, "Intelligence (g) can be described as the ability to deal with cognitive complexity. . . . The vast majority of intelligence researchers take these findings for granted" (Gottfredson 1998: 24). One popular explication of this view sees intelligence as a hierarchy with g at the apex of the hierarchy:

more specific aptitudes are arrayed at successively lower levels: the so-called group factors, such as verbal ability, mathematical reasoning, spatial visualization and memory, are just below g, and below these are skills that are more dependent on knowledge or experience, such as the principles and practices of a particular job or profession. (Gottfredson 1998: 3)

The view of Gardner (and some other cognitive scientists) "contrasts markedly with the view that intelligence is based on a unitary or 'general' ability for problem solving" (Teele 2000: 27). In the Gardner view, there exists a cluster of mental abilities that are separate but equal and that share the pinnacle at the top of the hierarchy called intelligence – thus, the eight Multiple Intelligences that Gardner has described. One way of look-

117

ing at the learning theoretical argument is to apply the logic of the single factor (g) model to the Multiple Intelligences model. The single factor model correlates higher intelligence (+g) with greater speed and efficiency of neural processing; that is, the higher the g factor in the individual, the greater the speed and efficiency of that individual's brain in performing cognitive operations (Gottfredson 1998: 3). If there is not one I but several I's, then one can assume that the speed and efficiency of neural processing will be greatest when a particular I is most fully exercised; that is, if a language learner has a high musical intelligence, that person will learn most quickly (e.g., a new language) when that content is embedded in a musical frame.

Design: Objectives, syllabus, learning activities, roles of learners, teachers, and materials

There are no goals stated for MI instruction in linguistic terms. MI pedagogy focuses on the language class as the setting for a series of educational support systems aimed at making the language learner a better designer of his/her own learning experiences. Such a learner is both better empowered and more fulfilled than a learner in traditional classrooms. A more goal-directed learner and happier person is held to be a likely candidate for being a better second language learner and user.

Also, there is no syllabus as such, either prescribed or recommended, in respect to MI-based language teaching. However, there is a basic developmental sequence that has been proposed (Lazear 1991) as an alternative to what we have elsewhere considered as a type of "syllabus" design. The sequence consists of four stages:

- *Stage 1:* Awaken the Intelligence. Through multisensory experiences – touching, smelling, tasting, seeing, and so on – learners can be sensitized to the many-faceted properties of objects and events in the world that surrounds them.
- *Stage 2:* Amplify the Intelligence. Students strengthen and improve the intelligence by volunteering objects and events of their own choosing and defining with others the properties and contexts of experience of these objects and events.
- *Stage 3:* Teach with/for the Intelligence. At this stage the intelligence is linked to the focus of the class, that is, to some aspect of language learning. This is done via worksheets and small-group projects and discussion.
- *Stage 4:* Transfer of the Intelligence. Students reflect on the learning experiences of the previous three stages and relate these to issues and challenges in the out-of-class world.

MI has been applied in many different types of classrooms. In some, there are eight self-access activity corners, each corner built around one of the eight intelligences. Students work alone or in pairs on intelligence foci of their own choosing. Nicholson-Nelson (1998: 73) describes how MI can be used to individualize learning through project work. She lists five types of projects:

1. *Multiple intelligence projects:* These are based on one or more of the intelligences and are designed to stimulate particular intelligences.
2. *Curriculum-based projects:* These are based on curriculum content areas but are categorized according to the particular intelligences they make use of.
3. *Thematic-based projects:* These are based on a theme from the curriculum or classroom but are divided into different intelligences.
4. *Resource-based projects:* These are designed to provide students with opportunities to research a topic using multiple intelligences.
5. *Student-choice projects:* These are designed by students and draw on particular intelligences.

In other, more fully teacher-fronted classrooms, the students move through a cycle of activities highlighting use of different intelligences in the activities that the teacher has chosen and orchestrated.

The following list summarizes several of the alternative views as to how the MI model can be used to serve the needs of language learners within a classroom setting:

– *Play to strength.* If you want an athlete or a musician (or a student having some of the these talents) to be an involved and successful language learner, structure the learning material for each individual (or similar group of individuals) around these strengths.
– *Variety is the spice.* Providing a teacher-directed rich mix of learning activities variously calling upon the eight different intelligences makes for an interesting, lively, and effective classroom for all students.
– *Pick a tool to suit the job.* Language has a variety of dimensions, levels, and functions. These different facets of language are best served instructionally by linking their learning to the most appropriate kind of MI activity.
– *All sizes fit one.* Every individual exercises all intelligences even though some of these may be out of awareness or undervalued. Pedagogy that appeals to all the intelligences speaks to the "whole person" in ways that more unifaceted approaches do not. An MI approach helps to develop the Whole Person within each learner, which best serves the person's language learning requirements as well.
– *Me and my people.* IQ testing is held to be badly biased in favor of Western views of intelligence. Other cultures may value other intelli-

gences more than the one measured in IQ testing. Since language learning involves culture learning as well, it is useful for the language learner to study language in a context that recognizes and honors a range of diversely valued intelligences.

Each of these views has strengths and weaknesses, some of a theoretical, some of a pedagogical, and some of a practical nature. It seems that potential MI teachers need to consider each of these possible applications of MI theory in light of their individual teaching situations.

Campbell notes that MI theory "is not prescriptive. Rather, it gives teachers a complex mental model from which to construct curriculum and improve themselves as educators" (Campbell 1997: 19). In this view, teachers are expected to understand, master, and be committed to the MI model. Teachers are encouraged to administer an MI inventory on themselves and thereby be able to "connect your life's experiences to your concept of Multiple Intelligences" (Christison 1997: 7). (The MI inventory is a short checklist that enables users to create their own MI profiles and use these as a guide to designing and reflecting upon their learning experiences [Christison 1997]). Teachers then become curriculum developers, lesson designers and analysts, activity finders or inventors, and, most critically orchestrators of a rich array of multisensory activities within the realistic constraints of time, space, and resources of the classroom. Teachers are encouraged not to think of themselves merely as language teachers. They have a role that is not only to improve the second language abilities of their students but to become major "contributors to the overall development of students' intelligences" (Christison 1999: 12).

Like teachers, learners need to see themselves engaged in a process of personality development above and beyond that of being successful language learners. The MI classroom is one designed to support development of the "whole person," and the environment and its activities are intended to enable students to become more well-rounded individuals and more successful learners in general. Learners are encouraged to see their goals in these broader terms. Learners are typically expected to take an MI inventory and to develop their own MI profiles based on the inventory. "The more awareness students have of their own intelligences and how they work, the more they will know how to use that intelligence [*sic*] to access the necessary information and knowledge from a lesson" (Christison 1997: 9). All of this is to enable learners to benefit from instructional approaches by reflecting on their own learning.

Where MI is richest is in proposals for lesson organization, multisensory activity planning, and in using realia. There are also now a number of reports of actual teaching experiences from an MI perspective that are both teacher-friendly and candid in their reportage. Activities and the materials that support them are often shown or suggested in tables in

Linguistic Intelligence

lectures	student speeches
small- and large-group discussions	storytelling
books	debates
worksheets	journal keeping
word games	memorizing
listening to cassettes or talking books	using word processors
publishing (creating class newspapers or collections of writing)	

Logical/Mathematical Intelligence

scientific demonstrations	creating codes
logic problems and puzzles	story problems
science thinking	calculations
logical-sequential presentation of subject matter	

Spatial Intelligence

charts, maps, diagrams	visualization
videos, slides, movies	photography
art and other pictures	using mind maps
imaginative storytelling	painting or collage
graphic organizers	optical illusions
telescopes, microscopes	student drawings
visual awareness activities	

Bodily/Kinesthetic Intelligence

creative movement	hands-on activities
Mother-may-I?	field trips
cooking and other "mess" activities	mime
role plays	

Musical Intelligence

playing recorded music	singing
playing live music (piano, guitar)	group singing
music appreciation	mood music
student-made instruments	Jazz Chants

Interpersonal Intelligence

cooperative groups	conflict mediation
peer teaching	board games
group brainstorming	pair work

Intrapersonal Intelligence

independent student work	reflective learning
individualized projects	journal keeping
options for homework	interest centers
inventories and checklists	self-esteem journals
personal journal keeping	goal setting
self-teaching/programmed instruction	

which a particular intelligence is paired with possible resources useful for working with this intelligence in class. Such a table from Christison (1997: 7–8) is reproduced in Table 1.

Procedure

Christison describes a low-level language lesson dealing with description of physical objects. The lesson plan recapitulates the sequence described earlier in the "Design" section.

- *Stage 1:* Awaken the Intelligence. The teacher brings many different objects to class. Students experience feeling things that are soft, rough, cold, smooth, and so on. They might taste things that are sweet, salty, sour, spicy, and so on. Experiences like this help activate and make learners aware of the sensory bases of experience.
- *Stage 2.* Amplify the Intelligence. Students are asked to bring objects to class or to use something in their possession. Teams of students describe each object attending to the five physical senses. They complete a worksheet including the information they have observed and discussed (Table 2).
- *Stage 3:* Teach with/for the Intelligence. At this stage, the teacher structures larger sections of lesson(s) so as to reenforce and emphasize sensory experiences and the language that accompanies these experiences. Students work in groups, perhaps completing a worksheet such as that shown in Table 3.
- *Stage 4:* Transfer of the Intelligence. This stage is concerned with application of the intelligence to daily living. Students are asked to reflect on both the content of the lesson and its operational procedures (working in groups, completing tables, etc.).

TABLE 2. THE SENSORY HANDOUT

Name of team _____
Team members _____
Sight _____
Sound _____
Feel _____
Smell _____
Size _____
What it's used for _____
Name of the object _____

TABLE 3. MULTIPLE INTELLIGENCES DESCRIPTION EXERCISE

What am I describing?
Directions: Work with your group. Listen as the teacher reads the description of the object. Discuss what you hear with your group. Together, decide which object in the class is being described.

Name of the object
Object 1 _____
Object 2 _____
Object 3 _____
Object 4 _____
Object 5 _____

Next have each group describe an object in the classroom using the formula given in Stage 2. Then, collect the papers and read them, one at a time. Ask each group to work together to write down the name of the object in the classroom that you are describing.

This particular lesson on describing objects is seen as giving students opportunities to "develop their linguistic intelligence (for example, describing objects), logical intelligence (for example, determining which object is being described), visual/spatial intelligence (for example, determining how to describe things), interpersonal intelligence (for example, working in groups), and intrapersonal intelligence (for example, reflecting on one's own involvement in the lesson)" (Christison 1997: 10–12).

Conclusion

Multiple Intelligences is an increasingly popular approach to characterizing the ways in which learners are unique and to developing instruction to respond to this uniqueness. MI is one of a set of such perspectives dealing with learner differences and borrows heavily from these in its recommendations and designs for lesson planning. The literature on MI provides a rich source of classroom ideas regardless of one's theoretical perspective and can help teachers think about instruction in their classes in unique ways. Some teachers may see the assumptions of identifying and responding to the variety of ways in which students differ to be unrealistic in their own settings and antithetical to the expectations of their students and administrators. There are, however entire schools as well as language programs being restructured around the MI perspective. Evaluation of how successful these innovations are will be needed to more fully evaluate the claims of MI in education and in second language teaching.

Bibliography and further reading

Armstrong, T. 1994. *Multiple Intelligences in the Classroom*. Alexandria, Va.: Association for Supervision and Curriculum Development.

Campbell, L. 1997. How teachers interpret MI theory. *Educational Leadership* 55(1): 15–19.

Christison, M. 1997. An introduction to multiple intelligences theory and second language learning. In J. Reid (ed.), Understanding Learning Styles in the Second Language Classroom. Englewood Cliffs, N.J.: Prentice Hall/Regents. 1–14.

Christison, M. 1998. Applying multiple intelligences theory in preservice and inservice TEFL education programs. *English Language Teaching Forum* 36(2) (April–June): 2–13.

Christison, M. 1999. Multiple Intelligences: Teaching the whole student. *ESL Magazine* 2(5): 10–13.

Christison, M. 2001. *Applying Multiple Intelligences Theory in the Second and Foreign Language Classroom*. Burlingame, Calif: Alta Book Center Publishers.

Gardner, H. 1985. *Frames of Mind: The Theory of Multiple Intelligences*. New York: Basic Books.

Gardner, H. 1993. *Multiple Intelligences: The Theory and Practice*. New York: Basic Books.

Gottfredson, L. 1998. The general intelligence factor. *Scientific American* 9(4) (Winter): 24–29.

Lazear, D. 1991. *Seven Ways of Teaching: The Artistry of Teaching with Multiple Intelligences*. Palatine, Ill.: IRI Skylight.

Marzano, R., R. Brandt, C. Hughes, B. Jones, B. Presseisen, and S. Rankin. 1988. *Dimensions of Thinking: A Framework for Curriculum and Instruction*. Alexandria, Va.: Association for Supervision and Curriculum Development.

Nicholson-Nelson, K. 1988. *Developing Students' Multiple Intelligences*. New York: Scholastic.

Reid, J. 1997. *Understanding Learning Styles in the Second Language Classroom*. Englewood Cliffs, N.J.: Prentice Hall/Regents.

Teele, S. 2000. *Rainbows of Intelligence: Exploring How Students Learn*. Thousand Oaks, Calif.: Corwin Press.

Weinreich-Haste, H. 1985. The varieties of intelligence: An interview with Howard Gardner. *New Ideas in Psychology* 3(4): 47–65.

11 Neurolinguistic Programming

Background

Neurolinguistic Programming (NLP) refers to a training philosophy and set of training techniques first developed by John Grindler and Richard Bandler in the mid-1970s as an alternative form of therapy. Grindler (a psychologist) and Bandler (a student of linguistics) were interested in how people influence each other and in how the behaviors of very effective people could be duplicated. They were essentially interested in discovering how successful communicators achieved their success. They studied successful therapists and concluded that they "followed similar patterns in relating to their clients and in the language they used, and that they all held similar beliefs about themselves and what they were doing" (Revell and Norman 1997: 14). Grindler and Bandler developed NLP as a system of techniques therapists could use in building rapport with clients, gathering information about their internal and external views of the world, and helping them achieve goals and bring about personal change. They sought to fill what they perceived to be a gap in psychological thinking and practice of the early 1970s by developing a series of step-by-step procedures that would enable people to improve themselves:

NLP is . . . a collection of techniques, patterns, and strategies for assisting effective communication, personal growth and change, and learning. It is based on a series of underlying assumptions about how the mind works and how people act and interact. (Revell and Norman 1997: 14)

The NLP model provides a theoretical framework and a set of working principles for directing or guiding therapeutic change, but the principles of NLP have been applied in a variety of other fields, including management training, sports training, communications sales and marketing, and language teaching. Since NLP is a set of general communication techniques, NLP practitioners generally are required to take training in how to use the techniques in their respective fields. NLP was not developed with any applications to language teaching in mind. However, because the assumptions of NLP refer to attitudes to life, to people, and to self-discovery and awareness, it has had some appeal within language teaching to those interested in what we have called humanistic approaches –

125

that is, approaches that focus on developing one's sense of self-actualization and self-awareness, as well as to those drawn to what has been referred to as New Age Humanism.

Approach: Theory of language and learning

The name "Neurolinguistic Programming" might lead one to expect that it is based on the science of neurolinguistics and that it also draws on behaviorist theories of learning (see Chapter 4). However, in NLP *neuro* refers to beliefs about the brain and how it functions: The literature on NLP does not refer to theory or research in neurolinguistics. In fact, research plays virtually no role in NLP. *Linguistic* has nothing to do with the field of linguistics but refers to a theory of communication, one that tries to explain both verbal and nonverbal information processing. *Programming* refers to observable patterns (referred to as "programs") of thought and behavior. NLP practitioners claim to be able to deprogram and program clients' behaviors with a precision close to computer programming. Learning effective behaviors is viewed as a problem of skill learning: It is dependent on moving from stages of controlled to automatic processing (O'Connor and McDermott 1996: 6). Modeling is also central to NLP views on learning:

Modeling a skill means finding out about it, and the beliefs and values that enable them to do it. You can also model emotions, experiences, beliefs and values. . . . Modeling successful performance leads to excellence. If one person can do something it is possible to model and teach others how to do it. (O'Connor and McDermott 1996: 71)

Revell and Norman offer the following explanation of the name:

The *neuro* part of NLP is concerned with how we experience the world through our five senses and represent it in our minds through our neurological processes.

The *linguistic* part of NLP is concerned with the way the language we use shapes, as well as reflects, our experience of the world. We use language – in thought as well as in speech – to represent the world to ourselves and to embody our beliefs about the world and about life. If we change the way we speak and think about things, we can change our behavior. We can also use language to help other people who want to change.

The *programming* part of NLP is concerned with training ourselves to think, speak, and act in new and positive ways in order to release our potential and reach those heights of achievement which we previously only dreamt of. (Revell and Norman 1997: 14)

Design: Objectives, syllabus, learning activities, roles of learners, teachers, and materials

Four key principles lie at the heart of NLP (O'Connor and McDermott 1996; Revell and Norman 1997).

1. *Outcomes:* the goals or ends. NLP claims that knowing precisely what you want helps you achieve it. This principle can be expressed as "know what you want."
2. *Rapport:* a factor that is essential for effective communication – maximizing similarities and minimizing differences between people at a nonconscious level. This principle can be expressed as "Establish rapport with yourself and then with others."
3. *Sensory acuity:* noticing what another person is communicating, consciously and nonverbally. This can be expressed as "Use your senses. Look at, listen to, and feel what is actually happening."
4. *Flexibility:* doing things differently if what you are doing is not working: having a range of skills to do something else or something different. This can be expressed as "Keep changing what you do until you get what you want."

Revell and Norman (1997) present thirteen presuppositions that guide the application of NLP in language learning and other fields. The idea is that these principles become part of the belief system of the teacher and shape the way teaching is conducted no matter what method the teacher is using:

1. Mind and body are interconnected: They are parts of the same system, and each affects the other.
2. The map is not the territory: We all have different maps of the world.
3. There is no failure, only feedback . . . and a renewed opportunity for success.
4. The map becomes the territory: What you believe to be true either is true or becomes true.
5. Knowing what you want helps you get it.
6. The resources we need are within us.
7. Communication is nonverbal as well as verbal.
8. The nonconscious mind is benevolent.
9. Communication is nonconscious as well as conscious.
10. All behavior has a positive intention.
11. The meaning of my communication is the response I get.
12. Modeling excellent behavior leads to excellence.
13. In any system, the element with the greatest flexibility will have the most influence on that system.

Revell and Norman's book (1997) on NLP in English-language teaching seeks to relate each of these principles to language teaching. For example, in discussing principle 7 – "Communication is nonverbal as well as verbal" – they discuss the kinds of nonverbal messages teachers consciously or unconsciously communicate to learners in the classroom.

As noted earlier, modeling is also central to NLP practice. Just as Bandler and Grinder modeled NLP on the practices of successful therapists, so teachers are expected to model their teaching on expert teachers they most admire. Similarly, learners are expected to find successful models for that person they themselves are striving to become:

If you want to be an excellent teacher, model excellent teachers. Look at that they do, how they act, what sort of relationship they have with their students and colleagues. Ask then how they feel about what they do. What are their beliefs? Second, position them. Imagine what it's like to be them. As you learn techniques and strategies, put them into practice. Share modeling strategies with students. Set the project of modeling good learners. Encourage them to share and try out strategies they learn. If you want to speak a language like a native speaker, model native speakers. (Revell and Norman 1997: 116)

What do NLP language teachers do that make them different from other language teachers? According to NLP, they seek to apply the principles in their teaching and this leads to different responses to many classroom events and processes. For example, one of the four central principles of NLP centers on the need for "rapport":

Rapport is meeting others in their world, trying to understand their needs, their values and their culture and communicating in ways that are congruent with those values. You don't necessarily have to agree with their values, simply recognize that they have a right to them and work within their framework, not against it. (Rylatt and Lohan 1995: 121)

Rylatt and Lohan give the following example of how a teacher might apply rapport in responding to the following statements from students:

a) I hate this stuff. It's such a waste of time.
b) Everyone says that. It makes me sick.
c) I can't do it.
d) This is all theory.

In establishing rapport, the teacher could respond:

a) Is a part of you saying that you want to be sure your time is well spent today?
b) Who says that?
c) What, specifically, can't you do?
d) Are you saying you want practical suggestions?

Likewise, principle 10 above – "All behavior has a positive intention" – would lead the teacher to seek for a positive intent in the following situations:

a) A learner disagrees strongly with the teacher.
b) A student frequently comes late to class.
c) A student seeks to dominate discussions.

The possible positive intents here could be:

a) wanting to have expertise acknowledged
b) having other important priorities
c) needing to vocalize thoughts in order to internalize them

Procedure

NLP principles can be applied to the teaching of all aspects of language, according to Revell and Norman. For example, the following suggested lesson sequence is "to help students become aware at a feeling level of the conceptual meaning of a grammatical structure." The primary focus of the sequence is awareness (and, indeed, production) of instances of the present perfect in English. The lesson begins with a guided fantasy of eating a food item and then reflecting on the experience.

1. Students are told that they are going on an "inner grammatical experience as you eat a biscuit."
2. Check that they understand vocabulary of the experience (smell, taste, chew, swallow, bite, lick, etc.).
3. Students are asked to relax, close their eyes, and "go inside." Once "inside," they listen to the teacher-produced fantasy, which is given as the following:
4. (An abbreviated version of the teacher text) "Imagine a biscuit. A delicious biscuit. The sort you really like. Pick it up and look at it closely. Notice how crisp and fresh it is. Smell it. Notice how your mouth is beginning to water. In a moment you are going to eat the biscuit. Say the words to yourself: 'I am going to eat this biscuit.'

   "Slowly chew the biscuit and notice how delicious it tastes on your tongue and in your mouth. . . . Say the words to yourself, 'I'm really enjoying eating this biscuit.'

   "Take another bite. Chew it. Taste it. Enjoy it. . . . And then swallow. Lick your lips, move your tongue all around the inside of your mouth to catch any last bits of biscuit, and swallow them.

   "Notice how you feel now. Notice the taste in your mouth. Notice how your stomach feels with a biscuit inside it. Notice how you feel emotionally. You have eaten a biscuit. Say the words to yourself, 'I've eaten a biscuit.'

"How are you feeling now? Think of the words to describe how you are feeling now. Take a deep breath and gently come back to the room, bringing the feeling with you. Open your eyes."

5. Ask the students to describe how they are feeling now – "the feeling of the present perfect." Listen for any statements that link the past experience of eating the biscuit with their present feelings (e.g., "I feel full," "I'm not hungry anymore," "I've got a nice taste in my mouth," "I feel fat").
6. Ask them to say again the sentence that describes the cause of the way they feel ("I've eaten a biscuit").
7. Put a large piece of paper on the wall with the words "I've eaten a biscuit" at the top. Have students write how they feel underneath.
8. On other pieces of paper, write sentences such as: I've painted a picture. I've had a row with my boy/girlfriend. I've finished my homework. I've cleaned my teeth.
9. Ask students to stand in front of each sentence, close their eyes, and strongly imagine what they have done in order to be saying that sentence now.
10. Students write on the paper how they feel now about these sentences.
11. Leave the papers on the wall as a reminder of the feeling link to the grammatical structure.
12. As follow-up, contrast the feeling of the present perfect with the feeling of the simple past. Ask students to remember the things they did in the last lesson ("I ate a biscuit"). Ask them to close their eyes and notice how they are feeling now. Contrast this feeling with the feeling they remember from the last lesson and which they wrote down on the papers.
13. Ask them to say the sentence "Yesterday, I ate a biscuit."
14. Discuss the comparison between the feelings ("I remember the taste, but I can't actually taste it").
15. You can do similar exercises to exemplify other tenses using different tastes and sensory experiences.

(Adapted from Revell and Norman 1999)

Conclusion

NLP is not a language teaching method. It does not consist of a set of techniques for teaching a language based on theories and assumptions at the levels of an approach and a design. Rather, it is a humanistic philosophy and a set of beliefs and suggestions based on popular psychology, designed to convince people that they have the power to control their own and other people's lives for the better, and practical prescriptions on how to do so. NLP practitioners believe that if language teachers adopt and use the principles of NLP, they will become more effective teachers. Workshops on NLP are hence typically short on theory and research to justify its claims and strong on creating positive expectations, bonding, and enthusiasm. As Revell and Norman comment, the assumptions on which NLP are based "need not be accepted as the absolute truth, but acting as if they were true can make a world of difference in your life and in your teaching" (1997: 15). In language teaching, the appeal of NLP to some teachers stems from the fact that it offers a set of humanistic principles that provide either a new justification for well-known techniques from the communicative or humanistic repertoire or a different interpretation of the role of the teacher and the learner, one in harmony with many learner-centered, person-centered views.

Bibliography and further reading

Bandler, R. 1985. *Using Your Brain for a Change.* Moab, Utah: Real People Press.

Bandler, R., and J. Grinder. 1982. *Reframing: NLP and the Transformation of Meaning.* Utah: Real People Press.

Betts, N. 1988. Neuro-Linguistic Programming: The new eclectic therapy. ERIC Document ED300711.

Grinder, M. 1991. *Righting the Educational Conveyor Belt.* Portland, Oreg.: Metamorphosis Press.

O'Connor, J., and I. McDermott. 1996. *Principles of NLP.* London: Thorsons.

O'Connor, J., and J. Seymour. 1993. *Introducing Neuro-Linguistic Programming.* Mandala: HarperCollins. rev ed. London: Aquarian/Thorsons, 1993.

Patridge, S. 1985. Neuro-Linguistic Programming: A discussion of why and how. ERIC Document ED265925.

Revell, J., and S. Norman. 1997. *In Your Hands: NLP in ELT.* London: Saffire Press.

Revell, J., and S. Norman. 1999. *Handing Over: NLP-Based Activities for Language Learning.* London: Saffire Press.

Rylatt, A., and K. Lohan. 1995. *Creating Training Miracles.* Sydney: Prentice Hall.

Turner, C., and P. Andrews. 1994. One to one: Interpersonal skills for managers. ERIC Document ED375759.

12 The lexical approach

Background

We have seen throughout this book that central to an approach or method in language teaching is a view of the nature of language, and this shapes teaching goals, the type of syllabus that is adopted, and the emphasis given in classroom teaching. A lexical approach in language teaching refers to one derived from the belief that the building blocks of language learning and communication are not grammar, functions, notions, or some other unit of planning and teaching but lexis, that is, words and word combinations. Lexical approaches in language teaching reflect a belief in the centrality of the lexicon to language structure, second language learning, and language use, and in particular to multiword lexical units or "chunks" that are learned and used as single items. Linguistic theory has also recognized a more central role for vocabulary in linguistic description. Formal transformational/generative linguistics, which previously took syntax as the primary focus, now gives more central attention to the lexicon and how the lexicon is formatted, coded, and organized. Chomsky, the father of contemporary studies in syntax, has recently adopted a "lexicon-is-prime" position in his Minimalist Linguistic theory.

The role of lexical units has been stressed in both first and second language acquisition research. These have been referred to by many different labels, including "holophrases" (Corder 1973), "prefabricated patterns" (Hakuta 1974), "gambits" (Keller 1979), "speech formulae" (Peters 1983), and "lexicalized stems" (Pawley and Syder 1983). Several approaches to language learning have been proposed that view vocabulary and lexical units as central in learning and teaching. These include *The Lexical Syllabus* (Willis 1990), *Lexical Phrases and Language Teaching* (Nattinger and DeCarrico 1992), and *The Lexical Approach* (Lewis 1993). Advances in computer-based studies of language (referred to as corpus linguistics) have also provided a huge, classroom-accessible database for lexically based inquiry and instruction. These studies have focused on collocations of lexical items and multiple word units. A number of lexically based texts and computer resources have become available to assist in organizing and teaching the lexicon.

Lexical approaches in language teaching seek to develop proposals for syllabus design and language teaching founded on a view of language in which lexis plays the central role.

Approach: Theory of language and learning

Whereas Chomsky's influential theory of language emphasized the capacity of speakers to create and interpret sentences that are unique and have never been produced or heard previously, in contrast, the lexical view holds that only a minority of spoken sentences are entirely novel creations and that multiword units functioning as "chunks" or memorized patterns form a high proportion of the fluent stretches of speech heard in everyday conversation (Pawley and Syder 1983). The role of collocation is also important in lexically based theories of language. Collocation refers to the regular occurrence together of words. For example, compare the following collocations of verbs with nouns:

do   my hair/the cooking/the laundry/my work
make   my bed/a promise/coffee/a meal

Many other lexical units also occur in language. For example:

binomials: clean and tidy, back to front
trinomials: cool, calm, and collected
idioms: dead drunk, to run up a bill
similes: as old as the hills
connectives: finally, to conclude
conversational gambits: Guess what!

These and other types of lexical units are thought to play a central role in learning and in communication. Studies based on large-scale computer databases of language corpora have examined patterns of phrase and clause sequences as they appear in samples of various kinds of texts, including spoken samples. Three important UK-based corpora are the COBUILD Bank of English Corpus, the Cambridge International Corpus, and the British National Corpus, the latter of which contains more than 300 million words. These and other corpora are important sources of information about collocations and other multiword units in English.

Lexis is also believed to play a central role in language learning. Nattinger commented:

Perhaps we should base our teaching on the assumption that, for a great deal of the time anyway, language production consists of piecing together the ready-made units appropriate for a particular situation and that comprehension relies on knowing which of these patterns to predict in these situations. Our teaching, therefore, would center on these patterns and the ways they can be pieced together, along with the ways they vary and the situations in which they occur. (Nattinger 1980: 341)

However, if as Pawley and Syder estimate, native speakers have hundreds of thousands of prepackaged phrases in their lexical inventory, the implications for second language learning are uncertain. How might second language learners, lacking the language experiential base of native speakers, approach the daunting task of internalizing this massive inventory of lexical usage?

Krashen suggests that massive amounts of "language input," especially through reading, is the only effective approach to such learning. Others propose making the language class a laboratory in which learners can explore, via computer concordance databases, the contexts of lexical use that occur in different kinds of texts and language data. A third approach to learning lexical chunks has been "contrastive": Some applied linguists have suggested that for a number of languages there is an appreciable degree of overlap in the form and meaning of lexical collocations. Bahns (1993: 58) suggests that "the teaching of lexical collocations in EFL should concentrate on items for which there is no direct translational equivalence in English and in the learners' respective mother tongues." Regardless of the learning route taken, a massive learning load seems an unavoidable consequence of a lexical approach in second language instruction.

Lewis (2000) acknowledges that the lexical approach has lacked a coherent learning theory and attempts to rectify this with the following assumptions about learning theory in the lexical approach (Lewis 2000: 184):

– Encountering new learning items on several occasions is a necessary but sufficient condition for learning to occur.
– Noticing lexical chunks or collocations is a necessary but not sufficient condition for "input" to become "intake."
– Noticing similarities, differences, restrictions, and examples contributes to turning input into intake, although formal description of rules probably does not help.
– Acquisition is based not on the application of formal rules but on an accumulation of examples from which learners make provisional generalizations. Language production is the product of previously met examples, not formal rules.
– No linear syllabus can adequately reflect the nonlinear nature of acquisition.

Design: Objectives, syllabus, learning activities, role of learners, teachers, and materials

The rationale and design for lexically based language teaching described in *The Lexical Syllabus* (Willis 1990) and the application of it in the Collins COBUILD English Course represent the most ambitious attempt to realize a syllabus and accompanying materials based on lexical rather than grammatical principles. (This may not, however, have been the reason for the lack of enthusiasm with which this course was received.) Willis notes that the COBUILD computer analyses of texts indicate that "the 700 most frequent words of English account for around 70% of all English text." This "fact" led to the decision that "word frequency would determine the contents of our course. Level 1 would aim to cover the most frequent 700 words together with their common patterns and uses" (Willis 1990: vi). In one respect, this work resembled the earlier frequency-based analyses of vocabulary by West (1953) and Thorndike and Longe (1944). The difference in the COBUILD course was the attention to word patterns derived from the computer analysis. Willis stresses, however, that "the lexical syllabus not only subsumes a structural syllabus, it also indicates how the structures which make up syllabus should be exemplified" since the computer corpus reveals the commonest structural patterns in which words are used (Willis 1990: vi).

Other proposals have been put forward as to how lexical material might be organized for instruction. Nation (1999) reviews a variety of criteria for classifying collocations and chunks and suggests approaches to instructional sequencing and treatment for different types of collocations. Nattinger and DeCarrico propose using a functional schema for organizing instruction:

Distinguishing lexical phrases as social interactions, necessary topics, and discourse devices seems to us the most effective distinction for pedagogical purposes, but that is not to say that a more effective way of grouping might not be found necessary in the wake of further research. (Nattinger and DeCarrico 1992: 185)

Nattinger and DeCarrico provide exemplification of the lexical phrases that exemplify these categories for English and several other languages.

Specific roles for teachers and learners are also assumed in a lexical approach. Lewis supports Krashen's Natural Approach procedures and suggests that teacher talk is a major source of learner input in demonstrating how lexical phrases are used for different functional purposes. Willis proposes that teachers need to understand and manage a classroom methodology based on stages composed of Task, Planning, and Report. In general terms, Willis views the teacher's role as one of creating an environment in which learners can operate effectively and then helping learners manage their own learning. This requires that teachers "abandon the idea of the teacher as 'knower' and concentrate instead on the idea of the learner as 'discoverer'" (Willis 1990: 131).

Others propose that learners make use of computers to analyze text data previously collected or made available "free-form" on the Internet. Here the learner assumes the role of data analyst constructing his or her own linguistic generalizations based on examination of large corpora of language samples taken from "real life." In such schemes, teachers have a major responsibility for organizing the technological system and providing scaffolding to help learners build autonomy in use of the system. The most popular computer-based applications using corpora are built on the presentation of concordance lines to the learner that illustrate the contexts of use of some words or structures. However, learners need training in how to use the concordancer effectively. Teaching assistance will be necessary in leading the learner, by example, through the different stages of lexical analysis such as observation, classification, and generalization.

Materials and teaching resources to support lexical approaches in language teaching are of at least four types. Type 1 consists of complete course packages including texts, tapes, teacher's manuals, and so on, such as the Collins COBUILD English Course (Willis and Willis 1989). Type 2 is represented by collections of vocabulary teaching activities such as those that appear in Lewis's *Implementing the Lexical Approach* (Lewis 1997). Type 3 consists of "printout" versions of computer corpora collections packaged in text format. Tribble and Jones (1990) include such materials with accompanying student exercises based on the corpora printouts. Type 4 materials are computer concordancing programs and attached data sets to allow students to set up and carry out their own analyses. These are typically packaged in CD-ROM form, such as Oxford's Micro Concord, or can be downloaded from sites on the Internet.

An example of the kinds of displays that appear in text materials and in the concordancing displays from which the printout materials derive is illustrated below. The difference between how the vocabulary items "predict" and "forecast" are used and how they collocate is not easy to explain. However, access to these items in context in the computer corpus allows students (and their teachers) to see how these words actually behave in authentic textual use. Corpus samples are usually presented in the limited context form exemplified here.

Some contexts of PREDICT
1. involved in copper binding. Our findings *predict* that examples of selective editing of mitocho

2. the stratosphere. The present models *predict* that a cooling of the winter polar vortex by
3. analysis of this DNA we are able to *predict* the complete amino-acid sequence of the polyp
4. or this problem use the survey data to *predict* values on the vertical profile; by contrast,
5. the calcium-voltage hypothesis would *predict* an increase in release, locked in time to the

Some contexts of FORECAST
1. calculations a second. The center makes *forecasts* 10 days ahead for 18 national meteorological
2. any action whose success hinges on a *forecast* being right. They might end up doing a lot
3. stands up in the House of Commons to *forecast* Britain's economic performance for the next
4. vice labor of its people. This gloomy *forecast* can be better understood by looking closely
5. But three months earlier the secret *forecast* carried out by Treasury economists suggested

Procedure

Procedural sequences for lexically based language teaching vary depending on which of the four types of materials and activities outlined in the preceding section are employed. However, all designers, to some degree, assume that the learner must take on the role of "discourse analyst," with the discourse being either packaged data or data "found" via one of the text search computer programs. Classroom procedures typically involve the use of activities that draw students' attention to lexical collocations and seek to enhance their retention and use of collocations. Woolard (2000) suggests that teachers should reexamine their course books for collocations, adding exercises that focus explicitly on lexical phrases. They should also develop activities that enable learners to discover collocations themselves, both in the classroom and in the language they encounter outside of the classroom. Woolard (2000: 35) comments:

The learning of collocations is one aspect of language development which is ideally suited to independent language learning. In a very real sense, we can teach students to teach themselves. Collocation is mostly a matter of noticing and recording, and trained students should be able to explore texts for themselves. Not only should they notice common collocations in the texts they meet, but more importantly, they should select those collocations which are crucial to their particular needs.

Hill (2000) suggests that classroom procedures involve (*a*) teaching individual collocations, (*b*) making students aware of collocation, (*c*) extending what students already know by adding knowledge of collocation restrictions to known vocabulary, and (*d*) storing collocations through encouraging students to keep a lexical notebook. Lewis (2000: 20–21) gives the following example of how a teacher extends learners' knowledge of collocations while giving feedback on a learner's error.

S: I have to make an exam in the summer.
    (T indicates mistake by facial expression.)
S: I have to make an exam.
T: (Writes 'exam' on the board.)
    What verb do we usually use with "exam"?
S2: Take.
T: Yes, that's right. (Writes "take" on the board.)
    What other verbs do we use with "exam"?
S2: Pass.
T: Yes. And the opposite?
S: Fail.
    (Writes "pass" and "fail" on the board.)
    And if you fail an exam, sometimes you can do it again.
    What's the verb for that? (Waits for response.)
    No? OK, retake. You can retake an exam.
    (Writes "retake" on the board.)
    If you pass an exam with no problems, what can you say? I . . . passed.
S2: Easily.
T: Yes, or we often say "comfortably." I passed comfortably.
    What about if you get 51 and the pass mark is 50?
    What can you say? I . . . (Waits for response.)
    No? I just passed. You can also just fail.

Conclusion

The status of lexis in language teaching has been considerably enhanced by developments in lexical and linguistic theory, by work in corpus analysis, and by recognition of the role of multiword units in language learning and communication. However, lexis still refers to only one component of communicative competence. Lewis and others have coined the term *lexical approach* to characterize their proposals for a lexis-based approach to language teaching. However, such proposals lack the full characterization of an approach or method as described in this book. It remains to be convincingly demonstrated how a lexically based theory of language and language learning can be applied at the levels of design and procedure in language teaching, suggesting that it is still an idea in search of an approach and a methodology.

Bibliography and further reading

Bahns, J. 1993. Lexical collocations: A contrastive view. *ELT Journal* 7(1): 56–63.

Corder, P. 1973. *Introducing Applied Linguistics*. Baltimore: Penguin Books.

Hakuta, K. 1974. Prefabricated patterns and the emergence of structure in second language acquisition. *Language Learning* 24, 287–297.

Hoey, M. 1983. *On the Surface of Discourse*. Boston: Allen and Unwin.

Hoey, M. 1991. *Patterns of Lexis in Text*. Oxford: Oxford University Press.

Keller, R. 1979. Gambits: Conversational strategy signals. *Journal of Pragmatics* 3, 219–237.

Leech, G. 1997. Teaching and language corpora: a convergence. In A. Wichmann, S. Fligelstone, T. McEnery, and G. Knowles (eds.), *Teaching and Language Corpora*. Harlow, Essex: Longman.

Lewis, M. 1993. *The Lexical Approach*. London: Language Teaching Publications.

Lewis, M. 1997. *Implementing the Lexical Approach*. London: Language Teaching Publications.

Lewis, M. (ed.). 2000. *Teaching Collocation: Further Developments in the Lexical Approach*. London: Language Teaching Publications.

Lewis, M. 2000. Learning in the lexical approach. In M. Lewis (ed.), *Teaching Collocation: Further Developments in the Lexical Approach*. London: Language Teaching Publications. 155–184.

Lewis, M. 2000. There is nothing as practical as a good theory. In M. Lewis (ed.), *Teaching Collocation: Further Developments in the Lexical Approach*. London: Language Teaching Publications. 10–27.

Murison-Bowie, S. 1996. Linguistic corpora and language teaching. *Annual Review of Applied Linguistics* 16: 182–199.

Nation, I. S. P. 1999. *Learning Vocabulary in Another Language*. ELI Occasional Publication No. 19, Victoria University of Wellington, New Zealand.

Nattinger, J. 1980. A lexical phrase grammar for ESL. *TESOL Quarterly* 14: 337–344.

Nattinger, J., and J. DeCarrico. 1992. *Lexical Phrases and Language Teaching*. Oxford: Oxford University Press.

Pawley, A., and F. Syder. 1983. Two puzzles for linguistic theory: Native-like selection and native-like fluency. In J. Richards and R. Schmidt (eds.), *Language and Communication*. London: Longman. 191–226.

Peters, A. 1983. *The Units of Language Acquisition*. Cambridge: Cambridge University Press.

Phillips, M. 1989. *Lexical Structure of Text*. Discourse Analysis Monograph No. 12, English Language Research, University of Birmingham (UK).

Thorndike, E. L., and I. Longe. 1944. *The Teacher's Word Book of 30,000 Words*. New York: Teachers College, Columbia University.

Tribble, C., and G. Jones. 1990. *Concordances in the Classroom: A Resource Book for Teachers*. Harlow, Essex: Longman.

West, M. 1953. *A General Service List of English Words*. London: Longman.

Willis, J., and D. Willis. 1989. *Collins COBUILD English Course*. London: Collins.

Willis, J. D. 1990. *The Lexical Syllabus*. London: Collins COBUILD.

Wood, M. 1981. *A Definition of Idiom*. Manchester, UK: Centre for Computational Linguistics, University of Manchester.

Woolard, G. 2000. Collocation-encouraging learner independence. In M. Lewis (ed.), *Teaching Collocation: Further Developments in the Lexical Approach*. London: Language Teaching Publications. 28–46.

13 Competency-Based Language Teaching

Background

Most of the methods and approaches described in this book focus on inputs to language learning. The assumption is that by improving syllabuses, materials, and activities or by changing the role of learners and teachers, more effective language learning will take place. Competency-Based Education (CBE) by comparison is an educational movement that focuses on the outcomes or outputs of learning in the development of language programs. CBE addresses what the learners are expected to do with the language, however they learned to do it. The focus on outputs rather than on inputs to learning is central to the competencies perspective. CBE emerged in the United States in the 1970s and refers to an educational movement that advocates defining educational goals in terms of precise measurable descriptions of the knowledge, skills, and behaviors students should possess at the end of a course of study. The characteristics of CBE are described by Schenck (1978: vi):

Competency-based education has much in common with such approaches to learning as performance-based instruction, mastery learning and individualized instruction. It is outcome-based and is adaptive to the changing needs of students, teachers and the community. . . . Competencies differ from other student goals and objectives in that they describe the student's ability to apply basic and other skills in situations that are commonly encountered in everyday life. Thus CBE is based on a set of outcomes that are derived from an analysis of tasks typically required of students in life role situations.

Competency-Based Language Teaching (CBLT) is an application of the principles of Competency-Based Education to language teaching. Such an approach had been widely adopted by the end of the 1970s, particularly as the basis for the design of work-related and survival-oriented language teaching programs for adults. It has recently reemerged in some parts of the world (e.g., Australia) as a major approach to the planning of language programs. The Center for Applied Linguistics called competency-based ESL curricula "the most important breakthrough in adult ESL" (1983). By the 1990s, CBLT had come to be accepted as "the state-of-the-art approach to adult ESL by national policymakers and leaders in curriculum development as well" (Auerbach 1986: 411): By 1986, any refugee in the United States who wished to receive federal assistance had to be enrolled in a competency-based program (Auerbach 1986: 412). Typically, such programs were based on

a performance outline of language tasks that lead to a demonstrated mastery of language associated with specific skills that are necessary for individuals to function proficiently in the society in which they live. (Grognet and Crandall 1982: 3)

Advocates of CBLT see it as a powerful and positive agent of change:

Competency-based approaches to teaching and assessment offer teachers an opportunity to revitalize their education and training programs. Not only will the quality of assessment improve, but the quality of teaching and student learning will be enhanced by the clear specification of expected outcomes and the continuous feedback that competency-based assessment can offer. These beneficial effects have been observed at all levels and kinds of education and training, from primary school to university, and from academic studies to workplace training. (Docking 1994: 15)

The most recent realization of a competency perspective in the United States is found in the "standards" movement, which has dominated educational discussions since the 1990s. As Glaser and Linn note:

In the recounting of our nation's drive towards educational reform, the last decade of this century will undoubtedly be identified as the time when a concentrated press for national educational standards emerged. The press for standards was evidenced by the efforts of federal and state legislators, presidential and gubernatorial candidates, teacher and subject-matter specialists, councils, governmental agencies, and private foundations. (Glaser and Linn 1993: xiii)

Second language teaching, especially ESL in the United States, was a late entry in the standards movement. As the ESL project director for ESL standards development noted in 1997:

It quickly became apparent to ESL educators in the United States at that time (1991) that the students we serve were not being included in the standards-setting movement that was sweeping the country. (Short 1997: 1)

The Washington, D.C.-based Center for Applied Linguistics under contract to the TESOL organization undertook to develop the K–12 "school" standards for ESL. These were completed in 1997. The ESL standards are framed around three goals and nine standards. Each standard is further explicated by descriptors, sample progress indicators, and classroom vignettes with discussions. The standards section is organized into grade-level clusters: pre-K–3, 4–8, and 9–12. Each cluster addresses all goals and standards with descriptors, progress indicators, and vignettes specific to that grade range.

CBLT also shares features of the graded objectives movement that was proposed as a framework for organizing foreign language teaching in Britain in the 1980s:

Graded objectives means the definition of a series of short-term goals, each building upon the one before, so that the learner advances in knowledge and skill. The setting up of graded objectives schemes in United Kingdom secondary schools has been one of the most remarkable phenomena in modern-language learning over the last five years. (Page 1983: 292)

Approach: Theory of language and learning

CBLT is based on a functional and interactional perspective on the nature of language. It seeks to teach language in relation to the social contexts in which it is used. Language always occurs as a medium of interaction and communication between people for the achievement of specific goals and purposes. CBLT has for this reason most often been used as a framework for language teaching in situations where learners have specific needs and are in particular roles and where the language skills they need can be fairly accurately predicted or determined. It also shares with behaviorist views of learning the notion that language form can be inferred from language function; that is, certain life encounters call for certain kinds of language. This assumes that designers of CBLT competencies can accurately predict the vocabulary and structures likely to be encountered in those particular situations that are central to the life of the learner and can state these in ways that can be used to organize teaching/learning units. Central to both language and learning theory is the view that language can be functionally analyzed into appropriate parts and subparts: that such parts and subparts can be taught (and tested) incrementally. CBLT thus takes a "mosaic" approach to language learning in that the "whole" (communicative competence) is constructed from smaller components correctly assembled. CBLT is also built around the notion of communicative competence and seeks to develop functional communication skills in learners. These skills are generally described in only the most general terms, however, rather than being linked to the performance of specific real-world tasks. CBLT thus shares some features with Communicative Language Teaching.

Design: Objectives, syllabus, learning activities, role of learners, teachers, and materials

Docking (1994) points out that the traditional approach to developing a syllabus involves using one's understanding of subject matter as the basis for syllabus planning. One starts with the field of knowledge that one is going to teach (e.g., contemporary European history, marketing, listening comprehension, or French literature) and then selects concepts, knowledge, and skills that constitute that field of knowledge. A syllabus and the course content are then developed around the subject. Objectives may also be specified, but these usually have little role in the teaching or assessing of the subject. Assessment of students is usually based on norm referencing, that is, students will be graded on a single scale with the expectation either that they be spread across a wide range of scores or that they conform to a preset distribution. A student receives a set of marks for his or her performance relative to other students, from which it is very difficult to make any form of judgment about the specific knowledge or skills a student has acquired. Indeed, two students may receive the same marks on a test but in fact have widely different capacities and knowledge in the subject:

CBT by comparison is designed not around the notion of subject knowledge but around the notion of competency. The focus moves from what students know about language to what they can do with it. The focus on competencies or learning outcomes underpins the curriculum framework and syllabus specification, teaching strategies, assessment and reporting. Instead of norm-referenced assessment, criterion-based assessment procedures are used in which learners are assessed according to how well they can perform on specific learning tasks. (Docking 1994: 16)

Competencies consist of a description of the essential skills, knowledge, attitudes, and behaviors required for effective performance of a real-world task or activity. These activities may be related to any domain of life, though have typically been linked to the field of work and to social survival in a new environment. For example, areas for which competencies have been developed in a vocationally oriented ESL curriculum for immigrants and refugees include:

Task Performance
Safety
General Word-Related
Work Schedules, Time Sheets, Paychecks
Social Language
Job Application
Job Interview

(Mrowicki 1986)

For the area of "Retaining a Job" the following competencies are described:

– Follow instructions to carry out a simple task.
– Respond appropriately to supervisor's comments about quality of work on the job, including mistakes, working too slowly, and incomplete work.

144

- Request supervisor to check work.
- Report completion of task to supervisor.
- Request supplies.
- Ask where object is located: Follow oral directions to locate an object.
- Follow simple oral directions to locate a place.
- Read charts, labels, forms, or written instructions to perform a task.
- State problem and ask for help if necessary.
- Respond to inquiry as to nature or progress of current task; state amount and type of work already competed.
- Respond appropriately to work interruption or modification.

(Mrowicki 1986)

Docking (1994: 11) points out the relationship between competencies and job performance:

A qualification or a job can be described as a collection of units of competency, each of which is composed on a number of elements of competency. A unit of competency might be a task, a role, a function, or a learning module. These will change over time, and will vary from context to context. An element of competency can be defined as any attribute of an individual that contributes to the successful performance of a task, job, function, or activity in an academic setting and/or a work setting. This includes specific knowledge, thinking processes, attitudes, and perceptual and physical skills. Nothing is excluded that can be shown to contribute to performance. An element of competency has meaning independent of context and time. It is the building block for competency specifications for education, training, assessment, qualifications, tasks, and jobs.

Tollefson (1986) observes that the analysis of jobs into their constituent functional competencies in order to develop teaching objectives goes back to the mid-nineteenth century. In the 1860s, Spencer "outlined the major areas of human activity he believed should be the basis for curricular objectives." Similarly, in 1926 Bobbitt developed curricular objectives according to his analysis of the functional competencies required for adults living in America. This approach has been picked up and refined as the basis for the development of CBLT since the 1960s. Northrup (1977) reports on a study commissioned by the U.S. Office of Education in which a wide variety of tasks performed by adults in American society were analyzed and the behaviors needed to carry out the tasks classified into five knowledge areas and four basic skill areas. From this analysis, sixty-five competencies were identified. Docking (1994) describes how he was involved in a project in Australia in 1968 that involved specifying the competencies of more than a hundred trades.

Auerbach (1986) provides a useful review of factors involved in the implementation of CBE programs in ESL, and identifies eight key features:

145

1. *A focus on successful functioning in society.* The goal is to enable students to become autonomous individuals capable of coping with the demands of the world.
2. *A focus on life skills.* Rather than teaching language in isolation, CBLT teaches language as a function of communication about concrete tasks. Students are taught just those language forms/skills required by the situations in which they will function. These forms are determined by "empirical assessment of language required" (Findley and Nathan 1980: 224).
3. *Task- or performance-centered orientation.* What counts is what students can do as a result of instruction. The emphasis is on overt behaviors rather than on knowledge or the ability to talk about language and skills.
4. *Modularized instruction.* "Language learning is broken down into manageable and immediately meaningful chunks" (Center for Applied Linguistics 1983: 2). Objectives are broken into narrowly focused subobjectives so that both teachers and students can get a clear sense of progress.
5. *Outcomes that are made explicit a priori.* Outcomes are public knowledge, known and agreed upon by both learner and teacher. They are specified in terms of behavioral objectives so that students know exactly what behaviors are expected of them.
6. *Continuous and ongoing assessment.* Students are pretested to determine what skills they lack and posttested after instruction in that skill. If they do not achieve the desired level of mastery, they continue to work on the objective and are retested. Program evaluation is based on test results and, as such, is considered objectively quantifiable.
7. *Demonstrated mastery of performance objectives.* Rather than the traditional paper-and-pencil tests, assessment is based on the ability to demonstrate prespecified behaviors.
8. *Individualized, student-centered instruction.* In content, level, and pace, objectives are defined in terms of individual needs; prior learning and achievement are taken into account in developing curricula. Instruction is not time-based; students progress at their own rates and concentrate on just those areas in which they lack competence.

(Auerbach 1986: 414–415)

There are said to be several advantages of a competencies approach from the learner's point of view:

1. The competencies are specific and practical and can be seen to relate to the learner's needs and interests.
2. The learner can judge whether the competencies seem relevant and useful.

3. The competencies that will be taught and tested are specific and public – hence the learner knows exactly what needs to be learned.
4. Competencies can be mastered one at a time so the learner can see what has been learned and what still remains to be learned.

Procedure

Examples of how many of these principles apply in practice is seen in the work of the Australian Migrant Education Program, one of the largest providers of language training to immigrants in the world. The program has undergone a number of philosophical reorientations since the mid-1970s, moving from "centralised curriculum planning with its content-based and structural curriculum in the late 1970s, to de-centralised learner-centred, needs-based planning with its multiplicity of methodologies and materials in the 1980s and yet more recently, to the introduction of competency-based curriculum frameworks" (Burns and Hood 1994: 76). In 1993, a competency-based curriculum, the Certificate in Spoken and Written English, was introduced as the framework for its programs. Learning outcomes are specified at three stages in the framework, leading to an Advanced Certificate in Spoken and Written English at Stage 4 of the framework. Hagan (1994: 22) describes how the framework operates:

After an initial assessment, students are placed within the framework on the basis of their current English proficiency level, their learning pace, their needs, and their social goals for learning English. The twelve core competencies at Stages 1 and 2 relate to general language development. . . . At stage 3, learners are more often grouped according to their goal focus and competencies are defined according to the three syllabus strands of Further Study, Vocational English, and Community Access. . . . The competency descriptions at each stage are divided into four domains . . . :

1. Knowledge and learning competencies
2. Oral competencies
3. Reading competencies
4. Writing competencies

All competencies are described in terms of:

– elements that break down the competency into smaller components and refer to the essential linguistic features of the text
– performance criteria that specify the minimal performance required to achieve a competency
– range of variables that sets limits for the performance of the competency
– sample texts and assessment tasks that provide examples of texts and assessment tasks that relate to the competency

Conclusion

Although CBLT has been embraced with enthusiasm by large sections of the ESL profession, it is not without its critics. These criticisms are both practical and philosophical. Tollefson (1986) argues that there are in fact no valid procedures available to develop competency lists for most programs. Many of the areas for which competencies are needed, such as "adult living," "survival," and "functioning proficiently in the community," are impossible to operationalize. Others have pointed out that dividing activities up into sets of competencies is a reductionist approach, and that the sum of the parts does not equal the complexity of the whole. Auerbach, summarizing the work of Paolo Friere and others, points out that CBLT reflects what Friere has characterized as a "banking" model of education. This assumes the following:

There is a structure of socially prescribed knowledge to be mastered by students. Here, the function of education is to transmit the knowledge and to socialise learners according to the values of the dominant socio-economic group. The teacher's job is to devise more and more effective ways to transmit skills: what counts is success in delivery. Educational progress is defined in terms of "improving" delivery systems. (Auerbach 1986: 416–417)

CBLT is therefore seen as prescriptivist in that it prepares students to fit into the status quo and maintain class relationships. In addition, teaching typically focuses on behavior and performance rather than on the development of thinking skills.

Because competencies are designed to enable learners to participate effectively in society, Tollefson and others have pointed out that they typically represent value judgments about what such participation involves. Competencies for refugee settlement programs in the United States, for example, attempt to inculcate attitudes and values that will make refugees passive citizens who accept the status quo rather than challenge it. Despite these criticisms, CBLT appears to be gaining strength internationally. Such outcomes-based approaches have, in particular, attracted a large political following from those seeking "accountability" for educational investment. As Rylatt and Lohan (1997: 18) conclude: "It can confidently be said, as we enter a new millennium, that the business of improving learning competencies and skills will remain one of the world's fastest growing industries and priorities."

Bibliography and further reading

Auerbach, E. R. 1986. Competency-based ESL: One step forward or two steps back? *TESOL Quarterly* 20(3): 411, 430.

Bottomley, Y., J. Dalton, and C. Corbel. 1994. *From Proficiency to Competencies*. Sydney: National Centre for English Teaching and Research.

Burns, A., and S. Hood. 1994. The competency-based curriculum in action: Investigating course design practices. *Prospect* 9(2): 76–89.

Center for Applied Linguistics. 1983. *From the Classroom to the Workplace: Teaching ESL to Adults.* Washington, D.C.: Center for Applied Linguistics.

Docking, R. 1994. Competency-based curricula – the big picture. *Prospect* 9(2): 8–17.

Findlay, C. A., and L. Nathan. 1980. Functional language objectives in a competency-based curriculum. *TESOL Quarterly* 14(2): 221–232.

Freed, B. 1984. Proficiency in context: The Pennsylvania experience. In S. Savignon and M. Berns (eds.), *Initiatives in Communicative Language Teaching.* Reading, Mass.: Addison-Wesley. 221-240.

Freire, P. 1970. *Pedagogy of the Oppressed.* Harmondsworth: Penguin Books.

Glaser, R., and R. Linn. 1993. Foreword. In L. Shephard, *Setting Performance Standards for Student Achievement.* Stanford, Calif.: National Academy of Education, Stanford University. xii–xiv.

Grognet, A. G., and J. Crandall. 1982. Competency-based curricula in adult ESL. ERIC/CLL New Bulletin 6: 3–4.

Hagan, P. 1994. Competency-based curriculum. The NSW AMES experience. *Prospect* 9(2): 19–30.

Harding, A., B. Page, and S. Rowell. 1980. *Graded Objectives in Modern Languages.* London: Centre for Information on Language Teaching and Research.

Higgs, T. V. (ed.). 1984. *Teaching for Proficiency, the Organizing Principle.* Skokie, Ill.: National Textbook Company.

Hood, S., and A. Burns. 1994. The competency-based curriculum in action: Investigating course design practices. *Prospect* 9(2): 76–89.

Ingram, D. E. 1982. Designing a language program. *RELC Journal* 13(2): 64–86.

Moore, H. 1996. Why has competency-based training become the "solution"? *Prospect* 11(2): 28–46.

Mrowicki, L. 1986. *Project Work English Competency-Based Curriculum.* Portland, Oreg.: Northwest Educational Cooperative.

Nitko, A. J. 1983. *Educational Tests and Measurement.* New York: Harcourt Brace Jovanovich.

Northrup, N. 1977. *The Adult Performance Level Study.* Austin: University of Texas Press.

Page, B. 1983. Graded objectives in modern-language learning. *Language Teaching* 16(4): 292–308.

Rylatt, A., and K. Lohan. 1997. *Creating Training Miracles.* Sydney: Prentice Hall.

Schneck, E. A. 1978. *A Guide to Identifying High School Graduation Competencies.* Portland, Oreg.: Northwest Regional Educational Laboratory.

Short, D. 1997. Revising the ESL standards. *TESOL Matters* (February–March): 1, 6.

Tollefson, J. 1986. Functional competencies in the U.S. refugee program: Theoretical and practical problems. *TESOL Quarterly* 20(4): 649–664.

III *Current communicative approaches*

The chapters in Part III bring the description of approaches and methods up to the present time and describe some of the directions mainstream language teaching has followed since the emergence of communicative methodologies in the 1980s.

Communicative Language Teaching (CLT) marks the beginning of a major paradigm shift within language teaching in the twentieth century, one whose ramifications continue to be felt today. The general principles of Communicative Language Teaching are today widely accepted around the world and we consider the reasons for this in Chapters 14 and 19. In Chapter 14 we present what we now might call the "Classical View of Communicative Language Teaching." The other chapters in this section trace how CLT philosophy has been molded into quite diverse teaching practices, although all would claim to embody basic principles of CLT.

Although the Natural Approach is not as widely established as CLT, Krashen's theories of language learning have had a wide impact, particularly in the United States, and the issues the Natural Approach addresses continue to be at the core of debates about teaching methods. Cooperative Language Learning originates outside of language teaching, but because it is compatible with many of the assumptions of Communicative Language Teaching it has become a popular and relatively uncontroversial approach to the organization of classroom teaching in many parts of the world.

Content-Based Teaching (CBT) can be regarded as a logical development of some of the core principles of Communicative Language Teaching, particularly those that relate to the role of meaning in language learning. Because CBT provides an approach that is particularly suited to prepare ESL students to enter elementary, secondary, or tertiary education, it is widely used in English-speaking countries around the world.

Task-Based Teaching can be regarded as a recent version of a communicative methodology and seeks to reconcile methodology with current theories of second language acquisition.

In the final chapter, we reflect on the history of approaches and methods in the recent history of language teaching and speculate as to why some approaches and methods have had a more lasting impact than others. We also characterize what has been termed the post-methods era and offer some suggestions about influences on language teaching in the future.

14 Communicative Language Teaching

Background

The origins of Communicative Language Teaching (CLT) are to be found in the changes in the British language teaching tradition dating from the late 1960s. Until then, Situational Language Teaching (see Chapter 3) represented the major British approach to teaching English as a foreign language. In Situational Language Teaching, language was taught by practicing basic structures in meaningful situation-based activities. But just as the linguistic theory underlying Audiolingualism was rejected in the United States in the mid-1960s, British applied linguists began to call into question the theoretical assumptions underlying Situational Language Teaching:

> By the end of the sixties it was clear that the situational approach . . . had run its course. There was no future in continuing to pursue the chimera of predicting language on the basis of situational events. What was required was a closer study of the language itself and a return to the traditional concept that utterances carried meaning in themselves and expressed the meanings and intentions of the speakers and writers who created them. (Howatt 1984: 280)

This was partly a response to the sorts of criticisms the prominent American linguist Noam Chomsky had leveled at structural linguistic theory in his now-classic book *Syntactic Structures* (1957). Chomsky had demonstrated that the current standard structural theories of language were incapable of accounting for the fundamental characteristic of language – the creativity and uniqueness of individual sentences. British applied linguists emphasized another fundamental dimension of language that was inadequately addressed in approaches to language teaching at that time – the functional and communicative potential of language. They saw the need to focus in language teaching on communicative proficiency rather than on mere mastery of structures. Scholars who advocated this view of language, such as Christopher Candlin and Henry Widdowson, drew on the work of British functional linguists (e.g., John Firth, M. A. K. Halliday), American work in sociolinguistics (e.g., Dell Hymes, John Gumperz, and William Labov), as well as work in philosophy (e.g., John Austin and John Searle).

Another impetus for different approaches to foreign language teaching

153

came from changing educational realities in Europe. With the increasing interdependence of European countries came the need for greater efforts to teach adults the major languages of the European Common Market. The Council of Europe, a regional organization for cultural and educational cooperation, examined the problem. Education was one of the Council of Europe's major areas of activity. It sponsored international conferences on language teaching, published books about language teaching, and was active in promoting the formation of the International Association of Applied Linguistics. The need to develop alternative methods of language teaching was considered a high priority.

In 1971, a group of experts began to investigate the possibility of developing language courses on a unit-credit system, a system in which learning tasks are broken down into "portions or units, each of which corresponds to a component of a learner's needs and is systematically related to all the other portions" (van Ek and Alexander 1980: 6). The group used studies of the needs of European language learners, and in particular a preliminary document prepared by a British linguist, D. A. Wilkins (1972), which proposed a functional or communicative definition of language that could serve as a basis for developing communicative syllabuses for language teaching. Wilkins's contribution was an analysis of the communicative meanings that a language learner needs to understand and express. Rather than describe the core of language through traditional concepts of grammar and vocabulary, Wilkins attempted to demonstrate the systems of meanings that lay behind the communicative uses of language. He described two types of meanings: notional categories (concepts such as time, sequence, quantity, location, frequency) and categories of communicative function (requests, denials, offers, complaints). Wilkins later revised and expanded his 1972 document into a book titled *Notional Syllabuses* (Wilkins 1976), which had a significant impact on the development of Communicative Language Teaching. The Council of Europe incorporated his semantic/communicative analysis into a set of specifications for a first-level communicative language syllabus. These threshold level specifications (van Ek and Alexander 1980) have had a strong influence on the design of communicative language programs and textbooks in Europe.

The work of the Council of Europe; the writings of Wilkins, Widdowson, Candlin, Christopher Brumfit, Keith Johnson, and other British applied linguists on the theoretical basis for a communicative or functional approach to language teaching; the rapid application of these ideas by textbook writers; and the equally rapid acceptance of these new principles by British language teaching specialists, curriculum development centers, and even governments gave prominence nationally and internationally to what came to be referred to as the Communicative Approach, or simply Communicative Language Teaching. (The terms *notional-*

154

functional approach and *functional approach* are also sometimes used.) Although the movement began as a largely British innovation, focusing on alternative conceptions of a syllabus, since the mid-1970s the scope of Communicative Language Teaching has expanded. Both American and British proponents now see it as an approach (and not a method) that aims to *(a)* make communicative competence the goal of language teaching and *(b)* develop procedures for the teaching of the four language skills that acknowledge the interdependence of language and communication. Its comprehensiveness thus makes it different in scope and status from any of the other approaches or methods discussed in this book. There is no single text or authority on it, nor any single model that is universally accepted as authoritative. For some, Communicative Language Teaching means little more than an integration of grammatical and functional teaching. Littlewood (1981: 1) states, "One of the most characteristic features of communicative language teaching is that it pays systematic attention to functional as well as structural aspects of language." For others, it means using procedures where learners work in pairs or groups employing available language resources in problem-solving tasks. A national primary English syllabus based on a communicative approach (*Syllabuses for Primary Schools* 1981), for example, defines the focus of the syllabus as the "communicative functions which the forms of the language serve" (p. 5). The introduction to the same document comments that "communicative purposes may be of many different kinds. What is essential in all of them is that at least two parties are involved in an interaction or transaction of some kind where one party has an intention and the other party expands or reacts to the intention" (p. 5). In her discussion of communicative syllabus design, Yalden (1983) discusses six Communicative Language Teaching design alternatives, ranging from a model in which communicative exercises are grafted onto an existing structural syllabus, to a learner-generated view of syllabus design (e.g., Holec 1980).

Howatt distinguishes between a "strong" and a "weak" version of Communicative Language Teaching:

There is, in a sense, a 'strong' version of the communicative approach and a 'weak' version. The weak version which has become more or less standard practice in the last ten years, stresses the importance of providing learners with opportunities to use their English for communicative purposes and, characteristically, attempts to integrate such activities into a wider program of language teaching. . . . The 'strong' version of communicative teaching, on the other hand, advances the claim that language is acquired through communication, so that it is not merely a question of activating an existing but inert knowledge of the language, but of stimulating the development of the language system itself. If the former could be described as 'learning to use' English, the latter entails 'using English to learn it.' (1984: 279)

Finocchiaro and Brumfit (1983) contrast the major distinctive features of the Audiolingual Method and the Communicative Approach, according to their interpretation:

Audiolingual

1. Attends to structure and form more than meaning.
2. Demands memorization of structure-based dialogues.
3. Language items are not necessarily contextualized.
4. Language learning is learning structures, sounds, or words.
5. Mastery, or "over-learning," is sought.
6. Drilling is a central technique.
7. Native-speaker-like pronunciation is sought.
8. Grammatical explanation is avoided.
9. Communicative activities only come after a long process of rigid drills and exercises.
10. The use of the student's native language is forbidden.
11. Translation is forbidden at early levels.
12. Reading and writing are deferred till speech is mastered.
13. The target linguistic system will be learned through the overt teaching of the patterns of the system.
14. Linguistic competence is the desired goal.

Communicative Language Teaching

Meaning is paramount.

Dialogues, if used, center around communicative functions and are not normally memorized.

Contextualization is a basic premise.

Language learning is learning to communicate.

Effective communication is sought.

Drilling may occur, but peripherally.

Comprehensible pronunciation is sought.

Any device that helps the learners is accepted – varying according to their age, interest, etc.

Attempts to communicate may be encouraged from the very beginning.

Judicious use of native language is accepted where feasible.

Translation may be used where students need or benefit from it.

Reading and writing can start from the first day, if desired.

The target linguistic system will be learned best through the process of struggling to communicate.

Communicative competence is the desired goal (i.e., the ability to use the linguistic system effectively and appropriately).

15. Varieties of language are recognized but not emphasized.	Linguistic variation is a central concept in materials and methodology.
16. The sequence of units is determined solely by principles of linguistic complexity.	Sequencing is determined by any consideration of content, function, or meaning that maintains interest.
17. The teacher controls the learners and prevents them from doing anything that conflicts with the theory.	Teachers help learners in any way that motivates them to work with the language.
18. "Language is habit" so errors must be prevented at all costs.	Language is created by the individual, often through trial and error.
19. Accuracy, in terms of formal correctness, is a primary goal.	Fluency and acceptable language is the primary goal: Accuracy is judged not in the abstract but in context.
20. Students are expected to interact with the language system, embodied in machines or controlled materials.	Students are expected to interact with other people, either in the flesh, through pair and group work, or in their writings.
21. The teacher is expected to specify the language that students are to use.	The teacher cannot know exactly what language the students will use.
22. Intrinsic motivation will spring from an interest in the structure of the language.	Intrinsic motivation will spring from an interest in what is being communicated by the language.

(1983: 91–93)

Apart from being an interesting example of how proponents of Communicative Language Teaching stack the cards in their favor, such a set of contrasts illustrates some of the major differences between communicative approaches and earlier traditions in language teaching. The wide acceptance of the Communicative Approach and the relatively varied way in which it is interpreted and applied can be attributed to the fact that practitioners from different educational traditions can identify with it, and consequently interpret it in different ways. One of its North American proponents, Savignon (1983), for example, offers as a precedent to CLT a commentary by Montaigne on his learning of Latin through conversation rather than through the customary method of formal analysis and translation. Writes Montaigne, "Without methods, without a book, without grammar or rules, without a whip and without tears, I had learned a Latin as proper as that of my schoolmaster" (Savignon 1983: 47). This antistructural view can be held to represent the language learning version of a more general learning perspective usually referred to as "learning by doing" or "the experience approach" (Hilgard and Bower 1966). This notion of direct rather than delayed practice of communicative acts is central to most CLT interpretations.

The focus on communicative and contextual factors in language use also has an antecedent in the work of the anthropologist Bronislaw Malinowski and his colleague, the linguist John Firth. British applied linguists usually credit Firth with focusing attention on discourse as subject and context for language analysis. Firth also stressed that language needed to be studied in the broader sociocultural context of its use, which included participants, their behavior and beliefs, the objects of linguistic discussion, and word choice. Both Michael Halliday and Dell Hymes, linguists frequently cited by advocates of Communicative Language Teaching, acknowledge primary debts to Malinowski and Firth.

Another frequently cited dimension of CLT, its learner-centered and experience-based view of second language teaching, also has antecedents outside the language teaching tradition per se. An important American national curriculum commission in the 1930s, for example, proposed the adoption of an Experience Curriculum in English. The report of the commission began with the premise that "experience is the best of all schools. . . . The ideal curriculum consists of well-selected experiences" (cited in Applebee 1974: 119). Like those who have urged the organization of Communicative Language Teaching around tasks and procedures, the committee tried to suggest "the means for selection and weaving appropriate experiences into a coherent curriculum stretching across the years of school English study" (Applebee 1974: 119). Individual learners were also seen as possessing unique interests, styles, needs, and goals, which should be reflected in the design of methods of instruction. Teachers were encouraged to develop learning materials "on the basis of the particular needs manifested by the class" (Applebee 1974: 150).

Common to all versions of Communicative Language Teaching is a theory of language teaching that starts from a communicative model of language and language use, and that seeks to translate this into a design for an instructional system, for materials, for teacher and learner roles and behaviors, and for classroom activities and techniques. Let us now consider how this is manifested at the levels of approach, design, and procedure.

Approach

Theory of language

The Communicative Approach in language teaching starts from a theory of language as communication. The goal of language teaching is to develop what Hymes (1972) referred to as "communicative competence." Hymes coined this term in order to contrast a communicative view of language and Chomsky's theory of competence. Chomsky held that

linguistic theory is concerned primarily with an ideal speaker-listener in a completely homogeneous speech community, who knows its language perfectly and is unaffected by such grammatically irrelevant conditions as memory limitation, distractions, shifts of attention and interest, and errors (random or characteristic) in applying his knowledge of the language in actual performance. (Chomsky 1965: 3)

For Chomsky, the focus of linguistic theory was to characterize the abstract abilities speakers possess that enable them to produce grammatically correct sentences in a language. Hymes held that such a view of linguistic theory was sterile, that linguistic theory needed to be seen as part of a more general theory incorporating communication and culture. Hymes's theory of communicative competence was a definition of what a speaker needs to know in order to be communicatively competent in a speech community. In Hymes's view, a person who acquires communicative competence acquires both knowledge and ability for language use with respect to

1. whether (and to what degree) something is formally possible
2. whether (and to what degree) something is feasible in virtue of the means of implementation available
3. whether (and to what degree) something is appropriate (adequate, happy, successful) in relation to a context in which it is used and evaluated
4. whether (and to what degree) something is in fact done, actually performed, and what its doing entails

(Hymes 1972: 281)

This theory of what knowing a language entails offers a much more comprehensive view than Chomsky's view of competence, which deals primarily with abstract grammatical knowledge. Another linguistic theory of communication favored in CLT is Halliday's functional account of language use. "Linguistics . . . is concerned . . . with the description of speech acts or texts, since only through the study of language in use are all the functions of language, and therefore all components of meaning, brought into focus" (Halliday 1970: 145). In a number of influential books and papers, Halliday has elaborated a powerful theory of the functions of language, which complements Hymes's view of communicative competence for many writers on CLT (e.g., Brumfit and Johnson 1979; Savignon 1983). He described (1975: 11–17) seven basic functions that language performs for children learning their first language:

1. the instrumental function: using language to get things
2. the regulatory function: using language to control the behavior of others
3. the interactional function: using language to create interaction with others
4. the personal function: using language to express personal feelings and meanings
5. the heuristic function: using language to learn and to discover
6. the imaginative function: using language to create a world of the imagination
7. the representational function: using language to communicate information

Learning a second language was similarly viewed by proponents of Communicative Language Teaching as acquiring the linguistic means to perform different kinds of functions.

Another theorist frequently cited for his views on the communicative nature of language is Henry Widdowson. In his book *Teaching Language as Communication* (1978), Widdowson presented a view of the relationship between linguistic systems and their communicative values in text and discourse. He focused on the communicative acts underlying the ability to use language for different purposes. A more pedagogically influential analysis of communicative competence is found in Canale and Swain (1980), in which four dimensions of communicative competence are identified: grammatical competence, sociolinguistic competence, discourse competence, and strategic competence. *Grammatical competence* refers to what Chomsky calls linguistic competence and what Hymes intends by what is "formally possible." It is the domain of grammatical and lexical capacity. *Sociolinguistic competence* refers to an understanding of the social context in which communication takes place, including role relationships, the shared information of the participants, and the communicative purpose for their interaction. *Discourse competence* refers to the interpretation of individual message elements in terms of their interconnectedness and of how meaning is represented in relationship to the entire discourse or text. *Strategic competence* refers to the coping strategies that communicators employ to initiate, terminate, maintain, repair, and redirect communication. The usefulness of the notion of communicative competence is seen in the many attempts that have been made to refine the original notion of communicative competence. Canale and Swain's extension of the Hymesian model of communicative competence discussed earlier was in turn elaborated in some complexity by Bachman (1991). The Bachman model has been, in turn, extended by Celce-Murcia, Dörnyei, and Thurrell (1997).

At the level of language theory, Communicative Language Teaching has a rich, if somewhat eclectic, theoretical base. Some of the characteristics of this communicative view of language follow:

1. Language is a system for the expression of meaning.
2. The primary function of language is to allow interaction and communication.
3. The structure of language reflects its functional and communicative uses.
4. The primary units of language are not merely its grammatical and structural features, but categories of functional and communicative meaning as exemplified in discourse.

Theory of learning

In contrast to the amount that has been written in Communicative Language Teaching literature about communicative dimensions of language, little has been written about learning theory. Neither Brumfit and Johnson (1979) nor Littlewood (1981), for example, offers any discussion of learning theory. Elements of an underlying learning theory can be discerned in some CLT practices, however. One such element might be described as the communication principle: Activities that involve real communication promote learning. A second element is the task principle: Activities in which language is used for carrying out meaningful tasks promote learning (Johnson 1982). A third element is the meaningfulness principle: Language that is meaningful to the learner supports the learning process. Learning activities are consequently selected according to how well they engage the learner in meaningful and authentic language use (rather than merely mechanical practice of language patterns). These principles, we suggest, can be inferred from CLT practices (e.g., Littlewood 1981; Johnson 1982). They address the conditions needed to promote second language learning, rather than the processes of language acquisition. These and a variety of other more recent learning principles relevant to the claims of Communicative Language Teaching are summarized in Skehan (1998), and are further discussed in relation to Task-Based Language Teaching in Chapter 18.

Other accounts of Communicative Language Teaching, however, have attempted to describe theories of language learning processes that are compatible with the Communicative Approach. Savignon (1983) surveys second language acquisition research as a source for learning theories and considers the role of linguistic, social, cognitive, and individual variables in language acquisition. Other theorists (e.g., Stephen Krashen, who is not directly associated with Communicative Language Teaching) have developed theories cited as compatible with the principles of CLT (see Chapter 15). Krashen sees acquisition as the basic process involved in developing language proficiency and distinguishes this process from learning. Acquisition refers to the unconscious development of the target-language system as a result of using the language for real communication. Learning is the conscious representation of grammatical knowledge that has resulted from instruction, and it cannot lead to acquisition. It is the acquired system that we call upon to create utterances during spontaneous language use. The learned system can serve only as a monitor of the output of the acquired system. Krashen and other second language acquisition theorists typically stress that language learning comes about through using language communicatively, rather than through practicing language skills.

Johnson (1984) and Littlewood (1984) consider an alternative learning theory that they also see as compatible with CLT – a skill-learning model of learning. According to this theory, the acquisition of communicative competence in a language is an example of skill development. This involves both a cognitive and a behavioral aspect:

The *cognitive* aspect involves the internalisation of plans for creating appropriate behaviour. For language use, these plans derive mainly from the language system – they include grammatical rules, procedures for selecting vocabulary, and social conventions governing speech. The *behavioural* aspect involves the automation of these plans so that they can be converted into fluent performance in real time. This occurs mainly through *practice* in converting plans into performance. (Littlewood 1984: 74)

This theory thus encourages an emphasis on practice as a way of developing communicative skills.

Design

Objectives

Piepho (1981) discusses the following levels of objectives in a communicative approach:

1. an integrative and content level (language as a means of expression)
2. a linguistic and instrumental level (language as a semiotic system and an object of learning)
3. an affective level of interpersonal relationships and conduct (language as a means of expressing values and judgments about oneself and others)
4. a level of individual learning needs (remedial learning based on error analysis)
5. a general educational level of extra-linguistic goals (language learning within the school curriculum)

(Piepho 1981: 8)

These are proposed as general objectives, applicable to any teaching situation. Particular objectives for CLT cannot be defined beyond this level of specification, since such an approach assumes that language teaching will reflect the particular needs of the target learners. These needs may be in the domains of reading, writing, listening, or speaking, each of which can be approached from a communicative perspective. Curriculum or instructional objectives for a particular course would reflect specific aspects of communicative competence according to the learner's proficiency level and communicative needs.

The syllabus

Discussions of the nature of the syllabus have been central in Communicative Language Teaching. We have seen that one of the first syllabus models to be proposed was described as a notional syllabus (Wilkins 1976), which specified the semantic-grammatical categories (e.g., frequency, motion, location) and the categories of communicative function that learners need to express. The Council of Europe expanded and developed this into a syllabus that included descriptions of the objectives of foreign language courses for European adults, the situations in which they might typically need to use a foreign language (e.g., travel, business), the topics they might need to talk about (e.g., personal identification, education, shopping), the functions they needed language for (e.g., describing something, requesting information, expressing agreement and disagreement), the notions made use of in communication (e.g., time, frequency, duration), as well as the vocabulary and grammar needed. The result was published as *Threshold Level English* (van Ek and Alexander 1980) and was an attempt to specify what was needed in order to be able to achieve a reasonable degree of communicative proficiency in a foreign language, including the language items needed to realize this "threshold level."

Discussion of syllabus theory and syllabus models in Communicative Language Teaching has been extensive. Wilkins's original notional syllabus model was soon criticized by British applied linguists as merely replacing one kind of list (e.g., a list of grammar items) with another (a list of notions and functions). It specified products, rather than communicative processes. Widdowson (1979) argued that notional-functional categories provide

only a very partial and imprecise description of certain semantic and pragmatic rules which are used for reference when people interact. They tell us nothing about the procedures people employ in the application of these rules when they are actually engaged in communicative activity. If we are to adopt a communicative approach to teaching which takes as its primary purpose the development of the ability to do things with language, then it is discourse which must be at the center of our attention. (Widdowson 1979: 254)

There are several proposals and models for what a syllabus might look like in Communicative Language Teaching. Yalden (1983) describes the major current communicative syllabus types. We summarize below a modified version of Yalden's classification of communicative syllabus types, with reference sources to each model:

Type	*Reference*
1. structures plus functions	Wilkins (1976)
2. functional spiral around a structural core	Brumfit (1980)
3. structural, functional, instrumental	Allen (1980)
4. functional	Jupp and Hodlin (1975)
5. notional	Wilkins (1976)
6. interactional	Widdowson (1979)
7. task-based	Prabhu (1983)
8. learner-generated	Candlin (1976), Henner-Stanchina and Riley (1978)

There is extensive documentation of attempts to create syllabus and proto-syllabus designs of Types 1–5. Descriptions of interactional strategies have been given, for example, for interactions of teacher and student (Sinclair and Coulthard 1975) and doctor and patient (Candlin, Bruton, and Leather 1974). Although interesting, these descriptions have restricted the field of inquiry to two-person interactions in which there exist reasonably rigid and acknowledged superordinate-to-subordinate role relationships.

Some designers of communicative syllabuses have also looked to task specification and task organization as the appropriate criteria for syllabus design.

The only form of syllabus which is compatible with and can support communicational teaching seems to be a purely procedural one – which lists, in more or less detail, the types of tasks to be attempted in the classroom and suggests an order of complexity for tasks of the same kind. (Prabhu 1983: 4)

An example of such a model that has been implemented nationally is the Malaysian communicational syllabus (English Language Syllabus in Malaysian Schools 1975) – a syllabus for the teaching of English at the upper secondary level in Malaysia. This was one of the first attempts to organize Communicative Language Teaching around a specification of communication tasks. In the organizational schema three broad communicative objectives are broken down into twenty-four more specific objectives determined on the basis of needs analysis. These objectives are organized into learning areas, for each of which are specified a number of outcome goals or products. A *product* is defined as a piece of comprehensible information, written, spoken, or presented in a nonlinguistic form. "A letter is a product, and so is an instruction, a message, a report or a map or graph produced through information gleaned through language" (*English Language Syllabus* 1975: 5). The products, then, result from successful completion of tasks. For example, the product called "relaying a message to others" can be broken into a number of tasks, such as *(a)* understanding the message, *(b)* asking questions to clear any doubts *(c)* asking questions to gather more information, *(d)* taking notes, *(e)* arranging the notes in a logical manner for presentation, and *(f)* orally presenting the message. For each product, a number of proposed situations are suggested. These situations consist of a set of specifications for learner interactions, the stimuli, communicative context, participants, desired outcomes, and constraints. These situations (and others constructed by individual teachers) constitute the means by which learner interaction and communicative skills are realized.

As discussion of syllabus models continues in the CLT literature, some have argued that the syllabus concept be abolished altogether in its accepted forms, arguing that only learners can be fully aware of their own needs, communicational resources, and desired learning pace and path, and that each learner must create a personal, albeit implicit, syllabus as part of learning. Others lean more toward the model proposed by Brumfit (1980), which favors a grammatically based syllabus around which notions, functions, and communicational activities are grouped.

Types of learning and teaching activities

The range of exercise types and activities compatible with a communicative approach is unlimited, provided that such exercises enable learners to attain the communicative objectives of the curriculum, engage learners in communication, and require the use of such communicative processes as information sharing, negotiation of meaning, and interaction. Classroom activities are often designed to focus on completing tasks that are mediated through language or involve negotiation of information and information sharing.

These attempts take many forms. Wright (1976) achieves it by showing out-of-focus slides which the students attempt to identify. Byrne (1978) provides incomplete plans and diagrams which students have to complete by asking for information. Allwright (1977) places a screen between students and gets one to place objects in a certain pattern: this pattern is then communicated to students behind the screen. Geddes and Sturtridge (1979) develop "jigsaw" listening in which students listen to different taped materials and then communicate their content to others in the class. Most of these techniques operate by providing information to some and withholding it from others. (Johnson 1982: 151)

Littlewood (1981) distinguishes between "functional communication activities" and "social interaction activities" as major activity types in Communicative Language Teaching. Functional communication activities include such tasks as learners comparing sets of pictures and noting similarities and differences; working out a likely sequence of events in a set of pictures; discovering missing features in a map or picture; one learner communicating behind a screen to another learner and giving instructions on how to draw a picture or shape, or how to complete a map; following directions; and solving problems from shared clues. Social interaction activities include conversation and discussion sessions, dialogues and role plays, simulations, skits, improvisations, and debates.

Learner roles

The emphasis in Communicative Language Teaching on the processes of communication, rather than mastery of language forms, leads to different roles for learners from those found in more traditional second language classrooms. Breen and Candlin describe the learner's role within CLT in the following terms:

The role of learner as negotiator – between the self, the learning process, and the object of learning – emerges from and interacts with the role of joint negotiator within the group and within the classroom procedures and activities which the group undertakes. The implication for the learner is that he should contribute as much as he gains, and thereby learn in an interdependent way. (1980: 110)

There is thus an acknowledgment, in some accounts of CLT, that learners bring preconceptions of what teaching and learning should be like. These constitute a "set" for learning, which when unrealized can lead to learner confusion and resentment (Henner-Stanchina and Riley 1978). Often there is no text, grammar rules are not presented, classroom arrangement is nonstandard, students are expected to interact primarily with each other rather than with the teacher, and correction of errors may be absent or infrequent. The cooperative (rather than individualistic) approach to learning stressed in CLT may likewise be unfamiliar to learners. CLT methodologists consequently recommend that learners learn to see that failed communication is a joint responsibility and not the fault of speaker or listener. Similarly, successful communication is an accomplishment jointly achieved and acknowledged.

Teacher roles

Several roles are assumed for teachers in Communicative Language Teaching, the importance of particular roles being determined by the view of CLT adopted. Breen and Candlin describe teacher roles in the following terms:

The teacher has two main roles: the first role is to facilitate the communication process between all participants in the classroom, and between these participants and the various activities and texts. The second role is to act as an independent participant within the learning-teaching group. The latter role is closely related to the objectives of the first role and arises from it. These roles imply a set of secondary roles for the teacher; first, as an organizer of resources and as a resource himself, second as a guide within the classroom procedures and activities. . . . A third role for the teacher is that of researcher and learner, with much to contribute in terms of appropriate knowledge and abilities, actual and observed experience of the nature of learning and organizational capacities. (1980: 99)

Other roles assumed for teachers are needs analyst, counselor, and group process manager.

NEEDS ANALYST

The CLT teacher assumes a responsibility for determining and responding to learner language needs. This may be done informally and personally through one-to-one sessions with students, in which the teacher talks through such issues as the student's perception of his or her learning style, learning assets, and learning goals. It may be done formally through administering a needs assessment instrument, such as those exemplified in Savignon (1983). Typically, such formal assessments contain items that attempt to determine an individual's motivation for studying the language. For example, students might respond on a 5-point scale (*strongly agree* to *strongly disagree*) to statements such as the following:

I want to study English because . . .
1. I think it will someday be useful in getting a good job.
2. it will help me better understand English-speaking people and their way of life.
3. one needs a good knowledge of English to gain other people's respect.
4. it will allow me to meet and converse with interesting people.
5. I need it for my job.
6. it will enable me to think and behave like English-speaking people.

On the basis of such needs assessments, teachers are expected to plan group and individual instruction that responds to the learners' needs.

167

COUNSELOR

Another role assumed by several CLT approaches is that of counselor, similar to the way this role is defined in Community Language Learning. In this role, the teacher-counselor is expected to exemplify an effective communicator seeking to maximize the meshing of speaker intention and hearer interpretation, through the use of paraphrase, confirmation, and feedback.

GROUP PROCESS MANAGER

CLT procedures often require teachers to acquire less teacher-centered classroom management skills. It is the teacher's responsibility to organize the classroom as a setting for communication and communicative activities. Guidelines for classroom practice (e.g., Littlewood 1981; Finocchiaro and Brumfit 1983) suggest that during an activity the teacher monitors, encourages, and suppresses the inclination to supply gaps in lexis, grammar, and strategy but notes such gaps for later commentary and communicative practice. At the conclusion of group activities, the teacher leads in the debriefing of the activity, pointing out alternatives and extensions and assisting groups in self-correction discussion. Critics have pointed out, however, that nonnative teachers may feel less than comfortable about such procedures without special training.

The focus on fluency and comprehensibility in Communicative Language Teaching may cause anxiety among teachers accustomed to seeing error suppression and correction as the major instructional responsibility, and who see their primary function as preparing learners to take standardized or other kinds of tests. A continuing teacher concern has been the possible negative effect in pair or group work of imperfect modeling and student error. Although this issue is far from resolved, it is interesting to note that some research findings suggest that "data contradicts the notion that other learners are not good conversational partners because they can't provide accurate input when it is solicited" (Porter 1983).

The role of instructional materials

A wide variety of materials have been used to support communicative approaches to language teaching. Unlike some contemporary methodologies, such as Community Language Learning, practitioners of Communicative Language Teaching view materials as a way of influencing the quality of classroom interaction and language use. Materials thus have the primary role of promoting communicative language use. We will consider three kinds of materials currently used in CLT and label these text-based, task-based, and realia.

TEXT-BASED MATERIALS

There are numerous textbooks designed to direct and support Communicative Language Teaching. Their tables of contents sometimes suggest a kind of grading and sequencing of language practice not unlike those found in structurally organized texts. Some of these are in fact written around a largely structural syllabus, with slight reformatting to justify their claims to be based on a communicative approach. Others, however, look very different from previous language teaching texts. Morrow and Johnson's *Communicate* (1979), for example, has none of the usual dialogues, drills, or sentence patterns and uses visual cues, taped cues, pictures, and sentence fragments to initiate conversation. Watcyn-Jones's *Pair Work* (1981) consists of two different texts for pair work, each containing different information needed to enact role plays and carry out other pair activities. Texts written to support the Malaysian *English Language Syllabus* (1975) likewise represent a departure from traditional textbook modes. A typical lesson consists of a theme (e.g., relaying information), a task analysis for thematic development (e.g., understanding the message, asking questions to obtain clarification, asking for more information, taking notes, ordering and presenting information), a practice situation description (e.g., "A caller asks to see your manager. He does not have an appointment. Gather the necessary information from him and relay the message to your manager."), a stimulus presentation (in the preceding case, the beginning of an office conversation scripted and on tape), comprehension questions (e.g., "Why is the caller in the office?"), and paraphrase exercises.

TASK-BASED MATERIALS

A variety of games, role plays, simulations, and task-based communication activities have been prepared to support Communicative Language Teaching classes. These typically are in the form of one-of-a-kind items: exercise handbooks, cue cards, activity cards, pair-communication practice materials, and student-interaction practice booklets. In pair-communication materials, there are typically two sets of material for a pair of students, each set containing different kinds of information. Sometimes the information is complementary, and partners must fit their respective parts of the "jigsaw" into a composite whole. Others assume different role relationships for the partners (e.g., an interviewer and an interviewee). Still others provide drills and practice material in interactional formats.

169

REALIA

Many proponents of Communicative Language Teaching have advocated the use of "authentic," "from-life" materials in the classroom. These might include language-based realia, such as signs, magazines, advertisements, and newspapers, or graphic and visual sources around which communicative activities can be built, such as maps, pictures, symbols, graphs, and charts. Different kinds of objects can be used to support communicative exercises, such as a plastic model to assemble from directions.

Procedure

Because communicative principles can be applied to the teaching of any skill, at any level, and because of the wide variety of classroom activities and exercise types discussed in the literature on Communicative Language Teaching, description of typical classroom procedures used in a lesson based on CLT principles is not feasible. Savignon (1983) discusses techniques and classroom management procedures associated with a number of CLT classroom procedures (e.g., group activities, language games, role plays), but neither these activities nor the ways in which they are used are exclusive to CLT classrooms. Finocchiaro and Brumfit offer a lesson outline for teaching the function "making a suggestion" for learners in the beginning level of a secondary school program that suggests that CLT procedures are evolutionary rather than revolutionary:

1. Presentation of a brief dialog or several mini-dialogs, preceded by a motivation (relating the dialog situation[s] to the learners' probable community experiences) and a discussion of the function and situation – people, roles, setting, topic, and the informality or formality of the language which the function and situation demand. (At beginning levels, where all the learners understand the same native language, the motivation can well be given in their native tongue.)
2. Oral practice of each utterance of the dialog segment to be presented that day (entire class repetition, half-class, groups, individuals) generally preceded by your model. If mini-dialogs are used, engage in similar practice.
3. Questions and answers based on the dialog topic(s) and situation itself. (Inverted *wh* or *or* questions.)
4. Questions and answers related to the students' personal experiences but centered around the dialog theme.
5. Study one of the basic communicative expressions in the dialog or one of the structures which exemplify the function. You will wish to give several additional examples of the communicative use of the expression or structure with familiar vocabulary in unambiguous utterances or mini-dialogs

(using pictures, simple real objects, or dramatization) to clarify the meaning of the expression or structure. . . .

6. Learner discovery of generalizations or rules underlying the functional expression or structure. This should include at least four points: its oral and written forms (the elements of which it is composed, e.g., "How about + verb + ing?"); its position in the utterance; its formality or informality in the utterance; and in the case of a structure, its grammatical function and meaning. . . .
7. Oral recognition, interpretative activities (two to five depending on the learning level, the language knowledge of the students, and related factors).
8. Oral production activities – proceeding from guided to freer communication activities.
9. Copying of the dialogs or mini-dialogs or modules if they are not in the class text.
10. Sampling of the written homework assignment, if given.
11. Evaluation of learning (oral only), e.g., "How would you ask your friend to _____? And how would you ask me to _____?"

(Finocchiaro and Brumfit 1983: 107–108)

Such procedures clearly have much in common with those observed in classes taught according to Structural-Situational and Audiolingual principles. Traditional procedures are not rejected but are reinterpreted and extended. A similar conservatism is found in many "orthodox" CLT texts, such as Alexander's *Mainline Beginners* (1978). Although each unit has an ostensibly functional focus, new teaching points are introduced with dialogues, followed by controlled practice of the main grammatical patterns. The teaching points are then contextualized through situational practice. This serves as an introduction to a freer practice activity, such as a role play or improvisation. Similar techniques are used in *Starting Strategies* (Abbs and Freebairn 1977). Teaching points are introduced in dialogue form, grammatical items are isolated for controlled practice, and then freer activities are provided. Pair and group work is suggested to encourage students to use and practice functions and forms. The methodological procedures underlying these texts reflect a sequence of activities represented in Littlewood (1981: 86) as follows:

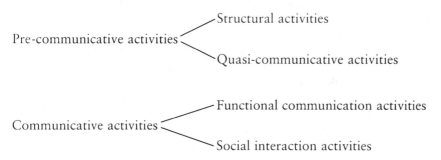

171

Savignon (1972, 1983), however, rejects the notion that learners must first gain control over individual skills (pronunciation, grammar, vocabulary) before applying them in communicative tasks; she advocates providing communicative practice from the start of instruction. How to implement the CLT principles at the level of classroom procedures thus remains central to discussions of the Communicative Approach. How can the range of communicative activities and procedures be defined, and how can the teacher determine a mix and timing of activities that best meets the needs of a particular learner or group of learners? These fundamental questions cannot be answered by proposing further taxonomies and classifications, but require systematic investigation of the use of different kinds of activities and procedures in L2 classrooms (see Chapter 19).

Conclusion

Communicative Language Teaching is best considered an approach rather than a method. It refers to a diverse set of principles that reflect a communicative view of language and language learning and that can be used to support a wide variety of classroom procedures.
These principles include:

- Learners learn a language through using it to communicate.
- Authentic and meaningful communication should be the goal of classroom activities.
- Fluency is an important dimension of communication.
- Communication involves the integration of different language skills.
- Learning is a process of creative construction and involves trial and error.

Communicative Language Teaching appeared at a time when language teaching in many parts of the world was ready for a paradigm shift. Situational Language Teaching and Audiolingualism were no longer felt to be appropriate methodologies. CLT appealed to those who sought a more humanistic approach to teaching, one in which the interactive processes of communication received priority. The rapid adoption and worldwide dissemination of the Communicative Approach also resulted from the fact that it quickly assumed the status of orthodoxy in British language teaching circles, receiving the sanction and support of leading applied linguists, language specialists, and publishers, as well as institutions such as the British Council (Richards 1985).

Since its inception CLT has passed through a number of different phases as its advocates have sought to apply its principles to different dimensions of the teaching/learning process. In its first phase, a primary concern was the need to develop a syllabus that was compatible with the notion of communicative competence. This led to proposals for the organization of syllabuses in terms of notions and functions rather than grammatical structures (Wilkins 1976). In the second phase, CLT focused on procedures for identifying learners' needs and this resulted in proposals to make needs analysis an essential component of communicative methodology (Munby 1978). In its third phase, CLT focused on the kinds of classroom activities that could be used as the basis of a communicative methodology, such as group work, task-work, and information-gap activities (Prabhu 1987).

Johnson and Johnson (1998) identify five core characteristics that underlie current applications of communicative methodology:

1. *Appropriateness:* Language use reflects the situations of its use and must be appropriate to that situation depending on the setting, the roles of the participants, and the purpose of the communication, for example. Thus learners may need to be able to use formal as well as casual styles of speaking.
2. *Message focus:* Learners need to be able to create and understand messages, that is, real meanings. Hence the focus on information sharing and information transfer in CLT activities.
3. *Psycholinguistic processing:* CLT activities seek to engage learners in the use of cognitive and other processes that are important factors in second language acquisition.
4. *Risk taking:* Learners are encouraged to make guesses and learn from their errors. By going beyond what they have been taught, they are encouraged to employ a variety of communication strategies.
5. *Free practice:* CLT encourages the use of "holistic practice" involving the simultaneous use of a variety of subskills, rather than practicing individual skills one piece at a time.

We noted in the introduction to Part III that the approaches considered in this section can be considered direct descendants of Communicative Language Teaching. However, the characteristics of communicative methodology just cited address very general aspects of language learning and teaching that are now largely accepted as self-evident and axiomatic throughout the profession. In some sense, then, almost all of the newer teaching proposals discussed in this book could claim to incorporate principles associated with Communicative Language Teaching. However, these proposals address different aspects of the processes of teaching and learning.

Some focus centrally on the *input* to the learning process. Thus Content-Based Teaching stresses that the content or subject matter of teaching is of primary importance in teaching. Not only should the language input be authentic but modes of learning should be authentic to the study of the subject as well. Lexical and corpus-based approaches to teaching start with a corpus of discourse relevant to learners' interests and needs and the goal of methodology is to engage learners directly with this material.

Some teaching proposals focus more directly on *instructional* factors. Cooperative Learning for example, which shares many of the characteristics of CLT, promotes learning through communication in pairs or small groups. Cooperative organization and activities are central with this approach. Task-Based Language Teaching advocates the importance of specially designed instructional tasks as the basis of learning.

Other more recent proposals take learners and *learning factors* as the primary issues to address in teaching and learning. Whole Language belongs to the humanistic tradition, which argues "Learner first, learning second." Learner engagement is a priority. Neurolinguistic Programming emerges from a therapeutic tradition in which individual growth and personal change are the focus, whereas Multiple Intelligences focuses on learner differences and how these can be accommodated in teaching.

Outcome is another dimension of the process of communication and is central in Competency-Based Language Teaching. Outcomes are the starting point in program planning with this approach.

Today, Communicative Language Teaching thus continues in its "classic" form, as is seen in the huge range of course books and other teaching resources based on the principles of CLT. In addition, it has influenced many other language teaching approaches and methods that subscribe to a similar philosophy of language teaching.

Bibliography and further reading

Abbs, B. A., and I. Freebairn. 1977. *Starting Strategies.* London: Longman.

Alexander, L. G. 1978. *Mainline Beginners.* London: Longman.

Allen, J. P. B. 1980. A three-level curriculum model for second language education. Mimeo, Modern Language Center, Ontario Institute for Studies in Education.

Allwright, R. L. 1977. Language learning through communication practice. *ELT Documents* 76(3). London: British Council.

Applebee, A. N. 1974. *Tradition and Reform in the Teaching of English: A History.* Urbana, Ill.: National Council of Teachers of English.

Austin, J. L. 1962. *How to Do Things with Words.* Oxford: Clarendon Press.

Bachman, L. 1991. *Fundamental Considerations in Language Testing.* Oxford: Oxford University Press.

Barnaby, B., and Sun, Y. 1989. Chinese teachers' views of Western language teaching: context informs paradigms. *TESOL Quarterly* 23(2): 219–238.

Breen, M., and C. N. Candlin. 1980. The essentials of a communicative curriculum in language teaching. *Applied Linguistics* 1(2): 89–112.

Brumfit, C. 1980. From defining to designing: Communicative specifications versus communicative methodology in foreign language teaching. In K. Muller (ed.), *The Foreign Language Syllabus and Communicative Ap-*

proaches to Teaching: Proceedings of a European-American Seminar. Special issue of *Studies in Second Language Acquisition* 3(1): 1–9.

Brumfit, C. J., and K. Johnson (eds.). 1979. *The Communicative Approach to Language Teaching.* Oxford: Oxford University Press.

Byrne, D. 1978. *Materials for Language Teaching: Interaction Packages.* London: Modern English Publications.

Canale, M., and M. Swain. 1980. Theoretical bases of communicative approaches to second language teaching and testing. *Applied Linguistics* 1(1): 1–47.

Candlin, C. N. 1976. Communicative language teaching and the debt to pragmatics. In C. Rameh (ed.), *Georgetown University Roundtable 1976.* Washington, D.C.: Georgetown University Press.

Candlin, C. N., C. J. Bruton, and J. H. Leather. 1974. Doctor-patient communication skills. Mimeo, University of Lancaster.

Celce-Murcia, M. A. Dörnyei, and S. Thurrell. 1997. Direct approaches in L2 instruction: A turning point in Communicative Language Teaching? *TESOL Quarterly* 31(1): 141–152.

Chomsky, N. 1957. *Syntactic Structures.* The Hague: Mouton.

Chomsky. N. 1965. *Aspects of the Theory of Syntax.* Cambridge: MIT Press.

Efstathiadis, S. 1987. A critique of the communicative approach to language learning and teaching. *Journal of Applied Linguistics* 3: 5–13.

English Language Syllabus in Malaysian Schools, Tingkatan 4–5. 1975. Kuala Lumpur: Dewan Bahasa Dan Pustaka.

Finocchiaro, M., and C. Brumfit. 1983. *The Functional-Notional Approach: From Theory to Practice.* New York: Oxford University Press.

Firth, R. 1957. *Papers in Linguistics: 1934–1951.* London: Oxford University Press.

Geddes, M., and G. Sturtridge. 1979. *Listening Links.* London: Heinemann.

Green, P. 1987. *Communicative Language Testing: A Resource Book for Teacher Trainers.* Strasbourg: Council of Europe.

Gumperz, J. J., and D. Hymes (eds.). 1972. *Directions in Sociolinguistics: The Ethnography of Communication.* New York: Holt, Rinehart and Winston.

Halliday, M. A. K. 1970. Language structure and language function. In J. Lyons (ed.), *New Horizons in Linguistics.* Harmondsworth: Penguin. 140–465.

Halliday, M. A. K. 1973. *Explorations in the Functions of Language.* London: Edward Arnold.

Halliday, M. A. K. 1975. *Learning How to Mean: Explorations in the Development of Language.* London: Edward Arnold.

Halliday, M. A. K. 1978. *Language as Social Semiotic.* London: Edward Arnold.

Henner-Stanchina, C., and P. Riley. 1978. Aspects of autonomous learning. In *ELT Documents 103: Individualization in Language Learning.* London: British Council. 75–97.

Hilgard, E. R., and G. H. Bower. 1966. *Theories of Learning.* New York: Appleton-Century-Crofts.

Holec, H. 1980. *Autonomy and Foreign Language Learning.* Strasbourg: Council of Europe.

Holliday, A. 1994. The house of TESEP and the communicative approach: The special needs of English language education. *ELT Journal* 48(1): 3–11.

Howatt, A. P. R. 1984. *A History of English Language Teaching.* Oxford: Oxford University Press.

Hymes, D. 1972. On communicative competence. In J. B. Pride and J. Holmes (eds.), *Sociolinguistics*. Harmondsworth: Penguin. 269–293.

Johnson, K. 1982. *Communicative Syllabus Design and Methodology*. Oxford: Pergamon.

Johnson, K. 1984. Skill psychology and communicative methodology. Paper presented at the RELC seminar, Singapore.

Johnson, K., and H. Johnson 1998. Communicative methodology. In K. Johnson and H. Johnson (eds.), *Encylopedic Dictionary of Applied Linguistics*. Oxford: Blackwell. 68–73.

Jones, N. 1995. Business writing, Chinese students and communicative language teaching. *TESOL Journal,* 4(3): 12–15.

Jupp, T. C., and S. Hodlin. 1975. *Industrial English: An Example of Theory and Practice in Functional Language Teaching*. London: Heinemann.

Lee, J., and B. Van Patten. 1995. *Making Communicative Language Teaching Happen*. San Francisco: McGraw Hill.

Littlewood, W. 1981. *Communicative Language Teaching*. Cambridge: Cambridge University Press.

Littlewood, W. 1984. *Foreign and Second Language Learning: Language Acquisition Research and Its Implications for the Classroom*. Cambridge: Cambridge University Press.

Met, M. 1993. Foreign language immersion programs. ERIC Document ED363141.

Morrow, K., and K. Johnson. 1979. *Communicate*. Cambridge: Cambridge University Press.

Munby, J. 1978. *Communicative Syllabus Design*. Cambridge: Cambridge University Press.

Oxford, R. 1989. Language learning strategies, the communicative approach and their classroom implications. *Foreign Language Annals,* 22(1): 29–39.

Pica, T. 1988. Communicative language teaching: An aid to second language acquisition? Some insights from classroom research. *English Quarterly* 21(2): 70–80.

Piepho, H.-E. 1981. Establishing objectives in the teaching of English. In C. Candlin (ed.), *The Communicative Teaching of English: Principles and an Exercise Typology*. London: Longman.

Porter, P. A. 1983. Variations in the conversations of adult learners of English as a function of the proficiency level of the participants. Ph.D. dissertation, Stanford University.

Prabhu, N. 1983. Procedural syllabuses. Paper presented at the RELC seminar, Singapore.

Prabhu, N.S. 1987. *Second Language Pedagogy*. Oxford: Oxford University Press.

Richards, J. C. 1985. The secret life of methods. In J. C. Richards, *The Context of Language Teaching*. Cambridge: Cambridge University Press. 32–45.

Savignon, S. 1972. Teaching for communicative competence: A research report. *Audiovisual Language Journal* 10(3): 153–162.

Savignon, S. 1983. *Communicative Competence: Theory and Classroom Practice*. Reading, Mass.: Addison-Wesley.

Savignon, S. 1991. Communicative language teaching: State of the art. *TESOL Quarterly* 25(2): 261–277.

Searle, J. R. 1969. *Speech Acts: An Essay in the Philosophy of Language.* Cambridge: Cambridge University Press.

Sinclair, J. McH., and R. M. Coulthard. 1975. *Towards an Analysis of Discourse.* Oxford: Oxford University Press.

Skehan, P. 1998. *A Cognitive Approach to Language Learning.* Oxford: Oxford University Press.

Swan, M. 1985. A critical look at the communicative approach. *English Language Teaching Journal,* pt. 1, 39(1): 2–12.

Syllabuses for Primary Schools. 1981. Hong Kong: Curriculum Development Committee Hong Kong.

van Ek, J. A. 1975. *The Threshold Level in a European Unit/Credit System for Modern Language Teaching by Adults.* Systems Development in Adult Language Learning. Strasbourg: Council of Europe.

van Ek, J., and L. G. Alexander. 1980. *Threshold Level English.* Oxford: Pergamon.

Watcyn-Jones, P. 1981. *Pair Work.* Harmondsworth: Penguin.

Widdowson, H. G. 1972. The teaching of English as communication. *English Language Teaching* 27(1): 15–18.

Widdowson, H. G. 1978. *Teaching Language as Communication.* Oxford: Oxford University Press.

Widdowson, H. G. 1979. The communicative approach and its applications. In H. G. Widdowson, *Explorations in Applied Linguistics.* Oxford: Oxford University Press. 251–264.

Wilkins, D. A. 1972. The linguistics and situational content of the common core in a unit/credit system. MS. Strasbourg: Council of Europe.

Wilkins, D. A. 1976. *Notional Syllabuses.* Oxford: Oxford University Press.

Wilkins, D. A. 1979. Notional syllabuses and the concept of a minimum adequate grammar. In C. J. Brumfit and K. Johnson (eds.), *The Communicative Approach to Language Teaching.* Oxford: Oxford University Press.

Wright, A. 1976. *Visual Material for the Language Teacher.* London: Longman.

Yalden, J. 1983. *The Communicative Syllabus: Evolution, Design and Implementation.* Oxford: Pergamon.

15 The Natural Approach

Background

In 1977, Tracy Terrell, a teacher of Spanish in California, outlined "a proposal for a 'new' philosophy of language teaching which [he] called the Natural Approach" (Terrell 1977; 1982: 121). This was an attempt to develop a language teaching proposal that incorporated the "naturalistic" principles researchers had identified in studies of second language acquisition. The Natural Approach grew out of Terrell's experiences teaching Spanish classes, although it has also been used in elementary- to advanced-level classes and with several other languages. At the same time, he joined forces with Stephen Krashen, an applied linguist at the University of Southern California, in elaborating a theoretical rationale for the Natural Approach, drawing on Krashen's influential theory of second language acquisition. Krashen and Terrell's combined statement of the principles and practices of the Natural Approach appeared in their book *The Natural Approach,* published in 1983. The Natural Approach attracted a wider interest than some of the other innovative language teaching proposals discussed in this book, largely because of its support by Krashen. Krashen and Terrell's book contains theoretical sections prepared by Krashen that outline his views on second language acquisition (Krashen 1981; 1982), and sections on implementation and classroom procedures, prepared largely by Terrell.

Krashen and Terrell identified the Natural Approach with what they call "traditional" approaches to language teaching. Traditional approaches are defined as "based on the use of language in communicative situations without recourse to the native language" – and, perhaps, needless to say, without reference to grammatical analysis, grammatical drilling, or a particular theory of grammar. Krashen and Terrell noted that such "approaches have been called natural, psychological, phonetic, new, reform, direct, analytic, imitative and so forth" (Krashen and Terrell 1983: 9). The fact that the authors of the Natural Approach relate their approach to the Natural Method (see Chapter 1) has led some people to assume that *Natural Approach* and *Natural Method* are synonymous terms. Although the tradition is a common one, there are important differences between the Natural Approach and the older Natural Method, which it will be useful to consider at the outset.

178

The Natural Method is another term for what by 1900 had become known as the Direct Method (see Chapter 1). It is described in a report on the state of the art in language teaching commissioned by the Modern Language Association in 1901 (the report of the "Committee of 12"):

In its extreme form the method consisted of a series of monologues by the teacher interspersed with exchanges of question and answer between the instructor and the pupil – all in the foreign language. . . . A great deal of pantomime accompanied the talk. With the aid of this gesticulation, by attentive listening and by dint of much repetition the learner came to associate certain acts and objects with certain combinations of the sounds and finally reached the point of reproducing the foreign words or phrases. . . . Not until a considerable familiarity with the spoken word was attained was the scholar allowed to see the foreign language in print. The study of grammar was reserved for a still later period. (Cole 1931: 58)

The term *natural*, used in reference to the Direct Method, merely emphasized that the principles underlying the method were believed to conform to the principles of naturalistic language learning in young children. Similarly, the Natural Approach, as defined by Krashen and Terrell, is believed to conform to the naturalistic principles found in successful second language acquisition. Unlike the Direct Method, however, it places less emphasis on teacher monologues, direct repetition, and formal questions and answers, and less focus on accurate production of target-language sentences. In the Natural Approach there is an emphasis on exposure, or *input*, rather than practice; optimizing emotional preparedness for learning; a prolonged period of attention to what the language learners hear before they try to produce language; and a willingness to use written and other materials as a source of comprehensible input. The emphasis on the central role of comprehension in the Natural Approach links it to other comprehension-based approaches in language teaching (see Chapter 5).

Approach

Theory of language

Krashen and Terrell see communication as the primary function of language, and since their approach focuses on teaching communicative abilities, they refer to the Natural Approach as an example of a communicative approach. The Natural Approach "is similar to other communicative approaches being developed today" (Krashen and Terrell 1983: 17). They reject earlier methods of language teaching, such as the Audiolingual Method, which viewed grammar as the central component of language. According to Krashen and Terrell, the major problem with these methods was that they were built not around "actual theories of language acquisition, but theories of something else; for example, the

179

structure of language" (1983: 1). Unlike proponents of Communicative Language Teaching (Chapter 14), however, Krashen and Terrell give little attention to a theory of language. Indeed, a critic of Krashen suggested that he has no theory of language at all (Gregg 1984). What Krashen and Terrell do describe about the nature of language emphasizes the primacy of meaning. The importance of the vocabulary is stressed, for example, suggesting the view that a language is essentially its lexicon and only inconsequently the grammar that determines how the lexicon is exploited to produce messages. Terrell quotes Dwight Bolinger to support this view:

The quantity of information in the lexicon far outweighs that in any other part of the language, and if there is anything to the notion of redundancy it should be easier to reconstruct a message containing just words than one containing just the syntactic relations. The significant fact is the subordinate role of grammar. The most important thing is to get the words in. (Bolinger, in Terrell 1977: 333)

Language is viewed as a vehicle for communicating meanings and messages. Hence Krashen and Terrell stated that "acquisition can take place only when people understand messages in the target language" (Krashen and Terrell 1983: 19). Yet despite their avowed communicative approach to language, they view language learning, as do audiolingualists, as mastery of structures by stages. "The input hypothesis states that in order for acquirers to progress to the next stage in the acquisition of the target language, they need to understand input language that includes a structure that is part of the next stage" (Krashen and Terrell 1983: 32). Krashen refers to this with the formula "I + 1" (i.e., input that contains structures slightly above the learner's present level). We assume that Krashen means by *structures* something at least in the tradition of what such linguists as Leonard Bloomfield and Charles Fries meant by *structures*. The Natural Approach thus assumes a linguistic hierarchy of structural complexity that one masters through encounters with "input" containing structures at the "I + 1" level.

We are left, then, with a view of language that consists of lexical items, structures, and messages. Obviously, there is no particular novelty in this view as such, except that messages are considered of primary importance in the Natural Approach. The lexicon for both perception and production is considered critical in the construction and interpretation of messages. Lexical items in messages are necessarily grammatically structured, and more complex messages involve more complex grammatical structure. Although they acknowledge such grammatical structuring, Krashen and Terrell feel that grammatical structure does not require explicit analysis or attention by the language teacher, by the language learner, or in language teaching materials.

Theory of learning

Krashen and Terrell make continuing reference to the theoretical and research base claimed to underlie the Natural Approach and to the fact that the method is unique in having such a base. "It is based on an empirically grounded theory of second language acquisition, which has been supported by a large number of scientific studies in a wide variety of language acquisition and learning contexts" (Krashen and Terrell 1983: 1). The theory and research are grounded on Krashen's views of language acquisition, which we will collectively refer to as *Krashen's language acquisition theory*. Krashen's views have been presented and discussed extensively elsewhere (e.g., Krashen 1982), so we will not try to present or critique Krashen's arguments here. (For a detailed critical review, see Gregg 1984 and McLaughlin 1978.) It is necessary, however, to present in outline form the principal tenets of the theory, since it is on these that the design and procedures in the Natural Approach are based.

THE ACQUISITION/LEARNING HYPOTHESIS

The Acquisition/Learning Hypothesis claims that there are two distinctive ways of developing competence in a second or foreign language. *Acquisition* is the "natural" way, paralleling first language development in children. Acquisition refers to an unconscious process that involves the naturalistic development of language proficiency through understanding language and through using language for meaningful communication. *Learning,* by contrast, refers to a process in which conscious rules about a language are developed. It results in explicit knowledge about the forms of a language and the ability to verbalize this knowledge. Formal teaching is necessary for "learning" to occur, and correction of errors helps with the development of learned rules. Learning, according to the theory, cannot lead to acquisition.

THE MONITOR HYPOTHESIS

The acquired linguistic system is said to initiate utterances when we communicate in a second or foreign language. Conscious learning can function only as a monitor or editor that checks and repairs the output of the acquired system. The Monitor Hypothesis claims that we may call upon learned knowledge to correct ourselves when we communicate, but that conscious learning (i.e., the *learned* system) has *only* this function. Three conditions limit the successful use of the monitor:

1. *Time.* There must be sufficient time for a learner to choose and apply a learned rule.

181

2. *Focus on form.* The language user must be focused on correctness or on the form of the output.
3. *Knowledge of rules.* The performer must know the rules. The monitor does best with rules that are simple in two ways. They must be simple to describe and they must not require complex movements and rearrangements.

THE NATURAL ORDER HYPOTHESIS

According to the Natural Order Hypothesis, the acquisition of grammatical structures proceeds in a predictable order. Research is said to have shown that certain grammatical structures or morphemes are acquired before others in first language acquisition of English, and a similar natural order is found in second language acquisition. Errors are signs of naturalistic developmental processes, and during acquisition (but not during learning), similar developmental errors occur in learners no matter what their native language is.

THE INPUT HYPOTHESIS

The Input Hypothesis claims to explain the relationship between what the learner is exposed to of a language (the input) and language acquisition. It involves four main issues.

First, the hypothesis relates to acquisition, and not to learning.

Second, people acquire language best by understanding input that is slightly beyond their current level of competence:

An acquirer can "move" from a stage I (where I is the acquirer's level of competence) to a stage I + 1 (where I + 1 is the stage immediately following I along some natural order) by understanding language containing I + 1. (Krashen and Terrell 1983: 32)

Clues based on the situation and the context, extralinguistic information, and knowledge of the world make comprehension possible.

Third, the ability to speak fluently cannot be taught directly; rather, it "emerges" independently in time, after the acquirer has built up linguistic competence by understanding input.

Fourth, if there is a sufficient quantity of comprehensible input, I + 1 will usually be provided automatically. Comprehensible input refers to utterances that the learner understands based on the context in which they are used as well as the language in which they are phrased. When a speaker uses language so that the acquirer understands the message, the speaker "casts a net" of structure around the acquirer's current level of competence, and this will include many instances of I + 1. Thus, input need not be finely tuned to a learner's current level of linguistic competence, and in fact cannot be so finely tuned in a language class, where learners will be at many different levels of competence.

Just as child acquirers of a first language are provided with samples of "caretaker speech," rough-tuned to their present level of understanding, so adult acquirers of a second language are provided with simple codes that facilitate second language comprehension. One such code is "foreigner talk," which refers to the speech native speakers use to simplify communication with foreigners. Foreigner talk is characterized by a slower rate of speech, repetition, restating, use of yes/no instead of *Wh*-questions, and other changes that make messages more comprehensible to persons of limited language proficiency.

THE AFFECTIVE FILTER HYPOTHESIS

Krashen sees the learner's emotional state or attitudes as an adjustable filter that freely passes, impedes, or blocks input necessary to acquisition. A low affective filter is desirable, since it impedes or blocks less of this necessary input. The hypothesis is built on research in second language acquisition, which has identified three kinds of affective or attitudinal variables related to second language acquisition:

1. *Motivation.* Learners with high motivation generally do better.
2. *Self-confidence.* Learners with self-confidence and a good self-image tend to be more successful.
3. *Anxiety.* Low personal anxiety and low classroom anxiety are more conducive to second language acquisition.

The Affective Filter Hypothesis states that acquirers with a low affective filter seek and receive more input, interact with confidence, and are more receptive to the input they receive. Anxious acquirers have a high affective filter, which prevents acquisition from taking place. It is believed that the affective filter (e.g., fear or embarrassment) rises in early adolescence, and this may account for children's apparent superiority to older acquirers of a second language.

These five hypotheses have obvious implications for language teaching. In sum, these are:

1. As much comprehensible input as possible must be presented.
2. Whatever helps comprehension is important. Visual aids are useful, as is exposure to a wide range of vocabulary rather than study of syntactic structure.
3. The focus in the classroom should be on listening and reading; speaking should be allowed to "emerge."
4. In order to lower the affective filter, student work should center on meaningful communication rather than on form; input should be interesting and so contribute to a relaxed classroom atmosphere.

Design

Objectives

The Natural Approach "is for beginners and is designed to help them become intermediates." It has the expectation that students

will be able to function adequately in the target situation. They will under-stand the speaker of the target language (perhaps with requests for clarifica-tion), and will be able to convey (in a non-insulting manner) their requests and ideas. They need not know every word in a particular semantic domain, nor is it necessary that the syntax and vocabulary be flawless – but their pro-duction does need to be understood. They should be able to make the mean-ing clear but not necessarily be accurate in all details of grammar. (Krashen and Terrell 1983: 71)

However, since the Natural Approach is offered as a general set of princi-ples applicable to a wide variety of situations, as in Communicative Language Teaching, specific objectives depend on learner needs and the skill (reading, writing, listening, or speaking) and level being taught.

Krashen and Terrell believe that it is important to communicate to learners what they can expect of a course as well as what they should not expect. They offer as an example a possible goal and nongoal statement for a beginning Natural Approach Spanish class:

After 100–150 hours of Natural Approach Spanish, you *will* be able to: "get around" in Spanish; you will be able to communicate with a monolingual na-tive speaker of Spanish without difficulty; read most ordinary texts in Spanish with some use of a dictionary; know enough Spanish to continue to improve on your own.

After 100–150 hours of Natural Approach Spanish you will *not* be able to: pass for a native speaker, use Spanish as easily as you use English, understand native speakers when they talk to each other (you will probably not be able to eavesdrop successfully); use Spanish on the telephone with great comfort; par-ticipate easily in a conversation with several other native speakers on un-familiar topics. (Krashen and Terrell 1983: 74)

The syllabus

Krashen and Terrell (1983) approach course organization from two points of view. First, they list some typical goals for language courses and suggest which of these goals are the ones at which the Natural Approach aims. They list such goals under four areas:

1. Basic personal communication skills: oral (e.g., listening to announce-ments in public places)
2. Basic personal communication skills: written (e.g., reading and writ-ing personal letters)

3. Academic learning skills: oral (e.g., listening to a lecture)
4. Academic learning skills: written (e.g., taking notes in class)

Of these, they note that the Natural Approach is primarily "designed to develop basic communication skills – both oral and written" (1983: 67). They then observe that communication goals "may be expressed in terms of situations, functions and topics" and proceed to order four pages of topics and situations "which are likely to be most useful to beginning students" (1983: 67). The functions are not specified or suggested but are felt to derive naturally from the topics and situations. This approach to syllabus design would appear to derive to some extent from threshold level specifications (see Chapter 14).

The second point of view holds that "the purpose of a language course will vary according to the needs of the students and their particular interests" (Krashen and Terrell (1983: 65):

The goals of a Natural Approach class are based on an assessment of student needs. We determine the situations in which they will use the target language and the sorts of topics they will have to communicate information about. In setting communication goals, we do not expect the students at the end of a particular course to have acquired a certain group of structures or forms. Instead we expect them to deal with a particular set of topics in a given situation. We do not organize the activities of the class about a grammatical syllabus. (Krashen and Terrell 1983: 71)

From this point of view, it is difficult to specify communicative goals that necessarily fit the needs of all students. Thus, any list of topics and situations must be understood as syllabus suggestions rather than as specifications.

As well as fitting the needs and interests of students, content selection should aim to create a low affective filter by being interesting and fostering a friendly, relaxed atmosphere, should provide a wide exposure to vocabulary that may be useful to basic personal communication, and should resist any focus on grammatical structures, since if input is provided "over a wider variety of topics while pursuing communicative goals, the necessary grammatical structures are automatically provided in the input" (Krashen and Terrell 1983: 71).

Types of learning and teaching activities

From the beginning of a class taught according to the Natural Approach, emphasis is on presenting comprehensible input in the target language. Teacher talk focuses on objects in the classroom and on the content of pictures, as with the Direct Method. To minimize stress, learners are not required to say anything until they feel ready, but they are expected to respond to teacher commands and questions in other ways.

When learners are ready to begin talking in the new language, the teacher provides comprehensible language and simple response opportunities. The teacher talks slowly and distinctly, asking questions and eliciting one-word answers. There is a gradual progression from Yes/No questions, through either-or questions, to questions that students can answer using words they have heard used by the teacher. Students are not expected to use a word actively until they have heard it many times. Charts, pictures, advertisements, and other realia serve as the focal point for questions, and when the students' competence permits, talk moves to class members. "Acquisition activities" – those that focus on meaningful communication rather than language form – are emphasized. Pair or group work may be employed, followed by whole-class discussion led by the teacher.

Techniques recommended by Krashen and Terrell are often borrowed from other methods and adapted to meet the requirements of Natural Approach theory. These include command-based activities from Total Physical Response; Direct Method activities in which mime, gesture, and context are used to elicit questions and answers; and even situation-based practice of structures and patterns. Group-work activities are often identical to those used in Communicative Language Teaching, where sharing information in order to complete a task is emphasized. There is nothing novel about the procedures and techniques advocated for use with the Natural Approach. A casual observer might not be aware of the philosophy underlying the classroom techniques he or she observes. What characterizes the Natural Approach is the use of familiar techniques within the framework of a method that focuses on providing comprehensible input and a classroom environment that cues comprehension of input, minimizes learner anxiety, and maximizes learner self-confidence.

Learner roles

There is a basic assumption in the Natural Approach that learners should not try to learn a language in the usual sense. The extent to which they can lose themselves in activities involving meaningful communication will determine the amount and kind of acquisition they will experience and the fluency they will ultimately demonstrate. The language acquirer is seen as a processor of comprehensible input. The acquirer is challenged by input that is slightly beyond his or her current level of competence and is able to assign meaning to this input through active use of context and extralinguistic information.

Learners' roles are seen to change according to their stage of linguistic development. Central to these changing roles are learner decisions on when to speak, what to speak about, and what linguistic expressions to use in speaking.

In the *pre-production stage,* students "participate in the language activity without having to respond in the target language" (Krashen and Terrell 1983: 76). For example, students can act out physical commands, identify student colleagues from teacher description, point to pictures, and so forth.

In the *early-production stage,* students respond to either-or questions, use single words and short phrases, fill in charts, and use fixed conversational patterns (e.g., How are you? What's your name?).

In the *speech-emergent phase,* students involve themselves in role play and games, contribute personal information and opinions, and participate in group problem solving.

Learners have four kinds of responsibilities in the Natural Approach classroom:

1. Provide information about their specific goals so that acquisition activities can focus on the topics and situations most relevant to their needs.
2. Take an active role in ensuring comprehensible input. They should learn and use conversational management techniques to regulate input.
3. Decide when to start producing speech and when to upgrade it.
4. Where learning exercises (i.e., grammar study) are to be a part of the program, decide with the teacher the relative amount of time to be devoted to them and perhaps even complete and correct them independently.

Learners are expected to participate in communication activities with other learners. Although communication activities are seen to provide naturalistic practice and to create a sense of camaraderie, which lowers the affective filter, they may fail to provide learners with well-formed and comprehensible input at the I + 1 level. Krashen and Terrell warn of these shortcomings but do not suggest means for their amelioration.

Teacher roles

The Natural Approach teacher has three central roles. First, the teacher is the primary source of comprehensible input in the target language. "Class time is devoted primarily to providing input for acquisition," and the teacher is the primary generator of that input. In this role, the teacher is required to generate a constant flow of language input while providing a multiplicity of nonlinguistic clues to assist students in interpreting the input. The Natural Approach demands a much more center-stage role for the teacher than do many contemporary communicative methods.

Second, the Natural Approach teacher creates a classroom atmosphere that is interesting, friendly, and in which there is a low affective filter for learning. This is achieved in part through such Natural Approach techniques as not demanding speech from the students before they are ready for it, not correcting student errors, and providing subject matter of high interest to students.

Finally, the teacher must choose and orchestrate a rich mix of classroom activities, involving a variety of group sizes, content, and contexts. The teacher is seen as responsible for collecting materials and designing their use. These materials, according to Krashen and Terrell, are based not just on teacher perceptions but on elicited student needs and interests.

As with other nonorthodox teaching systems, the Natural Approach teacher has a particular responsibility to communicate clearly and compellingly to students the assumptions, organization, and expectations of the method, since in many cases these will violate student views of what language learning and teaching are supposed to be.

The role of instructional materials

The primary goal of materials in the Natural Approach is to make classroom activities as meaningful as possible by supplying "the extralinguistic context that helps the acquirer to understand and thereby to acquire" (Krashen and Terrell 1983: 55), by relating classroom activities to the real world, and by fostering real communication among the learners. Materials come from the world of realia rather than from textbooks. The primary aim of materials is to promote comprehension and communication. Pictures and other visual aids are essential, because they supply the content for communication. They facilitate the acquisition of a large vocabulary within the classroom. Other recommended materials include schedules, brochures, advertisements, maps, and books at levels appropriate to the students, if a reading component is included in the course. Games, in general, are seen as useful classroom materials, since "games by their very nature, focus the students on what it is they are doing and use the language as a tool for reaching the goal rather than as a goal in itself" (Terrell 1982: 121). The selection, reproduction, and collection of materials places a considerable burden on the Natural Approach teacher. Since Krashen and Terrell suggest a syllabus of topics and situations, it is likely that at some point collections of materials to supplement teacher presentations will be published, built around the "syllabus" of topics and situations recommended by the Natural Approach.

Procedure

We have seen that the Natural Approach adopts techniques and activities freely from various method sources and can be regarded as innovative only with respect to the purposes for which they are recommended and the ways they are used. Krashen and Terrell (1983) provide suggestions for the use of a wide range of activities, all of which are familiar components of Situational Language Teaching, Communicative Language Teaching, and other methods discussed in this book. To illustrate procedural aspects of the Natural Approach, we will cite examples of how such activities are to be used in the Natural Approach classroom to provide comprehensible input, without requiring production of responses or minimal responses in the target language.

1. Start with TPR [Total Physical Response] commands. At first the commands are quite simple: "Stand up. Turn around. Raise your right hand."
2. Use TPR to teach names of body parts and to introduce numbers and sequence. "Lay your right hand on your head, put both hands on your shoulder, first touch your nose, then stand up and turn to the right three times" and so forth.
3. Introduce classroom terms and props into commands. "Pick up a pencil and put it under the book, touch a wall, go to the door and knock three times." Any item which can be brought to the class can be incorporated. "Pick up the record and place it in the tray. Take the green blanket to Larry. Pick up the soap and take it to the woman wearing the green blouse."
4. Use names of physical characteristics and clothing to identify members of the class by name. The instructor uses context and the items themselves to make the meanings of the key words clear: hair, long, short, etc. Then a student is described. "What is your name?" (selecting a student). "Class. Look at Barbara. She has long brown hair. Her hair is long and brown. Her hair is not short. It is long." (Using mime, pointing and context to ensure comprehension.) "What's the name of the student with long brown hair?" (Barbara). Questions such as "What is the name of the woman with the short blond hair?" or "What is the name of the student sitting next to the man with short brown hair and glasses?" are very simple to understand by attending to key words, gestures and context. And they require the students only to remember and produce the name of a fellow student. The same can be done with articles of clothing and colors. "Who is wearing a yellow shirt? Who is wearing a brown dress?"
5. Use visuals, typically magazine pictures, to introduce new vocabulary and to continue with activities requiring only student names as response. The instructor introduces the pictures to the entire class one at a time focusing usually on one single item or activity in the picture. He may introduce one to five new words while talking about the picture. He then passes the picture to a particular student in the class. The students' task is to remember the name of the student with a particular picture. For example, "Tom has the picture of the sailboat. Joan has the picture of the family watching television" and so forth. The instructor will ask questions like "Who has the picture with the sailboat? Does Susan or Tom have the picture of the people on the beach?" Again the students need only produce a name in response.

6. Combine use of pictures with TPR. "Jim, find the picture of the little girl with her dog and give it to the woman with the pink blouse."
7. Combine observations about the pictures with commands and conditionals. "If there is a woman in your picture, stand up. If there is something blue in your picture, touch your right shoulder."
8. Using several pictures, ask students to point to the picture being described. Picture 1. "There are several people in this picture. One appears to be a father, the other a daughter. What are they doing? Cooking. They are cooking a hamburger." Picture 2. "There are two men in this picture. They are young. They are boxing." Picture 3 . . .

(Krashen and Terrell 1983: 75–77)

In all these activities, the instructor maintains a constant flow of "comprehensible input," using key vocabulary items, appropriate gestures, context, repetition, and paraphrase to ensure the comprehensibility of the input.

Conclusion

The Natural Approach belongs to a tradition of language teaching methods based on observation and interpretation of how learners acquire both first and second languages in nonformal settings. Such methods reject the formal (grammatical) organization of language as a prerequisite to teaching. They hold with Newmark and Reibel that "an adult can effectively be taught by grammatically unordered materials" and that such an approach is, indeed, "the *only* learning process which we know for certain will produce mastery of the language at a native level" (1968: 153). In the Natural Approach, a focus on comprehension and meaningful communication as well as the provision of the right kinds of comprehensible input provide the necessary and sufficient conditions for successful classroom second and foreign language acquisition. This has led to a new rationale for the integration and adaptation of techniques drawn from a wide variety of existing sources. Like Communicative Language Teaching, the Natural Approach is hence evolutionary rather than revolutionary in its procedures. Its greatest claim to originality lies not in the techniques it employs but in their use in a method that emphasizes comprehensible and meaningful practice activities, rather than production of grammatically perfect utterances and sentences.

Bibliography and further reading

Baltra, A. 1992. On breaking with tradition: The significance of Terrell's Natural Approach. *Canadian Modern Language Review* 49(3): 565–593.
Berne, J. 1990. A comparison of teaching for proficiency with the natural approach: Procedure, design and approach. *Hispania* 73(4): 147–153.

Brown, J. M., and A. Palmer. 1988. *Listening Approach: Methods and Materials for Applying Krashen's Input Hypothesis*. Harlow, UK: Longman.

Cole, R. 1931. *Modern Foreign Languages and Their Teaching*. New York: Appleton-Century-Crofts.

Ellis, R. 1997. *Second Language Acquisition*. Oxford: Oxford University Press.

Gregg, K. 1984. Krashen's monitor and Occam's razor. *Applied Linguistics* 5(2): 79–100.

Hashemipor, P., R. Maldonado, and M. van Naerssen (eds.). 1995. *Studies in Language Learning and Spanish Linguistics: Festschrift in Honor of Tracy D. Terrell*. New York: McGraw-Hill.

Krashen, S. 1981. *Second Language Acquisition and Second Language Learning*. Oxford: Pergamon.

Krashen, S. 1982. *Principles and Practices in Second Language Acquisition*. Oxford: Pergamon

Krashen. S. 1985. *The Input Hypothesis: Issues and Implications*. London: Longman.

Krashen, S. 1989. We acquire vocabulary and spelling by reading: Additional evidence for the input hypothesis. *Modern Language Journal*. 73(4): 440–464.

Krashen, S. 1992. *Fundamentals of Language Education*. Beverley Hills, Calif.: Laredo.

Krashen, S. 1993. The case for free voluntary reading. *Canadian Modern Language Review* 50(1): 72–82.

Krashen, S. 1996. The case for narrow listening. *System* 24(1): 97–100.

Krashen, S. 1997. The comprehension hypothesis: Recent evidence. *English Teachers' Journal* (Israel). 51: 17–29.

Krashen, S. 1996. Principles of English as a foreign language. *English Teachers' Journal* (Israel) 49: 11–19.

Krashen, S., and T. Terrell. 1983. *The Natural Approach: Language Acquisition in the Classroom*. Oxford: Pergamon.

McLaughlin, B. 1978. The Monitor Model: Some methodological considerations. *Language Learning* 28(2): 309–332.

Newmark, L., and D. A. Reibel. 1968. Necessity and sufficiency in language learning. *International Review of Applied Linguistics* 6(2): 145–164.

Rivers, W. 1981. *Teaching Foreign-Language Skills*. 2nd ed. Chicago: University of Chicago Press.

Skehan, P. 1998. *A Cognitive Approach to Language Learning*. Oxford: Oxford University Press.

Stevick, E. W. 1976. *Memory, Meaning and Method: Some Psychological Perspectives on Language Learning*. Rowley, Mass.: Newbury House.

Terrell, T. D. 1977. A natural approach to second language acquisition and learning. *Modern Language Journal* 61: 325–336.

Terrell, T. D. 1981. The natural approach in bilingual education. MS. California Office of Bilingual Education.

Terrell, T. D. 1982. The natural approach to language teaching: An update. *Modern Language Journal* 66: 121–132.

16 Cooperative Language Learning

Background

Cooperative Language Learning (CLL) is part of a more general instructional approach also known as Collaborative Learning (CL). Cooperative Learning is an approach to teaching that makes maximum use of cooperative activities involving pairs and small groups of learners in the classroom. It has been defined as follows:

Cooperative learning is group learning activity organized so that learning is dependent on the socially structured exchange of information between learners in groups and in which each learner is held accountable for his or her own learning and is motivated to increase the learning of others. (Olsen and Kagan 1992: 8)

Cooperative Learning has antecedents in proposals for peer-tutoring and peer-monitoring that go back hundreds of years and longer. The early twentieth century U.S. educator John Dewey is usually credited with promoting the idea of building cooperation in learning into regular classrooms on a regular and systematic basis (Rodgers 1988). It was more generally promoted and developed in the United States in the 1960s and 1970s as a response to the forced integration of public schools and has been substantially refined and developed since then. Educators were concerned that traditional models of classroom learning were teacher-fronted, fostered competition rather than cooperation, and favored majority students. They believed that minority students might fall behind higher-achieving students in this kind of learning environment. Cooperative Learning in this context sought to do the following:

- raise the achievement of all students, including those who are gifted or academically handicapped
- help the teacher build positive relationships among students
- give students the experiences they need for healthy social, psychological, and cognitive development
- replace the competitive organizational structure of most classrooms and schools with a team-based, high-performance organizational structure

(Johnson, Johnson, and Holubec 1994: 2)

192

In second language teaching, CL (where it is often referred to as Cooperative Language Learning–CLL) has been embraced as a way of promoting communicative interaction in the classroom and is seen as an extension of the principles of Communicative Language Teaching. It is viewed as a learner-centered approach to teaching held to offer advantages over teacher-fronted classroom methods. In language teaching its goals are:

- to provide opportunities for naturalistic second language acquisition through the use of interactive pair and group activities
- to provide teachers with a methodology to enable them to achieve this goal and one that can be applied in a variety of curriculum settings (e.g., content-based, foreign language classrooms; mainstreaming)
- to enable focused attention to particular lexical items, language structures, and communicative functions through the use of interactive tasks
- to provide opportunities for learners to develop successful learning and communication strategies
- to enhance learner motivation and reduce learner stress and to create a positive affective classroom climate

CLL is thus an approach that crosses both mainstream education and second and foreign language teaching.

Approach

Theory of language

We outlined an "Interactive" view of language structuring in Chapter 2. Cooperative Language Learning is founded on some basic premises about the interactive/cooperative nature of language and language learning and builds on these premises in several ways.

Premise 1 mirrors the title of a book on child language titled *Born to Talk* (Weeks 1979). The author holds (along with many others) that "all normal children growing up in a normal environment learn to talk. We are born to talk . . . we may think of ourselves as having been programmed to talk . . . communication is generally considered to be the primary purpose of language" (Weeks 1979: 1).

Premise 2 is that most talk/speech is organized as conversation. "Human beings spend a large part of their lives engaging in conversation and for most of them conversation is among their most significant and engrossing activities" (Richards and Schmidt 1983: 117).

Premise 3 is that conversation operates according to a certain agreed-upon set of cooperative rules or "maxims" (Grice 1975).

Premise 4 is that one learns how these cooperative maxims are realized in one's native language through casual, everyday conversational interaction.

Premise 5 is that one learns how the maxims are realized in a second language through participation in cooperatively structured interactional activities. This involves using

a progressive format or sequencing of strategies in the conversation class which carefully prepares students, that systematically breaks down stereotypes of classroom procedure and allows them to begin interacting democratically and independently. Through this approach, students learn step-by-step, functional interaction techniques at the same time the group spirit or trust is being built. (Christison and Bassano 1981: xvi).

Practices that attempt to organize second language learning according to these premises, explicitly or implicitly, are jointly labeled Cooperative Language Learning. In its applications, CLL is used to support both structural and functional models as well as interactional models of language, since CLL activities may be used to focus on language form as well as to practice particular language functions.

Theory of learning

Cooperative learning advocates draw heavily on the theoretical work of developmental psychologists Jean Piaget (e.g., 1965) and Lev Vygotsky (e.g., 1962), both of whom stress the central role of social interaction in learning. As we have indicated, a central premise of CLL is that learners develop communicative competence in a language by conversing in socially or pedagogically structured situations. CLL advocates have proposed certain interactive structures that are considered optimal for learning the appropriate rules and practices in conversing in a new language. CLL also seeks to develop learners' critical thinking skills, which are seen as central to learning of any sort. Some authors have even elevated critical thinking to the same level of focus as that of the basic language skills of reading, writing, listening, and speaking (Kagan 1992). One approach to integrating the teaching of critical thinking adopted by CLL advocates is called the *Question Matrix* (Wiederhold 1995). Wiederhold has developed a battery of cooperative activities built on the matrix that encourages learners to ask and respond to a deeper array of alternative question types. Activities of this kind are believed to foster the development of critical thinking. (The matrix is based on the well-known Taxonomy of Educational Objectives devised by Bloom [1956], which assumes a hierarchy of learning objectives ranging from simple recall of information to forming conceptual judgments.) Kagan and other CL theorists have adopted this framework as an underlying learning theory for Cooperative Learning.

194

The word *cooperative* in Cooperative Learning emphasizes another important dimension of CLL: It seeks to develop classrooms that foster cooperation rather than competition in learning. Advocates of CLL in general education stress the benefits of cooperation in promoting learning:

Cooperation is working together to accomplish shared goals. Within cooperative situations, individuals seek outcomes beneficial to themselves and all other group members. Cooperative learning is the instructional use of small groups through which students work together to maximize their own and each other's learning. It may be contrasted with competitive learning in which students work against each other to achieve an academic goal such as a grade of "A." (Johnson et al., 1994: 4)

From the perspective of second language teaching, McGroarty (1989) offers six learning advantages for ESL students in CLL classrooms:

1. increased frequency and variety of second language practice through different types of interaction
2. possibility for development or use of language in ways that support cognitive development and increased language skills
3. opportunities to integrate language with content-based instruction
4. opportunities to include a greater variety of curricular materials to stimulate language as well as concept learning
5. freedom for teachers to master new professional skills, particularly those emphasizing communication
6. opportunities for students to act as resources for each other, thus assuming a more active role in their learning

Design

Objectives

Since CLL is an approach designed to foster cooperation rather than competition, to develop critical thinking skills, and to develop communicative competence through socially structured interaction activities, these can be regarded as the overall objectives of CLL. More specific objectives will derive from the context in which it is used.

The syllabus

CLL does not assume any particular form of language syllabus, since activities from a wide variety of curriculum orientations can be taught via cooperative learning. Thus we find CLL used in teaching content classes, ESP, the four skills, grammar, pronunciation, and vocabulary. What

195

defines CLL is the systematic and carefully planned use of group-based procedures in teaching as an alternative to teacher-fronted teaching.

Types of learning and teaching activities

Johnson et al., (1994: 4–5) describe three types of cooperative learning groups.

1. *Formal cooperative learning groups.* These last from one class period to several weeks. These are established for a specific task and involve students working together to achieve shared learning goals.
2. *Informal cooperative learning groups.* These are ad-hoc groups that last from a few minutes to a class period and are used to focus student attention or to facilitate learning during direct teaching.
3. *Cooperative base groups.* These are long term, lasting for at least a year and consist of heterogeneous learning groups with stable membership whose primary purpose is to allow members to give each other the support, help, encouragement, and assistance they need to succeed academically.

The success of CL is crucially dependent on the nature and organization of group work. This requires a structured program of learning carefully designed so that learners interact with each other and are motivated to increase each other's learning. Olsen and Kagan (1992) propose the following key elements of successful group-based learning in CL:

– Positive interdependence
– Group formation
– Individual accountability
– Social skills
– Structuring and structures

Positive interdependence occurs when group members feel that what helps one member helps all and what hurts one member hurts all. It is created by the structure of CL tasks and by building a spirit of mutual support within the group. For example, a group may produce a single product such as an essay or the scores for members of a group may be averaged.

Group formation is an important factor in creating positive interdependence. Factors involved in setting up groups include:

– deciding on the size of the group: This will depend on the tasks they have to carry out, the age of the learners, and time limits for the lesson. Typical group size is from two to four.
– assigning students to groups: Groups can be teacher-selected, random,

or student-selected, although teacher-selected is recommended as the usual mode so as to create groups that are heterogeneous on such variables as past achievement, ethnicity, or sex.
– student roles in groups: Each group member has a specific role to play in a group, such as noise monitor, turn-taker monitor, recorder, or summarizer.

Individual accountability involves both group and individual performance, for example, by assigning each student a grade on his or her portion of a team project or by calling on a student at random to share with the whole class, with group members, or with another group.

Social skills determine the way students interact with each other as teammates. Usually some explicit instruction in social skills is needed to ensure successful interaction.

Structuring and Structures refer to ways of organizing student interaction and different ways students are to interact such as Three-step interview or Round Robin (discussed later in this section).

Numerous descriptions exist of activity types that can be used with CLL. Coelho (1992b: 132) describes three major kinds of cooperative learning tasks and their learning focus, each of which has many variations.

1. Team practice from common input – skills development and mastery of facts
– All students work on the same material.
– Practice could follow a traditional teacher-directed presentation of new material and for that reason is a good starting point for teachers and/or students new to group work.
– The task is to make sure that everyone in the group knows the answer to a question and can explain how the answer was obtained or understands the material. Because students want their team to do well, they coach and tutor each other to make sure that any member of the group could answer for all of them and explain their team's answer.
– When the teacher takes up the question or assignment, anyone in a group may be called on to answer for the team.
– This technique is good for review and for practice tests; the group takes the practice test together, but each student will eventually do an assignment or take a test individually.
– This technique is effective in situations where the composition of the groups is unstable (in adult programs, for example). Students can form new groups every day.

2. Jigsaw: differentiated but predetermined input – evaluation and synthesis of facts and opinions
– Each group member receives a different piece of the information.

197

- Students regroup in topic groups (expert groups) composed of people with the same piece to master the material and prepare to teach it.
- Students return to home groups (Jigsaw groups) to share their information with each other.
- Students synthesize the information through discussion.
- Each student produces an assignment of part of a group project, or takes a test, to demonstrate synthesis of all the information presented by all group members.
- This method of organization may require team-building activities for both home groups and topic groups, long-term group involvement, and rehearsal of presentation methods.
- This method is very useful in the multilevel class, allowing for both homogeneous and heterogeneous grouping in terms of English proficiency.
- Information-gap activities in language teaching are jigsaw activities in the form of pair work. Partners have data (in the form of text, tables, charts, etc.) with missing information to be supplied during interaction with another partner.

3. Cooperative projects: topics/resources selected by students – discovery learning
- Topics may be different for each group.
- Students identify subtopics for each group member.
- Steering committee may coordinate the work of the class as a whole.
- Students research the information using resources such as library reference, interviews, visual media.
- Students synthesize their information for a group presentation: oral and/or written. Each group member plays a part in the presentation.
- Each group presents to the whole class.
- This method places greater emphasis on individualization and students' interests. Each student's assignment is unique.
- Students need plenty of previous experience with more structured group work for this to be effective.

Olsen and Kagan (1992: 88) describes the following examples of CLL activities:

Three-step interview: (1) Students are in pairs; one is interviewer and the other is interviewee. (2) Students reverse roles. (3) Each shares with team member what was learned during the two interviews.

Roundtable: There is one piece of paper and one pen for each team. (1) One student makes a contribution and (2) passes the paper and pen to the student of his or her left. (3) Each student makes contributions in turn. If done orally, the structure is called Round Robin.

Think-Pair-Share: (1) Teacher poses a question (usually a low-consensus question). (2) Students think of a response. (3) Students discuss their responses with a partner. (4) Students share their partner's response with the class.

Solve-Pair-Share: (1) Teacher poses a problem (a low-consensus or high-consensus item that may be resolved with different strategies). (2) Students work out solutions individually. (3) Students explain how they solved the problem in Interview or Round Robin structures.

Numbered Heads: (1) Students number off in teams. (2) Teacher asks a question (usually high-consensus). (3) Heads Together – students literally put their heads together and make sure everyone knows and can explain the answer. (4) Teacher calls a number and students with that number raise their hands to be called on, as in traditional classroom.

Learner roles

The primary role of the learner is as a member of a group who must work collaboratively on tasks with other group members. Learners have to learn teamwork skills. Learners are also directors of their own learning. They are taught to plan, monitor, and evaluate their own learning, which is viewed as a compilation of lifelong learning skills. Thus, learning is something that requires students' direct and active involvement and participation. Pair grouping is the most typical CLL format, ensuring the maximum amount of time both learners spend engaged on learning tasks. Pair tasks in which learners alternate roles involve partners in the role of tutors, checkers, recorders, and information sharers.

Teacher roles

The role of the teacher in CLL differs considerably from the role of teachers in traditional teacher-fronted lesson. The teacher has to create a highly structured and well-organized learning environment in the classroom, setting goals, planning and structuring tasks, establishing the physical arrangement of the classroom, assigning students to groups and roles, and selecting materials and time (Johnson et al. 1994). An important role for the teacher is that of facilitator of learning. In his or her role as facilitator, the teacher must move around the class helping students and groups as needs arise:

During this time the teacher interacts, teaches, refocuses, questions, clarifies, supports, expands, celebrates, empathizes. Depending on what problems evolve, the following supportive behaviors are utilized. Facilitators are giving feedback, redirecting the group with questions, encouraging the group to solve its own problems, extending activity, encouraging thinking, managing conflict, observing students, and supplying resources. (Harel 1992: 169)

Teachers speak less than in teacher-fronted classes. They provide broad questions to challenge thinking, they prepare students for the tasks they will carry out, they assist students with the learning tasks, and they give few commands, imposing less disciplinary control (Harel 1992). The teacher may also have the task of restructuring lessons so that students can work on them cooperatively. This involves the following steps, according to Johnson et al. (1994: 9):

1. Take your existing lessons, curriculum, and sources and structure them cooperatively.
2. Tailor cooperative learning lessons to your unique instructional needs, circumstances, curricula, subject areas, and students.
3. Diagnose the problems some students may have in working together and intervene to increase learning groups' effectiveness.

The role of instructional materials

Materials play an important part in creating opportunities for students to work cooperatively. The same materials can be used as are used in other types of lessons but variations are required in how the materials are used. For example, if students are working in groups, each might have one set of materials (or groups might have different sets of materials), or each group member might need a copy of a text to read and refer to. Materials may be specially designed for CLL learning (such as commercially sold jigsaw and information-gap activities), modified from existing materials, or borrowed from other disciplines.

Procedure

Johnson et al. (1994: 67–68) give the following example of how a collaborative learning lesson would be carried out when students are required to write an essay, report, poem, or story, or review something that they have read. A cooperative writing and editing pair arrangement is used. Pairs verify that each member's composition matches the criteria that have been established by the teacher; they then receive an individual score on the quality of their compositions. They can also be given a group score based on the total number of errors made by the pair in their individual compositions. The procedure works in the following way:

1. The teacher assigns students to pairs with at least one good reader in each pair.
2. Student A describes what he or she is planning to write to Student B, who listens carefully, probes with a set of questions, and outlines Student A's ideas. Student B gives the written outline to Student A.
3. This procedure is reversed, with Student B describing what he or she is

going to write and Student A listening and completing an outline of Student B's ideas, which is then given to Student B.

4. The students individually research the material they need for their compositions, keeping an eye out for material useful to their partner.
5. The students work together to write the first paragraph of each composition to ensure that they both have a clear start on their compositions.
6. The students write their compositions individually.
7. When the students have completed their compositions, they proofread each other's compositions, making corrections in capitalization, punctuation, spelling, language usage, and other aspects of writing the teacher specifies. Students also give each other suggestions for revision.
8. The students revise their compositions.
9. The students then reread each other's compositions and sign their names to indicate that each composition is error-free.

During this process, the teacher monitors the pairs, intervening when appropriate to help students master the needed writing and cooperative skills.

Conclusions

The use of discussion groups, group work, and pair work has often been advocated both in teaching languages and in other subjects. Typically, such groups are used to provide a change from the normal pace of classroom events and to increase the amount of student participation in lessons. Such activities, however, are not necessarily cooperative. In Cooperative Learning, group activities are the major mode of learning and are part of a comprehensive theory and system for the use of group work in teaching. Group activities are carefully planned to maximize students' interaction and to facilitate students' contributions to each other's learning. CLL activities can also be used in collaboration with other teaching methods and approaches.

Unlike most language teaching proposals, CLL has been extensively researched and evaluated and research findings are generally supportive (see Slavin 1995; Baloche 1998), although little of this research was conducted in L2 classrooms. CLL is not without its critics, however. Some have questioned its use with learners of different proficiency levels, suggesting that some groups of students (e.g., intermediate and advanced learners) may obtain more benefits from it than others. In addition, it places considerable demands on teachers, who may have difficulty adapting to the new roles required of them. Proponents of CLL stress that it enhances both learning and learners' interaction skills.

Bibliography and further reading

Baloche, L. 1998. *The Cooperative Classroom*. Englewood Cliffs, N.J.: Prentice Hall.

Bloom, S. 1956. *Taxonomy of Educational Objectives*. New York: David McKay.

Brody, C., and N. Davidson (eds). 1998. Professional Development for Cooperative Learning. New York: State University of New York Press.

Christison, M., and S. Bassano. 1981. *Look Who's Talking*. San Fransisco: Alemany Press.

Coelho, E. 1992a. Cooperative learning: Foundation for a communicative curriculum. In C. Kessler (ed.), *Cooperative Language Learning: A Teacher's Resource Book*. New York: Prentice Hall. 31–51.

Coelho, E. 1992b. Jigsaw: Integrating language and content. In C. Kessler 129–152.

Coelho, E. 1994. *Learning Together in the Multicultural Classroom*. Scarborough, Ont.: Pippin.

Dishon, D., and P. W. O'Leary. 1998. *A Guidebook for Cooperative Learning*. Holmes Beach, Fla.: Learning Publications.

Fathman, A., and C. Kessler. 1992. Cooperative language learning in school contexts. *Annual Review of Applied Linguistics* 13: 127–140.

Grice, H. P. 1975. Logic and conversation. In P. Cole and J. Morgan (eds.), *Syntax and Semantics,* vol 3, *Speech Acts*. New York: Academic Press. 41–58.

Harel, Y. 1992. Teacher talk in the cooperative learning classroom. In C. Kessler (ed.), *Cooperative Language Learning: A Teacher's Resource Book*. New York: Prentice Hall. 153–162.

Jacobs, G. M., G. Lee, and J. Ball. 1995. *Learning Cooperative Learning via Cooperative Learning*. Singapore: Regional Language Centre.

Johnson, D., R. Johnson, and E. Holubec. 1994. *Cooperative Learning in the Classroom*. Alexandria, Va.: Association for Supervision and Curriculum Development.

Kagan, S. 1992. *Cooperative Learning*. San Juan Capistrano, Calif.: Kagan Cooperative Learning.

Kessler, C. 1992 (ed.). *Cooperative Language Learning: A Teacher's Resource Book*. New York: Prentice Hall.

McGroarty, M. 1989. The benefits of cooperative learning arrangements in second lnguage instruction. *NABE Journal* 13(2) (winter): 127–143.

Olsen, J. W. B. 1978. Communication Starters and Other Activities for the ESL Classroom. San Fransisco: Alemany Press.

Olsen, R., and S. Kagan. 1992. About cooperative learning. In C. Kessler (ed.), *Cooperative Language Learning: A Teacher's Resource Book*. New York: Prentice Hall. 1–30.

Palmer, A., and T. Rodgers. 1986. *Back and Forth: Pair Activities for Language Development*. San Fransisco: Alemany Press.

Piaget, J. 1965. *The Language and Thought of the Child*. New York: World Publishing Co.

Richards, J., and R. Schmidt. 1983. *Language and Communication*. London: Longman.

Rodgers, T. 1988. Cooperative language learning: What's new? *PASAA: A Journal of Language Teaching and Learning* 18(2): 12–23.

Sharan, S. (ed.). 1994. *Handbook of Cooperative Learning Methods.* Westport, Conn.: Greenwood Press.

Skehan, P. 1998. *A Cognitive Approach to Language Learning.* Oxford: Oxford University Press.

Slavin, R. 1995. *Cooperative Learning: Theory, Research and Practice.* 2nd ed. New York: Prentice Hall.

Vygotsky, L. 1962. *Thought and Language.* Cambridge: MIT Press.

Weeks, T. 1979. *Born to Talk.* Rowley, Mass.: Newbury House.

Wiederhold, C. 1995. *The Question Matrix.* San Juan Capistrano, Calif.: Kagan Cooperative Learning.

17   Content-Based Instruction

Background

Content-Based Instruction (CBI) refers to an approach to second language teaching in which teaching is organized around the content or information that students will acquire, rather than around a linguistic or other type of syllabus. Krahnke offers the following definition:

It is the teaching of content or information in the language being learned with little or no direct or explicit effort to teach the language itself separately from the content being taught. (Krahnke, 1987: 65)

The term *content* has become a popular one both within language teaching and in the popular media. *New York Times* columnist and linguistic pundit William Safire addressed it in one of his columns in 1998 and noted:

If any word in the English language is hot, buzzworthy and finger-snappingly with it, surpassing even millennium in both general discourse and insiderese, that word is content. Get used to it, because we won't soon get over it. (*New York Times*, August 19, 1998, 15)

Although *content* is used with a variety of different meanings in language teaching, it most frequently refers to the substance or subject matter that we learn or communicate through language rather than the language used to convey it. Attempts to give priority to meaning in language teaching are not new. Approaches encouraging demonstration, imitation, miming, those recommending the use of objects, pictures, and audiovisual presentations, and proposals supporting translation, explanation, and definition as aids to understanding meaning have appeared at different times in the history of language teaching. Brinton, Snow, and Wesche (1989) propose that Saint Augustine was an early proponent of Content-Based Language Teaching and quote his recommendations regarding focus on meaningful content in language teaching. Kelly's history of language teaching cites a number of such meaning-based proposals (Kelly 1969). Content-Based Instruction likewise draws on the principles of Communicative Language Teaching, as these emerged in the 1980s. If, as it was argued, classrooms should focus on real communication and the exchange of information, an ideal situation for second language learning would be one where the subject matter of language teaching was not grammar or functions or some other language-based unit of organization, but content, that is, subject matter from outside the domain of language. The language that is being taught could be used to present subject matter, and the students would learn the language as a by-product of learning about real-world content. Widdowson commented (1978: 16):

I would argue, then, that a foreign language can be associated with those areas of use which are represented by the other subjects on the school curriculum and that this not only helps to ensure the link with reality and the pupil's own experience but also provides us with the most certain means we have of teaching the language as communication, as use, rather than simply as usage. The kind of language course that I envisage is one which deals with a selection of topics taken from the other subjects: simple experiments in physics and chemistry, biological processes in plants and animals, map-drawing, descriptions of historical events and so on. . . . It is easy to see that if such a procedure were adopted, the difficulties associated with the presentation of language use in the classroom would, to a considerable degree, disappear. The presentation would essentially be the same as the methodological techniques used for introducing the topics in the subjects from which they are drawn.

Other educational initiatives since the late 1970s that also emphasize the principle of acquiring content through language rather than the study of language for its own sake include Language across the Curriculum, Immersion Education, Immigrant On-Arrival Programs, Programs for Students with Limited English Proficiency, and Language for Specific Purposes. Content-Based Instruction draws some of its theory and practice from these curriculum approaches. We will briefly consider the role of content in these curriculum models before looking at the specific claims of Content-Based Instruction.

The role of content in other curriculum designs

Language across the Curriculum was a proposal for native-language education that grew out of recommendations of a British governmental commission in the mid-1970s. The report of the commission recommended a focus on reading and writing in all subject areas in the curriculum, and not merely in the subject called language arts. Language skills should also be taught in the content subjects and not left exclusively for the English teacher to deal with. This report influenced American education as well, and the slogan "Every teacher, an English teacher" became familiar to every teacher. Like other cross-disciplinary proposals, this one never had the classroom impact that its advocates had hoped for. Nevertheless, subject-matter texts appeared that included exercises dealing with language practice, and the need for collaboration between subject-matter teachers and language teachers was emphasized. In some cases, curricular material was produced that integrated subject matter and language teaching goals, such as the Singaporean Primary Pilot Project in the 1970s – classroom texts integrating science, math, and language study.

Immersion Education has also had a strong influence on the theory of Content-Based Instruction. Immersion Education is a type of foreign language instruction in which the regular school curriculum is taught through the medium of the foreign language. The foreign language is the vehicle for content instruction; it is not the subject of instruction. Thus, for example, an English-speaking child might enter a primary school in which the medium of instruction for all the content subjects is French. Student goals of an immersion program include: (1) developing a high level of proficiency in the foreign language; (2) developing positive attitudes toward those who speak the foreign language and toward their culture(s); (3) developing English language skills commensurate with expectations for a student's age and abilities; (4) gaining designated skills and knowledge in the content areas of the curriculum.

The first immersion programs were developed in Canada in the 1970s to provide English-speaking students with the opportunity to learn French. Since that time, immersion programs have been adopted in many parts of North America, and alternative forms of immersion have been devised. In the United States, immersion programs can be found in a number of languages, including French, German, Spanish, Japanese, and Chinese.

Immigrant On-Arrival Programs typically focus on the language newly arrived immigrants in a country need for survival. Such learners typically need to learn how to deal with differing kinds of real-world content as a basis for social survival. Design of such courses in Australia was among the first attempts to integrate notional, functional, grammatical, and lexical specifications built around particular themes and situations. A typical course would cover language needed to deal with immigration bureaucracies, finding accommodations, shopping, finding a job, and so forth. The methodology of the Australian on-arrival courses was based on the Direct Method (Ozolins 1993) but included role play and simulations based on the language needed to function in specific situations. In current on-arrival programs, a competency-based approach is often used in which a teaching syllabus is developed around the competencies learners are presumed to need in different survival situations (see Chapter 13).

Programs for Students with Limited English Proficiency (SLEP) are governmentally mandated programs to serve especially those children whose parents might be served by the on-arrival programs, but more generally designed to provide in-class or pullout instruction for any school-age children whose language competence is insufficient to participate fully in normal school instruction. Early versions of such programs were largely grammar-based. More recent SLEP programs focus on giving students the language and other skills needed to enter the regular school curriculum. Such skills often involve learning how to carry out academic tasks and understand academic content through a second language.

Language for Specific Purposes (LSP) is a movement that seeks to serve the language needs of learners who need language in order to carry out specific roles (e.g., student, engineer, technician, nurse) and who thus need to acquire content and real-world skills through the medium of a second language rather than master the language for its own sake. LSP has focused particularly on English for Science and Technology (EST). An institution offering English for Science and Technology courses would have specialized courses to support its clients in learning to read technical articles in computer science or to write academic papers in chemical engineering. LSP/EST have given rise to a number of subfields, such as ESP (English for Specific Purposes), EOP (English for Occupational Purposes), and EAP (English for Academic Purposes).

Content-based courses are now common in many different settings and content is often used as the organizing principle in ESL/EFL courses of many different kinds. In this chapter we will examine the principles underlying Content-Based Instruction and how these are applied in language teaching programs and teaching materials.

Approach

Content-Based Instruction is grounded on the following two central principles: (as we examine how these principles are applied in CBI, a number of other issues will also be considered):

1. *People learn a second language more successfully when they use the language as a means of acquiring information, rather than as an end in itself.* This principle reflects one of the motivations for CBI noted earlier – that it leads to more effective language learning.

2. *Content-Based Instruction better reflects learners' needs for learning a second language.* This principle reflects the fact that many content-based programs serve to prepare ESL students for academic studies or for mainstreaming; therefore, the need to be able to access the content of academic learning and teaching as quickly as possible, as well as the processes through which such learning and teaching are realized, are a central priority.

Theory of language

A number of assumptions about the nature of language underlie Content-Based Instruction.

207

LANGUAGE IS TEXT- AND DISCOURSE-BASED

CBI addresses the role of language as a vehicle for learning content. This implies the centrality of linguistic entities longer than single sentences, because the focus of teaching is how meaning and information are communicated and constructed through texts and discourse. The linguistic units that are central are not limited to the level of sentences and subsentential units (clauses and phrases) but are those that account for how longer stretches of language are used and the linguistic features that create coherence and cohesion within speech events and text types. This involves study of the textual and discourse structure of written texts such as letters, reports, essays, descriptions, or book chapters, or of speech events such as meetings, lectures, and discussions.

LANGUAGE USE DRAWS ON INTEGRATED SKILLS

CBI views language use as involving several skills together. In a content-based class, students are often involved in activities that link the skills, because this is how the skills are generally involved in the real world. Hence students might read and take notes, listen and write a summary, or respond orally to things they have read or written. And rather than viewing grammar as a separate dimension of language, in CBI grammar is seen as a component of other skills. Topic- or theme-based courses provide a good basis for an integrated skills approach because the topics selected provide coherence and continuity across skill areas and focus on the use of language in connected discourse rather than isolated fragments. They seek to bring together knowledge, language, and thinking skills. Grammar can also be presented through a content-based approach. The teacher or course developer has the responsibility to identify relevant grammatical and other linguistic focuses to complement the topic or theme of the activities.

LANGUAGE IS PURPOSEFUL

Language is used for specific purposes. The purpose may be academic, vocational, social, or recreational but it gives direction, shape, and ultimately meaning to discourse and texts. When learners focus on the purpose of the language samples they are exposed to, they become engaged in following through and seeing if the purpose is attained and how their own interests relate to this purpose (or purposes). For learners to receive maximum benefit from CBI they need to be clearly in tune with its purposes and the language codes that signal and link these expressions of purpose.

Language contains great potential for communicating meaning. In order to make content comprehensible to learners, teachers need to make

208

the same kinds of adjustments and simplifications that native speakers make in communicating with second language learners. The discourse that results from these simplifications is often referred to as "foreigner talk." Teachers and lecturers operating within CBI consciously and unconsciously make such "foreigner talk" modifications in the language they use in teaching, in order to make the content they are focusing on more comprehensible to their students. These modifications include simplification (e.g., use of shorter T units and clauses), well-formedness (e.g., using few deviations from standard usage), explicitness (e.g., speaking with nonreduced pronunciation), regularization (e.g., use of canonical word order), and redundancy (e.g., highlighting important material through simultaneous use of several linguistic mechanisms) (Stryker and Leaver, 1993).

Theory of learning

We earlier described one of the core principles of CBI as follows: *People learn a second language more successfully when they use the language as a means of acquiring information, rather than as an end in itself.* Regardless of the type of CBI model that is used, they all "share the fact that content is the point of departure or organizing principle of the course – a feature that grows out of the common underlying assumption that successful language learning occurs when students are presented with target language material in a meaningful, contextualized form with the primary focus on acquiring information" (Brinton et al., Wesche, 1989: 17). This assumption is backed by a number of studies (e.g., Scott 1974; Collier 1989; Grandin 1993; Wesche 1993) that support the position that in formal educational settings, second languages are best learned when the focus is on mastery of content rather than on mastery of language per se. CBI thus stands in contrast to traditional approaches to language teaching in which language form is the primary focus of the syllabus and of classroom teaching.

A number of additional assumptions that derive from the core principles of CBI just discussed will now be described. One important corollary can be stated as follows:

People learn a second language most successfully when the information they are acquiring is perceived as interesting, useful, and leading to a desired goal.

To justify this claim, CBI advocates refer to ESP studies that "note that for successful learning to occur, the language syllabus must take into account the eventual uses the learner will make of the target language" and further that "the use of informational content which is perceived as relevant by the learner is assumed by many to increase motivation in the

209

language course, and thus to promote more effective learning" (Brinton et al. 1989: 3).

Language learning is also believed to be more motivating when students are focusing on something other than language, such as ideas, issues, and opinions. "The student can most effectively acquire a second language when the task of language learning becomes incidental to the task of communicating with someone . . . about some topic . . . which is inherently interesting to the student" (D'Anglejan and Tucker 1975: 284). If content with a high level of interest is chosen, learners may acquire the language more willingly. This can be expressed as:

Some content areas are more useful as a basis for language learning than others.

Certain areas of content are thought to be more effective as a basis for CBI than others. For example, geography is often the "first choice" of subject matter. Geography is "highly visual, spatial and contextual; it lends itself to the use of maps, charts, and realia, and the language tends to be descriptive in nature with use of the 'to be,' cognates and proper names" (Stryker and Leaver 1993: 288). For somewhat different reasons, "Introduction to Psychology offered an ideal situation in which to introduce CBI at the bilingual University of Ottawa, since it has the largest enrollment of any introductory course in the university" and thus was likely to "attract a large enough number of second language speakers to justify special lecture or discussion sections" (Brinton et al., 1989: 46). This course was further recommended because of student interest in the course topics and because of "the highly structured nature of the content, the emphasis on receptive learning of factual information, the availability of appropriate textbooks and video study material" (Brinton et al., 1989: 46).

On the other hand, CBI courses have been created around a rich variety of alternative kinds of content. Case studies of CBI in foreign language education report content selection as wide-ranging as "Themes of Soviet Life and Worldview" (Russian), "Aphorisms, Proverbs, and Popular Sayings" (Italian), "Religion and Change in Twentieth-Century Latin America" (Spanish), and "French Media" (French). Eleven such case studies using a variety of course content in a variety of foreign language teaching situations are reported in Stryker and Leaver (1993).

Students learn best when instruction addresses students' needs.

This principle emphasizes that in CBI the content that students study is selected according to their needs. Hence, if the program is at a secondary school, the academic needs of students across the curriculum form the basis for the content curriculum. Authentic texts, both written and spoken, that students will encounter in the real world (e.g., at school or at work) provide the starting point for developing a syllabus, so relevance to learners' needs is assured. In the case of an academically focused program, "the language curriculum is based directly on the academic needs of the students and generally follows the sequence determined by a particular subject matter in dealing with the language problems which students encounter" (Brinton et al., 1989: 2).

Teaching builds on the previous experience of the learners.

Another assumption of CBI is that it seeks to build on students' knowledge and previous experience. Students do not start out as blank slates but are treated as bringing important knowledge and understanding to the classroom. The starting point in presenting a theme-based lesson is therefore what the students already know about the content.

Design

Objectives

In CBI, language learning is typically considered incidental to the learning of content. Thus the objectives in a typical CBI course are stated as objectives of the content course. Achievement of content course objectives is considered as necessary and sufficient evidence that language learning objectives have been achieved as well. An exception to this generalization is with the theme-based instructional model of CBI. In theme-based CBI, language learning objectives drive the selection of theme topics; that is, "there are often set linguistic objectives in the curriculum, and thematic modules are selected for the degree to which they provide compatible contexts for working towards these objectives." It is possible for theme-based courses to be directed toward single-skill objectives; however, most often theme-based instruction "lends itself well to four-skills courses, since the topic selected provides coherence and continuity across skill areas and allows work on higher-level language skills (e.g., integrating reading and writing skills)" (Brinton et al., 1989: 26).

An example of objectives in CBI comes from the theme-based Intensive Language Course (ILC) at the Free University of Berlin. Four objectives were identified for its yearlong, multitheme program. These objectives were linguistic, strategic, and cultural. Objectives were:

1. to activate and develop existing English language skills
2. to acquire learning skills and strategies that could be applied in future language development opportunities
3. to develop general academic skills applicable to university studies in all subject areas
4. to broaden students' understanding of English-speaking peoples

(Brinton et al., 1989: 32)

211

Syllabus

In most CBI courses, the syllabus is derived from the content area, and these obviously vary widely in detail and format. It is typically only CBI following the theme-based model in which content and instructional sequence is chosen according to language learning goals. The theme-based model uses the syllabus type referred to as a topical syllabus, the organization of which is built around specific topics and subtopics, as the name implies.

The organization of the Intensive Language Course at the Free University of Berlin consists of a sequence of modules spread over the academic year. The topical themes of the modules are:

1. Drugs
2. Religious Persuasion
3. Advertising
4. Drugs
5. Britain and the Race Question
6. Native Americans
7. Modern Architecture
8. Microchip Technology
9. Ecology
10. Alternative Energy
11. Nuclear Energy
12. Dracula in Myth, Novel, and Films
13. Professional Ethics

There is both macro- and micro-structuring of the yearlong syllabus for this course. At the macro-level, the syllabus consists of a sequence of modules selected to reflect student interests and a multidisciplinary perspective. The modules are designed and sequenced so that they "relate to one another so as to create a cohesive transition of certain skills, vocabulary, structures, and concepts." The first six modules are ordered so that early modules have easily accessible, high-interest themes. "Later modules deal with more technical processes and assume mastery of certain skills, vocabulary, structures, and concepts" (Brinton et al., 1989: 35). The internal design of the modules (the micro-structure) is such that:

All modules move from an initial exercise intended to stimulate student interest in the theme through a variety of exercises aimed at developing comprehension and the students' ability to manipulate the language appropriate to the situation and use the language of the texts. The final activities of each module require the students themselves to choose the language appropriate for the situation and use it in communicative interaction. (Brinton et al., 1989: 34)

Types of learning and teaching activities

There are a number of descriptions of activity types in CBI. Stoller (1997) provides a list of activities classified according to their instructional focus. The classification categories she proposes are:

– language skills improvement

- vocabulary building
- discourse organization
- communicative interaction
- study skills
- synthesis of content materials and grammar.

Mohan (1986) describes an approach to content-based ESL instruction at the secondary level that is built around the notion of knowledge structures. This refers to the structures of knowledge across the curriculum in terms of frameworks and schemas that apply to a wide range of topics. The framework consists of six universal knowledge structures, half of which represent specific, practical elements (Description, Sequence, and Choice) and the other half of which represent general, theoretical elements (Concepts/Classification, Principles, and Evaluation). A variety of CBI courses have been developed based on Mohan's knowledge framework.

Learner roles

One goal of CBI is for learners to become autonomous so that they come to "understand their own learning process and . . . take charge of their own learning from the very start" (Stryker and Leaver 1993: 286). In addition, most CBI courses anticipate that students will support each other in collaborative modes of learning. This may be a challenge to those students who are accustomed to more whole-class or independent learning and teaching modes. CBI is in the "learning by doing" school of pedagogy. This assumes an active role by learners in several dimensions. Learners are expected to be active interpreters of input, willing to tolerate uncertainty along the path of learning, willing to explore alternative learning strategies, and willing to seek multiple interpretations of oral and written texts.

Learners themselves may be sources of content and joint participants in the selection of topics and activities. Such participation "has been found to be highly motivating and has resulted in a course changing its direction in order to better meet the needs of students" (Stryker and Leaver 1993: 11). Learners need commitment to this new kind of approach to language learning, and CBI advocates warn that some students may not find this new set of learner roles to their liking and may be less than ready and willing participants in CBI courses. Some students are overwhelmed by the quantity of new information in their CBI courses and may flounder. Some students are reported to have experienced frustration and have asked to be returned to more structured, traditional classrooms. Students need to be prepared both psychologically and cognitively for CBI and, if they are not adequately primed, then "missing schemata needs to be provided or students need to be kept from enrolling until they are 'ready'" (Stryker and Leaver 1993: 292).

The role of teachers

CBI anticipates a change in the typical roles of language teachers. "Instructors must be more than just good language teachers. They must be knowledgeable in the subject matter and able to elicit that knowledge from their students" (Stryker and Leaver 1993: 292). At a more detailed level, teachers have to keep context and comprehensibility foremost in their planning and presentations, they are responsible for selecting and adapting authentic materials for use in class, they become student needs analysts, and they have to create truly learner-centered classrooms. As Brinton et al. (1989: 3) note:

They are asked to view their teaching in a new way, from the perspective of truly contextualizing their lessons by using content as the point of departure. They are almost certainly committing themselves to materials adaptation and development. Finally, with the investment of time and energy to create a content-based language course comes even greater responsibility for the learner, since learner needs become the hub around which the second language curriculum and materials, and therefore teaching practices, revolve.

Stryker and Leaver suggest the following essential skills for any CBI instructor:

1. Varying the format of classroom instruction
2. Using group work and team-building techniques
3. Organizing jigsaw reading arrangements
4. Defining the background knowledge and language skills required for student success
5. Helping students develop coping strategies
6. Using process approaches to writing
7. Using appropriate error correction techniques
8. Developing and maintaining high levels of student esteem
(Stryker and Leaver 1993: 293)

Content-Based Instruction places different demands on teachers from regular ESL teaching. Brinton et al. (1989) identify the following issues:

– Are adequately trained instructors available to teach the selected courses?
– Will there be any incentives offered to instructors who volunteer to teach in the proposed program (e.g., salary increases, release time, smaller class sizes)?
– How will faculty not willing or qualified to participate in the new program be reassigned?

- How will teachers and other support staff be oriented to the model (e.g., pre-service, in-service)?
- What is the balance of language and content teaching (i.e., focus on content teaching, focus on language teaching, equal attention to both)?
- What are the roles of the teacher (e.g., facilitator, content-area expert, language expert)? What is the anticipated workload (e.g., contact hours, curriculum duties)?
- Who is responsible for selecting the teaching materials?
- Are teachers expected to develop content-specific language-teaching materials? If yes, will materials development training and guidelines be provided?
- Will alternate staffing configurations (e.g., curriculum and materials specialists, team teaching) be used?

Almost all participating instructors comment on the large amounts of time and energy involved in Content-Based Instruction and many describe it as "a major challenge. Taking up this challenge requires a highly motivated and dedicated individual – or group of individuals" (Stryker and Leaver 1993: 311).

The role of materials

As with other elements in CBI, the materials that facilitate language learning are the materials that are used typically with the subject matter of the content course. It is recommended that a rich variety of materials types be identified and used with the central concern being the notion that the materials are "authentic." In one sense, authenticity implies that the materials are like the kinds of materials used in native-language instruction. In another sense, authenticity refers to introduction of, say, newspaper and magazine articles and any other media materials "that were not originally produced for language teaching purposes" (Brinton et al., 1989: 17). Many CBI practitioners recommend the use of realia such as tourist guidebooks, technical journals, railway timetables, newspaper ads, radio and TV broadcasts, and so on, and at least one cautions that "textbooks are contrary to the very concept of CBI – and good language teaching in general" (Stryker and Leaver 1993: 295).

However, comprehensibility is as critical as authenticity and it has been pointed out that CBI courses are often "characterized by a heavy use of instructional media (e.g., videotapes and/or audiotapes) to further enrich the context provided by authentic readings selected to form the core of the thematic unit" (Brinton et al. 1989: 31). Although authenticity is considered critical, CBI proponents do note that materials (as well as lecturer presentations) may need modification in order to ensure maximum comprehensibility. This may mean linguistic simplification or adding redundancy to text materials. It will certainly mean "providing guides and strategies to assist them [students] in comprehending the materials" (Brinton et al., 1989: 17).

Contemporary models of content-based instruction

The principles of CBI can be applied to the design of courses for learners at any level of language learning. The following are examples of different applications of CBI.

Courses at the university level

Several different approaches to Content-Based Instruction have been developed at the university level.

Theme-based language instruction. This refers to a language course in which the syllabus is organized around themes or topics such as "pollution" or "women's rights." The language syllabus is subordinated to the more general theme. A general theme such as "business and marketing" or "immigrants in a new city" might provide organizing topics for 2 weeks of integrated classroom work. Language analysis and practice evolve out of the topics that form the framework for the course. A topic might be introduced through a reading, vocabulary developed through guided discussion, audio or video material on the same topic used for listening comprehension, followed by written assignments integrating information from several different sources. Most of the materials used will typically be teacher-generated and the topic treated will cross all skills (Brinton et al., 1989).

Sheltered content instruction. This refers to content courses taught in the second language by a content area specialist, to a group of ESL learners who have been grouped together for this purpose. Since the ESL students are not in a class together with native speakers, the instructor will be required to present the content in a way which is comprehensible to second language learners and in the process use language and tasks at an appropriate level of difficulty. Typically, the instructor will choose texts of a suitable difficulty level for the learners and adjust course requirements to accommodate the learners' language capacities (e.g., by making fewer demands for written assignments). Shih cites examples of such an approach in sheltered psychology courses for English and French immersion students at the University of Ottawa, courses in English for business and economics offered at Oregon State University, and ESP courses in English for business, economics, and computer science at Western Illinois University (Shih 1986: 638).

Adjunct language instruction. In this model, students are enrolled in two linked courses, one a content course and one a language course, with both courses sharing the same content base and complementing each other in terms of mutually coordinated assignments. Such a program requires a large amount of coordination to ensure that the two curricula are interlocking and this may require modifications to both courses.

Team-teach approach. This is a variation on the adjunct approach. Shih (1986) describes two examples of this approach. One (developed at the University of Birmingham) focuses on lecture comprehension and the writing of examination questions in fields such as transportation and plant biology. The work of recording lectures and preparing comprehension checks (including exam questions) is shared between the subject teacher and the language teacher, and during class time, both help students with problems that arise. A second example is from a polytechnic program in Singapore. An English-for-occupational-purposes writing course was designed to prepare students for writing tasks they might have to carry out in future jobs in building maintenance and management (e.g., writing of specifications, memos, accident reports, progress reports, and meeting reports). The subject teacher finds authentic or realistic situations that are the basis for report assignments. As students work on these assignments, both teachers acts as consultants. Models written by the subject teacher or based on the best student work are later presented and discussed (Shih 1986: 638).

Skills-based approach. This is characterized by a focus on a specific academic skill area (e.g., academic writing) that

is linked to concurrent study of specific subject matter in one or more academic disciplines. This may mean that students write about material they are currently studying in an academic course or that the language or composition course itself simulates the academic process (e.g. mini-lectures, readings, and discussion on a topic lead into writing assignments). Students write in a variety of forms (e.g. short-essay tests, summaries, critiques, research reports) to demonstrate understanding of the subject matter and to extend their knowledge to new areas. Writing is integrated with reading, listening, and discussion about the core content and about collaborative and independent research growing form the core material. (Shih, 1986: 617–618)

Courses at the elementary and secondary level

Variations of the approaches discussed in the preceding section are also found at the secondary and elementary level.

Theme-based approach. A common model at this level is one in which students complete theme-based modules that are designed to facilitate their entry into the regular subject-areas classroom. These models do not provide a substitute for mainstream content classes but focus on learning strategies, concepts, tasks, and skills that are needed in subject areas in the mainstream curriculum, grouped around topics and themes such as consumer education, map skills, foods, and nutrition.

217

Current communicative approaches

Two critical elements are necessary in developing an approach in which language proficiency and academic content are developed in parallel: integration of second language development into regular content-area instruction and creation of appropriate conditions for providing input. Success for this model rests on cooperative learning in heterogeneous small-group settings. This entails:

– grouping strategies
– alternative ways for providing input
– techniques for making subject matter comprehensible
– opportunities to develop language proficiency for academic purposes

(Kessler and Quinn 1989: 75)

This approach acknowledges that preparing ESL students for main-streaming is a responsibility not only for ESL teachers but also for content teachers. The latter have to increasingly acknowledge the crucial role language plays in content learning.

An example of this approach is described by Wu (1996) in a program prepared for ESL students in an Australian high school. Topics from a range of mainstream subjects were chosen as the basis for the course and to provide a transition to mainstream classes. Topics were chosen primarily to cater to the widest variety of students' needs and interests. Linguistic appropriateness was another factor taken into account when choosing topics as some involved more technical terms and complex grammatical constructions. The topics were also chosen for relevance to the Australian sociopolitical and cultural climate. Topics that fulfilled these criteria included multiculturalism, the nuclear age, sports, the Green movement, street kids, and teenage smoking (Wu 1996: 23).

Adjunct approach. Parallel to the theme-based component described by Wu was an adjunct course focusing on science. Both ESL teachers and science teachers were involved in this aspect of the course, which focused on preparing students to make the transition to learning science through English. The adjunct course focused on the following:

1. Understanding specialized science terminologies and concepts
2. Report writing skills
3. Grammar for science
4. Note-taking skills

(Wu 1996: 24)

Courses in private language institutes

Theme-based courses also provide a framework for courses and materials in many programs outside the public school and university sector, such as the private language-school market. With theme-based courses, a set of themes might be selected as the basis for a semester's work, and each

218

theme used as the basis for 6 or more hours of work in which the four skills and grammar are taught drawing on the central theme. Such an approach also provides the basis for many published ESL texts (e.g., Richards and Sandy 1998).

Procedure

Since Content-Based Instruction refers to an approach rather than a method, no specific techniques or activities are associated with it. At the level of procedure, teaching materials and activities are selected according to the extent to which they match the type of program it is. Stryker and Leaver (1997: 198–199) describe a typical sequence of classroom procedures in a content-based lesson. The lesson is a Spanish lesson built around the viewing of the film *El Norte*.

Preliminary preparation: Students read reference materials regarding U.S. immigration laws as well as an extract from Octavio Paz's *El Laberinto de la Soledad*.

1. Linguistic analysis: discussion of grammar and vocabulary based on students' analysis of oral presentations done the day before.
2. Preparation for film: activities previewing vocabulary in the film, including a vocabulary worksheet.
3. Viewing a segment of the movie.
4. Discussion of the film: The teacher leads a discussion of the film.
5. Discussion of the reading.
6. Videotaped interview: Students see a short interview in which immigration matters are discussed.
7. Discussion: a discussion of immigration reform.
8. Preparation of articles: Students are given time to read related articles and prepare a class presentation.
9. Presentation of articles: Students make presentations, which may be taped so that they can later listen for self-correction.
10. Wrap-up discussion.

Conclusion

Content-based approaches in language teaching have been widely used in a variety of different settings since the 1980s. From its earliest applications in ESP, EOP, and immersion programs, it is now widely used in K–12 programs for ESL students, in university foreign language programs, and in business and vocational courses in EFL settings. Its advocates claim that it leads to more successful program outcomes than alternative language teaching approaches. Because it offers unlimited opportunities for teachers to match students' interests and needs with interesting and meaningful content, it offers many practical advantages for teachers and course designers. Brinton et al., (1989: 2) observe:

In a content-based approach, the activities of the language class are specific to the subject being taught, and are geared to stimulate students to think and learn through the target language. Such an approach lends itself quite naturally to the integrated teaching of the four traditional language skills. For example, it employs authentic reading materials which require students not only to understand information but to interpret and evaluate it as well. It provides a forum in which students can respond orally to reading and lecture materials. It recognizes that academic writing follows from listening, and reading, and thus requires students to synthesize facts and ideas from multiple sources as preparation for writing. In this approach, students are exposed to study skills and learn a variety of language skills which prepare then for a range of academic tasks they will encounter.

Critics have noted that most language teachers have been trained to teach language as a skill rather than to teach a content subject. Thus, language teachers may be insufficiently grounded to teach subject matter in which they have not been trained. Team-teaching proposals involving language teachers and subject-matter teachers are often considered unwieldy and likely to reduce the efficiency of both. However, because CBI is based on a set of broad principles that can be applied in many different ways and is widely used as the basis for many different kinds of successful language programs, we can expect to see CBI continue as one of the leading curricular approaches in language teaching.

Bibliography and further reading

Brinton, D. M., M. A. Snow, and M. B. Wesche. 1989. *Content-Based Second Language Instruction*. New York: Newbury House.

Brinton, D. M., and P. Master (eds.). 1997. *New Ways in Content-Based Instruction*. Alexandria, Va.: TESOL Inc.

Burger, S. 1989. Content-based ESL in a sheltered psychology course: Input, output and outcomes. *TESL Canada Journal* 6: 45–49.

Cantoni-Harvey, G. 1987. *Content-Area Language Instruction*. Reading, Mass.: Addison-Wesley.

Collier, V. 1989. How long? A synthesis of research on academic achievement in a second language. *TESOL Quarterly* 23: 509–531.

Crandall, J. (ed.). 1987. *ESL through Content-Area Instruction: Mathematics, Science, Social Studies*. Englewood Cliffs, N.J.: Prentice Hall.

D'Anglejan, A., and R. Tucker. 1975. The acquisition of complex English structures by adult learners. *Language Learning* 25(2): 281–296.

Dudley-Evans, T., and M. J. St John (eds.). 1998. *Developments in English for Specific Purposes: A Multidisciplinary Approach*. Cambridge: Cambridge University Press.

Gass, S., and C. Madden (eds.). 1985. *Input in Second Language Acquisition.* New York: Newbury House.

Grabe, W., and F. Stoller. 1997. Content-Based Instruction: Research foundations. In M. Snow and D. M. Brinton (eds.), *The Content-Based Classroom.* New York: Longman.

Grandin, J. 1993. The University of Rhode Island's International Engineering Program. In M. Krueger and F. Ryan (eds.), *Language and Content.* Lexington, Mass.: D. C. Heath. 57–79.

Hutchison, T., and A. Waters. 1987. *English for Specific Purposes.* Cambridge: Cambridge University Press.

Jordan, R. R. 1997. *English for Academic Purposes.* Cambridge: Cambridge University Press.

Kelly, L. G. 1969. *25 Centuries of Language Teaching.* Rowley, Mass.: Newbury House.

Kessler, C., and M. Quinn. 1987. ESL and science learning. In J. Crandall (ed.), *ESL through Content Area Instruction: Mathematics, Science, and Social Studies.* Englewood Cliffs, N.Y. Prentice Hall. 55–88.

Krahnke, K. 1987. *Approaches to Syllabus Design for Foreign Language Teaching.* New York: Prentice Hall.

Mohan, B. 1986. *Language and Content.* Reading, Mass.: Addison-Wesley.

Mohan, B. 1993. A common agenda for language and content integration. In N. Bird, J. Harris, and M. Ingram (eds.), *Language and Content.* Hong Kong: Institute of Language in Education. 4–19.

Ozolins, U. 1993. *The Politics of Language in Australia.* Melbourne: Cambridge University Press.

Richards, J. C., and C. Sandy. 1998. *Passages.* New York: Cambridge University Press.

Richards, J. C., and D. Hurley. 1990. Language and content: Approaches to curriculum alignment. In J. C. Richards, *The Language Teaching Matrix.* New York: Cambridge University Press. 144–162.

Robinson, P. 1980. *ESP (English for Specific Purposes).* Oxford: Pergamon.

Safire, W. 1998. On language: The summer of this content. *New York Times,* August 19, 1998, 15.

Scott, M. S. 1974. A note on the relationship between English proficiency, years of language study and the medium of instruction. *Language Learning* 24: 99–104.

Shih, M. 1986. Content-based approaches to teaching academic writing. *TESOL Quarterly* 20(4) (December): 617–648.

Snow, M., and D. M. Brinton (eds.). 1998. *The Content-Based Classroom.* New York: Longman.

Snow, M., M. Met, and F. Genesee. 1989. A conceptual framework for the integration of language and content in second/foreign language instruction. *TESOL Quarterly* 23: 201–217.

Stoller, F. 1997. Project work: a means to promote language and content. *English Teaching Forum.* 35(4): 2–9, 37.

Stoller, F., and W. Grabe. 1997. A Six-T's Approach to Content-Based Instruction. In M. Snow and D. Brinton (eds.), *The Content-Based Classroom: Perspectives on Integrating Language and Content.* White Plains, N.Y.: Longman. 78–94.

Stryker, S., and B. Leaver. 1993. *Content-Based Instruction in Foreign Language Education.* Washington, D.C.: Georgetown University Press.

Wesche, M. 1993. Discipline-based approaches to language study: Research issues and outcomes. In M. Krueger and F. Ryan (eds.), *Language and Content.* Lexington, Mass.: D. C. Heath. 80–95.

Widdowson, H. 1978. *Teaching Language as Communication.* Oxford: Oxford University Press.

Widdowson, H. 1983. *Learning Purpose and Learning Use.* Oxford: Oxford University Press.

Wu, S.-M. 1996. Content-based ESL at high school level: A case study. *Prospect* 11(1): 18–36.

18 Task-Based Language Teaching

Background

Task-Based Language Teaching (TBLT) refers to an approach based on the use of tasks as the core unit of planning and instruction in language teaching. Some of its proponents (e.g., Willis 1996) present it as a logical development of Communicative Language Teaching since it draws on several principles that formed part of the communicative language teaching movement from the 1980s. For example:

- Activities that involve real communication are essential for language learning.
- Activities in which language is used for carrying out meaningful tasks promote learning.
- Language that is meaningful to the learner supports the learning process.

Tasks are proposed as useful vehicles for applying these principles. Two early applications of a task-based approach within a communicative framework for language teaching were the Malaysian Communicational Syllabus (1975) and the Bangalore Project (Beretta and Davies 1985; Prabhu 1987; Beretta 1990) both of which were relatively short-lived.

The role of tasks has received further support from some researchers in second language acquisition, who are interested in developing pedagogical applications of second language acquisition theory (e.g., Long and Crookes 1993). An interest in tasks as potential building blocks of second language instruction emerged when researchers turned to tasks as SLA research tools in the mid-1980s. SLA research has focused on the strategies and cognitive processes employed by second language learners. This research has suggested a reassessment of the role of formal grammar instruction in language teaching. There is no evidence, it is argued, that the type of grammar-focused teaching activities used in many language classrooms reflects the cognitive learning processes employed in naturalistic language learning situations outside the classroom. Engaging learners in task work provides a better context for the activation of learning processes than form-focused activities, and hence ultimately provides better opportunities for language learning to take place. Language learning is believed to depend on immersing students not merely in

223

"comprehensible input" but in tasks that require them to negotiate meaning and engage in naturalistic and meaningful communication.

The key assumptions of task-based instruction are summarized by Feez (1998: 17) as:

- The focus is on process rather than product.
- Basic elements are purposeful activities and tasks that emphasize communication and meaning.
- Learners learn language by interacting communicatively and purposefully while engaged in the activities and tasks.
- Activities and tasks can be either:
  those that learners might need to achieve in real life;
  those that have a pedagogical purpose specific to the classroom.
- Activities and tasks of a task-based syllabus are sequenced according to difficulty.
- The difficulty of a task depends on a range of factors including the previous experience of the learner, the complexity of the task, the language required to undertake the task, and the degree of support available.

Because of its links to Communicative Language Teaching methodology and support from some prominent SLA theorists, TBLT has gained considerable attention within applied linguistics, though there have been few large-scale practical applications of it and little documentation concerning its implications or effectiveness as a basis for syllabus design, materials development, and classroom teaching.

Task-Based Language Teaching proposes the notion of "task" as a central unit of planning and teaching. Although definitions of task vary in TBLT, there is a commonsensical understanding that a task is an activity or goal that is carried out using language, such as finding a solution to a puzzle, reading a map and giving directions, making a telephone call, writing a letter, or reading a set of instructions and assembling a toy:

Tasks . . . are activities which have meaning as their primary focus. Success in tasks is evaluated in terms of achievement of an outcome, and tasks generally bear some resemblance to real-life language use. So task-based instruction takes a fairly strong view of communicative language teaching. (Skehan 1996b: 20)

Nunan (1989: 10) offers this definition:

the communicative task [is] a piece of classroom work which involves learners in comprehending, manipulating, producing or interacting in the target language while their attention is principally focused on meaning rather than form. The task should also have a sense of completeness, being able to stand alone as a communicative act in its own right.

224

Although advocates of TBLT have embraced the concept of task with enthusiasm and conviction, the use of tasks as a unit in curriculum planning has a much older history in education. It first appeared in the vocational training practices of the 1950s. Task focus here first derived from training design concerns of the military regarding new military technologies and occupational specialties of the period. *Task analysis* initially focused on solo psychomotor tasks for which little communication or collaboration was involved. In task analysis, on-the-job, largely manual tasks were translated into training tasks. The process is outlined by Smith:

The operational system is analyzed from the human factors point of view, and a mission profile or flow chart is prepared to provide a basis for developing the task inventory. The task inventory (an outline of the major duties in the job and the more specific job tasks associated with each duty) is prepared, using appropriate methods of job analysis. Decisions are made regarding tasks to be taught and the level of proficiency to be attained by the students. A detailed task description is prepared for those tasks to be taught. Each task is broken down into the specific acts required for its performance. The specific acts, or task elements, are reviewed to identify the knowledge and skill components involved in task performance. Finally, a hierarchy of objectives is organized. (Smith 1971: 584)

A similar process is at the heart of the curriculum approach known as Competency-Based Language Teaching (see Chapter 13). Task-based training identified several key areas of concern.

1. analysis of real-world task-use situations
2. the translation of these into teaching tasks descriptions
3. the detailed design of instructional tasks
4. the sequencing of instructional tasks in classroom training/teaching

These same issues remain central in current discussions of task-based instruction in language teaching. Although task analysis and instructional design initially dealt with solo job performance on manual tasks, attention then turned to team tasks, for which communication is required. Four major categories of team performance function were recognized:

1. *orientation functions* (processes for generating and distributing information necessary to task accomplishment to team members)
2. *organizational functions* (processes necessary for members to coordinate actions necessary for task performance)
3. *adaptation functions* (processes occurring as team members adapt their performance to each other to complete the task)

4. motivational functions (defining team objectives and "energizing the group" to complete the task)

(Nieva, Fleishman, and Rieck [1978], cited in Crookes 1986)

Advocates of TBLT have made similar attempts to define and validate the nature and function of tasks in language teaching. Although studies of the kind just noted have focused on the nature of occupational tasks, academic tasks have also been the focus of considerable attention in general education since the early 1970s. Doyle noted that in elementary education, "the academic task is the mechanism through which the curriculum is enacted for students" (Doyle 1983: 161). Academic tasks are defined as having four important dimensions:

1. the products students are asked to produce
2. the operations they are required to use in order to produce these products
3. the cognitive operations required and the resources available
4. the accountability system involved

All of the questions (and many of the proposed answers) that were raised in these early investigations of tasks and their role in training and teaching mirror similar discussions in relation to Task-Based Language Teaching. In this chapter, we will outline the critical issues in Task-Based Language Teaching and provide examples of what task-based teaching is supposed to look like.

Approach

Theory of language

TBLT is motivated primarily by a theory of learning rather than a theory of language. However, several assumptions about the nature of language can be said to underlie current approaches to TBLT. These are:

LANGUAGE IS PRIMARILY A MEANS OF MAKING MEANING

In common with other realizations of communicative language teaching, TBLT emphasizes the central role of meaning in language use. Skehan notes that in task-based instruction (TBI), "meaning is primary . . . the assessment of the task is in terms of outcome" and that task-based instruction is *not* "concerned with language display" (Skehan 1998: 98).

MULTIPLE MODELS OF LANGUAGE INFORM TBI

Advocates of task-based instruction draw on structural, functional, and interactional models of language, as defined in Chapter 1. This seems to be more a matter of convenience than of ideology. For example, *structural* criteria are employed by Skehan in discussing the criteria for determining the linguistic complexity of tasks:

Language is simply seen as less-to-more complex in fairly traditional ways, since linguistic complexity is interpretable as constrained by structural syllabus considerations. (Skehan 1998: 99)

Other researchers have proposed *functional* classifications of task types. For example, Berwick uses "task goals" as one of two distinctions in classification of task types. He notes that task goals are principally "educational goals which have clear didactic function" and "social (phatic) goals which require the use of language simply because of the activity in which the participants are engaged." (Berwick 1988, cited in Skehan 1998: 101). Foster and Skehan (1996) propose a three-way functional distinction of tasks – personal, narrative, and decision-making tasks. These and other such classifications of task type borrow categories of language function from models proposed by Jakobson, Halliday, Wilkins, and others.

Finally, task classifications proposed by those coming from the SLA research tradition of interaction studies focus on *interactional* dimensions of tasks. For example, Pica (1994) distinguishes between interactional activity and communicative goal.

TBI is therefore not linked to a single model of language but rather draws on all three models of language theory.

LEXICAL UNITS ARE CENTRAL IN LANGUAGE USE AND LANGUAGE LEARNING

In recent years, vocabulary has been considered to play a more central role in second language learning than was traditionally assumed. Vocabulary is here used to include the consideration of lexical phrases, sentence stems, prefabricated routines, and collocations, and not only words as significant units of linguistic lexical analysis and language pedagogy. Many task-based proposals incorporate this perspective. Skehan, for example (1996b: 21–22), comments:

Although much of language teaching has operated under the assumption that language is essentially structural, with vocabulary elements slotting in to fill structural patterns, many linguists and psycholinguists have argued that native language speech processing is very frequently lexical in nature. This means that speech processing is based on the production and reception of whole phrase units larger than the word (although analyzable by linguists into words) which do not require any internal processing when they are 'reeled off'. . . . . Fluency concerns the learner's capacity to produce language in real time without undue pausing for hesitation. It is likely to rely upon more lexicalized modes of communication, as the pressures of real-time speech production met only by avoiding excessive rule-based computation.

"CONVERSATION" IS THE CENTRAL FOCUS OF LANGUAGE AND THE KEYSTONE OF LANGUAGE ACQUISITION

Speaking and trying to communicate with others through the spoken language drawing on the learner's available linguistic and communicative resources is considered the basis for second language acquisition in TBI; hence, the majority of tasks that are proposed within TBLT involve conversation. We will consider further the role of conversation later in this chapter.

Theory of learning

TBI shares the general assumptions about the nature of language learning underlying Communicative Language Teaching (see Chapter 14). However some additional learning principles play a central role in TBLT theory. These are:

TASKS PROVIDE BOTH THE INPUT AND OUTPUT PROCESSING NECESSARY FOR LANGUAGE ACQUISITION

Krashen has long insisted that comprehensible input is the one necessary (and sufficient) criterion for successful language acquisition (see Chapter 15). Others have argued, however, that productive output and not merely input is also critical for adequate second language development. For example, in language immersion classrooms in Canada, Swain (1985) showed that even after years of exposure to comprehensible input, the language ability of immersion students still lagged behind native-speaking peers. She claimed that adequate opportunities for productive use of language are critical for full language development. Tasks, it is said, provide full opportunities for both input and output requirements, which are believed to be key processes in language learning. Other researchers have looked at "negotiation of meaning" as the necessary element in second language acquisition. "It is meaning negotiation which focuses a learner's attention on some part of an [the learner's] utterance (pronunciation, grammar, lexicon, etc.) which requires modification. That is, negotiation can be viewed as the trigger for acquisition" (Plough and Gass 1993: 36).

Tasks are believed to foster processes of negotiation, modification, rephrasing, and experimentation that are at the heart of second language learning. This view is part of a more general focus on the critical importance of conversation in language acquisition (e.g., Sato 1988). Drawing on SLA research on negotiation and interaction, TBLT proposes that the task is the pivot point for stimulation of input–output practice, negotiation of meaning, and transactionally focused conversation.

TASK ACTIVITY AND ACHIEVEMENT ARE MOTIVATIONAL

Tasks are also said to improve learner motivation and therefore promote learning. This is because they require the learners to use authentic language, they have well-defined dimensions and closure, they are varied in format and operation, they typically include physical activity, they involve partnership and collaboration, they may call on the learner's past experience, and they tolerate and encourage a variety of communication styles. One teacher trainee, commenting on an experience involving listening tasks, noted that such tasks are "genuinely authentic, easy to understand because of natural repetition; students are motivated to listen because they have just done the same task and want to compare how they did it" (quoted in Willis 1996: 61–62). (Doubtless enthusiasts for other teaching methods could cite similar "evidence" for their effectiveness.)

LEARNING DIFFICULTY CAN BE NEGOTIATED AND FINE-TUNED FOR PARTICULAR PEDAGOGICAL PURPOSES

Another claim for tasks is that specific tasks can be designed to facilitate the use and learning of particular aspects of language. Long and Crookes (1991: 43) claim that tasks

provide a vehicle for the presentation of appropriate target language samples to learners – input which they will inevitably reshape via application of general cognitive processing capacities – and for the delivery of comprehension and production opportunities of negotiable difficulty.

In more detailed support of this claim, Skehan suggests that in selecting or designing tasks there is a trade-off between cognitive processing and focus on form. More difficult, cognitively demanding tasks reduce the amount of attention the learner can give to the formal features of messages, something that is thought to be necessary for accuracy and grammatical development. In other words if the task is too difficult, fluency may develop at the expense of accuracy. He suggests that tasks can be designed along a cline of difficulty so that learners can work on tasks that enable them to develop both fluency and an awareness of language form (Skehan 1998: 97). He also proposes that tasks can be used to "channel" learners toward particular aspects of language:

Such channeled use might be towards some aspect of the discourse, or accuracy, complexity, fluency in general, or even occasionally, the use of particular sets of structures in the language. (Skehan 1998: 97–98)

Design

Objectives

There are few published (or perhaps, fully implemented) examples of complete language programs that claim to be fully based on most recent formulations of TBLT. The literature contains mainly descriptions of examples of task-based activities. However, as with other communicative approaches, goals in TBLT are ideally to be determined by the specific needs of particular learners. Selection of tasks, according to Long and Crookes (1993), should be based on a careful analysis of the real-world needs of learners. An example of how this was done with a national English curriculum is the *English Language Syllabus in Schools Malaysian* (1975) – a national, task-based communicative syllabus. A very broad goal for English use was determined by the Ministry of Education at a time when Malay was systematically replacing English-medium instruction at all levels of education. An attempt to define the role of English, given the new role for national Malay language, led to the broad goal of giving all Malaysian secondary school leavers *the ability to communicate accurately and effectively in the most common English-language activities they may be involved in.* Following this broad statement, the syllabus development team identified a variety of work situations in which English use was likely. The anticipated vocational (and occasionally recreational) uses of English for nontertiary-bound, upper secondary school leavers were stated as a list of general English use objectives. The resulting twenty-four objectives then became the framework within which a variety of related activities were proposed. The components of these activities were defined in the syllabus under the headings of Situation, Stimulus, Product, Tasks, and Cognitive Process. An overview of the syllabus that resulted from this process is given in Chapter 14.

The syllabus

The differences between a conventional language syllabus and a task-based one are discussed below. A conventional syllabus typically specifies the content of a course from among these categories:

- language structures
- functions
- topics and themes
- macro-skills (reading, writing, listening, speaking)
- competencies
- text types
- vocabulary targets

The syllabus specifies content and learning outcomes and is a document that can be used as a basis for classroom teaching and the design of teaching materials. Although proponents of TBLT do not preclude an interest in learners' development of any of these categories, they are more concerned with the process dimensions of learning than with the specific content and skills that might be acquired through the use of these processes. A TBLT syllabus, therefore, specifies the tasks that should be carried out by learners within a program.

Nunan (1989) suggests that a syllabus might specify two types of tasks:

1. real-world tasks, which are designed to practice or rehearse those tasks that are found to be important in a needs analysis and turn out to be important and useful in the real world
2. pedagogical tasks, which have a psycholinguistic basis in SLA theory and research but do not necessarily reflect real-world tasks

Using the telephone would be an example of the former, and an information-gap task would be an example of the latter. (It should be noted that a focus on Type 1 tasks, their identification through needs analysis, and the use of such information as the basis for the planning and delivery of teaching are identical with procedures used in Competency-Based Instruction; see Chapter 13.)

In the Bangalore Project (a task-based design for primary age learners of English), both types of tasks were used, as is seen from the following list of the first ten task types:

Task type	*Example*
1. Diagrams and formations	Naming parts of a diagram with numbers and letters of the alphabet as instructed.
2. Drawing	Drawing geometrical figures/formations from sets of verbal instructions
3. Clock faces	Positioning hands on a clock to show a given time
4. Monthly calendar	Calculating duration in days and weeks in the context of travel, leave, and so on
5. Maps	Constructing a floor plan of a house from a description
6. School timetables	Constructing timetables for teachers of particular subjects
7. Programs and itineraries	Constructing itineraries from descriptions of travel

8. Train timetables	Selecting trains appropriate to given needs
9. Age and year of birth	Working out year of birth from age
10. Money	Deciding on quantities to be bought given the money available

(Adapted from Prabhu and cited in Nunan 1989: 42–44)

Norris, Brown, Hudson, and Yoshioka (1998) provide examples of representative real-world tasks grouped according to themes. For example:

Theme: planning a vacation

Tasks
– decide where you can go based on the "advantage miles"
– booking a flight
– choosing a hotel
– booking a room

Theme: application to a university

Tasks
– applying to the university
– corresponding with the department chair
– inquiring about financial support
– selecting the courses you want and are eligible to take, using advice from your adviser
– registering by phone
– calculating and paying your fees

It is hard to see that this classification offers much beyond the intuitive impressions of the writers of Situational Language Teaching materials of the 1960s or the data-free taxonomies that are seen in Munby's *Communicative Syllabus Design* (1978). Nor have subsequent attempts at describing task dimensions and task difficulty gone much beyond speculation (see Skehan 1998: 98–99).

In addition to selecting tasks as the basis for a TBLT syllabus, the ordering of tasks also has to be determined. We saw that the intrinsic difficulty of tasks has been proposed as a basis for the sequencing of tasks, but task difficulty is itself a concept that is not easy to determine. Honeyfield (1993: 129) offers the following considerations:

1. Procedures, or what the learners have to do to derive output from input
2. Input text
3. Output required
   a) Language items: vocabulary, structures, discourse structures, processability, and so on

b) Skills, both macro-skills and subskills
c) World knowledge or "topic content"
d) Text handling or conversation strategies
4. Amount and type of help given
5. Role of teachers and learners
6. Time allowed
7. Motivation
8. Confidence
9. Learning styles

This list illustrates the difficulty of operationalizing the notion of task difficulty: One could add almost anything to it, such as time of day, room temperature, or the aftereffects of breakfast!

Types of learning and teaching activities

We have seen that there are many different views as to what constitutes a task. Consequently, there are many competing descriptions of basic task types in TBLT and of appropriate classroom activities. Breen gives a very broad description of a task (1987: 26):

A language learning task can be regarded as a springboard for learning work. In a broad sense, it is a structured plan for the provision of opportunities for the refinement of knowledge and capabilities entailed in a new language and its use during communication. Such a work plan will have its own particular objective, appropriate content which is to be worked upon, and a working procedure. . . . A simple and brief exercise is a task, and so also are more complex and comprehensive work plans which require spontaneous communication of meaning or the solving of problems in learning and communicating. Any language test can be included within this spectrum of tasks. All materials designed for language teaching – through their particular organization of content and the working procedures they assume or propose for the learning of content – can be seen as compendia of tasks.

For Prabhu, a task is "an activity which requires learners to arrive at an outcome from given information through some process of thought, and which allows teachers to control and regulate that process" (Prabhu 1987: 17). Reading train timetables and deciding which train one should take to get to a certain destination on a given day is an appropriate classroom task according to this definition. Crookes defines a task as "a piece of work or an activity, usually with a specified objective, undertaken as part of an educational course, at work, or used to elicit data for research" (Crookes 1986: 1). This definition would lead to a very different set of "tasks" from those identified by Prahbu, since it could include not only summaries, essays, and class notes, but presumably, in some language classrooms, drills, dialogue readings, and any of the other "tasks" that teachers use to attain their teaching objectives.

In the literature on TBLT, several attempts have been made to group tasks into categories, as a basis for task design and description. Willis (1996) proposes six task types built on more or less traditional knowledge hierarchies. She labels her task examples as follows:

1. listing
2. ordering and sorting
3. comparing
4. problem solving
5. sharing personal experiences
6. creative tasks

Pica, Kanagy, and Falodun (1993) classify tasks according to the type of interaction that occurs in task accomplishment and give the following classification:

1. *Jigsaw tasks:* These involve learners combining different pieces of information to form a whole (e.g., three individuals or groups may have three different parts of a story and have to piece the story together).
2. *Information-gap tasks:* One student or group of students has one set of information and another student or group has a complementary set of information. They must negotiate and find out what the other party's information is in order to complete an activity.
3. *Problem-solving tasks:* Students are given a problem and a set of information. They must arrive at a solution to the problem. There is generally a single resolution of the outcome.
4. *Decision-making tasks:* Students are given a problem for which there are a number of possible outcomes and they must choose one through negotiation and discussion.
5. *Opinion exchange tasks:* Learners engage in discussion and exchange of ideas. They do not need to reach agreement.

Other characteristics of tasks have also been described, such as the following:

1. one-way or two-way: whether the task involves a one-way exchange of information or a two-way exchange
2. convergent or divergent: whether the students achieve a common goal or several different goals
3. collaborative or competitive: whether the students collaborate to carry out a task or compete with each other on a task

4. single or multiple outcomes: whether there is a single outcome or many different outcomes are possible
5. concrete or abstract language: whether the task involves the use of concrete language or abstract language
6. simple or complex processing: whether the task requires relatively simple or complex cognitive processing
7. simple or complex language: whether the linguistic demands of the task are relatively simple or complex
8. reality-based or not reality-based: whether the task mirrors a real-world activity or is a pedagogical activity not found in the real world

Learner roles

A number of specific roles for learners are assumed in current proposals for TBI. Some of these overlap with the general roles assumed for learners in Communicative Language Teaching while others are created by the focus on task completion as a central learning activity. Primary roles that are implied by task work are:

GROUP PARTICIPANT

Many tasks will be done in pairs or small groups. For students more accustomed to whole-class and/or individual work, this may require some adaptation.

MONITOR

In TBLT, tasks are not employed for their own sake but as a means of facilitating learning. Class activities have to be designed so that students have the opportunity to notice how language is used in communication. Learners themselves need to "attend" not only to the message in task work, but also to the form in which such messages typically come packed. A number of learner-initiated techniques to support learner reflection on task characteristics, including language form, are proposed in Bell and Burnaby (1984).

RISK-TAKER AND INNOVATOR

Many tasks will require learners to create and interpret messages for which they lack full linguistic resources and prior experience. In fact, this is said to be the point of such tasks. Practice in restating, paraphrasing, using paralinguistic signals (where appropriate), and so on, will often be needed. The skills of guessing from linguistic and contextual clues, asking for clarification, and consulting with other learners may also need to be developed.

Teacher roles

Additional roles are also assumed for teachers in TBI, including:

SELECTOR AND SEQUENCER OF TASKS

A central role of the teacher is in selecting, adapting, and/or creating the tasks themselves and then forming these into an instructional sequence in keeping with learner needs, interests, and language skill level.

PREPARING LEARNERS FOR TASKS

Most TBLT proponents suggest that learners should not go into new tasks "cold" and that some sort of pretask preparation or cuing is important. Such activities might include topic introduction, clarifying task instructions, helping students learn or recall useful words and phrases to facilitate task accomplishment, and providing partial demonstration of task procedures. Such cuing may be inductive and implicit or deductive and explicit.

CONSCIOUSNESS-RAISING

Current views of TBLT hold that if learners are to acquire language through participating in tasks they need to attend to or notice critical features of the language they use and hear. This is referred to as "Focus on Form." TBLT proponents stress that this does not mean doing a grammar lesson before students take on a task. It does mean employing a variety of form-focusing techniques, including attention-focusing pretask activities, text exploration, guided exposure to parallel tasks, and use of highlighted material.

The role of instructional materials

PEDAGOGIC MATERIALS

Instructional materials play an important role in TBLT because it is dependent on a sufficient supply of appropriate classroom tasks, some of which may require considerable time, ingenuity, and resources to develop. Materials that can be exploited for instruction in TBLT are limited only by the imagination of the task designer. Many contemporary language teaching texts cite a "task focus" or "task-based activities" among their credentials, though most of the tasks that appear in such books are familiar classroom activities for teachers who employ collaborative learning, Communicative Language Teaching, or small-group activities. Several teacher resource books are available that contain representative sets of sample task activities (e.g., Willis 1996) that can be adapted for a variety of situations. A number of task collections have also been put into textbook form for students use. Some of these are in more or less traditional text format (e.g., *Think Twice,* Hover 1986), some are multimedia (e.g., *Challenges,* Candlin and Edelhoff 1982), and some are published as task cards (e.g., Malaysian Upper Secondary Communicational Syllabus Resource Kit, 1979). A wide variety of realia can also be used as a resource for TBI.

REALIA

TBI proponents favor the use of authentic tasks supported by authentic materials wherever possible. Popular media obviously provide rich resources for such materials. The following are some of the task types that can be built around such media products.

Newspapers
- Students examine a newspaper, determine its sections, and suggest three new sections that might go in the newspaper.
- Students prepare a job-wanted ad using examples from the classified section.
- Students prepare their weekend entertainment plan using the entertainment section.

Television
- Students take notes during the weather report and prepare a map with weather symbols showing likely weather for the predicted period.
- In watching an infomercial, students identify and list "hype" words and then try to construct a parallel ad following the sequence of the hype words.
- After watching an episode of an unknown soap opera, students list the characters (with known or made-up names) and their possible relationship to other characters in the episode.

Internet
- Given a book title to be acquired, students conduct a comparative shopping analysis of three Internet booksellers, listing prices, mailing times, and shipping charges, and choose a vendor, justifying their choice.
- Seeking to find an inexpensive hotel in Tokyo, students search with three different search engines (e.g., Yahoo, Netscape, Snap), comparing search times and analyzing the first ten hits to determine most useful search engine for their purpose.
- Students initiate a "chat" in a chat room, indicating a current interest in their life and developing an answer to the first three people to respond. They then start a diary with these text-sets, ranking the responses.

Procedure

The way in which task activities are designed into an instructional bloc can be seen from the following example from Richards (1985). The example comes from a language program that contained a core component built around tasks. The program was an intensive conversation course for Japanese college students studying on a summer program in the United States. Needs analysis identified target tasks the students needed to be able to carry out in English, including:

– basic social survival transactions
– face-to-face informal conversations
– telephone conversations
– interviews on the campus
– service encounters

A set of role-play activities was then developed focusing on situations students would encounter in the community and transactions they would have to carry out in English. The following format was developed for each role-play task:

Pretask activities
1. Learners first take part in a preliminary activity that introduces the topic, the situation, and the "script" that will subsequently appear in the role-play task. Such activities are of various kinds, including brainstorming, ranking exercises, and problem-solving tasks. The focus is on thinking about a topic, generating vocabulary and related language, and developing expectations about the topic. This activity therefore prepares learners for the role-play task by establishing schemata of different kinds.
2. Learners then read a dialogue on a related topic. This serves both to model the kind of transaction the learner will have to perform in the role-play task and to provide examples of the kind of language that could be used to carry out such a transaction.

Task activity
3. Learners perform a role play. Students work in pairs with a task and cues needed to negotiate the task.

Posttask activities
4. Learners then listen to recordings of native speakers performing the same role-play task they have just practiced and compare differences between the way they expressed particular functions and meanings and the way native speakers performed.

Willis (1996: 56–57) recommends a similar sequence of activities:

Pretask

Introduction to topic and task
- T helps Ss to understand the theme and objectives of the task, for example, brainstorming ideas with the class, using pictures, mime, or personal experience to introduce the topic.
- Ss may do a pretask, for example, topic-based odd-word-out games.
- T may highlight useful words and phrases, but would not preteach new structures.
- Ss can be given preparation time to think about how to do the task.
- Ss can hear a recording of a parallel task being done (so long as this does not give away the solution to the problem).
- If the task is based on a text, Ss read part of it.

The task cycle

Task
- The task is done by Ss (in pairs or groups) and gives Ss a chance to use whatever language they already have to express themselves and say whatever they want to say. This may be in response to reading a text or hearing a recording.
- T walks round and monitors, encouraging in a supportive way everyone's attempts at communication in the target language.
- T helps Ss to formulate what they want to say, but will not intervene to correct errors of form.
- The emphasis is on spontaneous, exploratory talk and confidence building, within the privacy of the small group.
- Success in achieving the goals of the task helps Ss' motivation.

Planning
- Planning prepares for the next stage, when Ss are asked to report briefly to the whole class how they did the task and what the outcome was.
- Ss draft and rehearse what they want to say or write.
- T goes round to advise students on language, suggesting phrases and helping Ss to polish and correct their language.
- If the reports are in writing, T can encourage peer editing and use of dictionaries.
- The emphasis is on clarity, organization, and accuracy, as appropriate for a public presentation.
- Individual students often take this chance to ask questions about specific language items.

Report
- T asks some pairs to report briefly to the whole class so everyone can compare findings, or begin a survey. (NB: There must be a purpose for

others to listen.) Sometimes only one or two groups report in full; others comment and add extra points. The class may take notes.
– T chairs, comments on the content of their reports, rephrases perhaps, but gives no overt public correction.

Posttask listening
– Ss listen to a recording of fluent speakers doing the same task, and compare the ways in which they did the task themselves.

The language focus

Analysis
– T sets some language-focused tasks, based on the texts students have read or on the transcripts of the recordings they have heard.
– Examples include the following:
  Find words and phrases related to the title of the topic or text.
  Read the transcript, find words ending in *s* or *'s,* and say what the *s* means.
  Find all the verbs in the simple past form. Say which refer to past time and which do not.
  Underline and classify the questions in the transcript.
– T starts Ss off, then Ss continue, often in pairs.
– T goes round to help; Ss can ask individual questions.
– In plenary, T then reviews the analysis, possibly writing relevant language up on the board in list form; Ss may make notes.

Practice
– T conducts practice activities as needed, based on the language analysis work already on the board, or using examples from the text or transcript.
– Practice activities can include:
  choral repetition of the phrases identified and classified
  memory challenge games based on partially erased examples or using lists already on blackboard for progressive deletion
  sentence completion (set by one team for another)
  matching the past-tense verbs (jumbled) with the subject or objects they had in the text
  Kim's game (in teams) with new words and phrases
  dictionary reference words from text or transcript

Conclusion

Few would question the pedagogical value of employing tasks as a vehicle for promoting communication and authentic language use in second language classrooms, and depending on one's definition of a task, tasks have long been part of the mainstream repertoire of language teaching techniques for teachers of many different methodological persuasions. TBLT, however, offers a different rationale for the use of tasks as well as different criteria for the design and use of tasks. It is the dependence on tasks as the primary source of pedagogical input in teaching and the absence of a systematic grammatical or other type of syllabus that characterizes current versions of TBLT, and that distinguishes it from the use of tasks in Competency-Based Language Teaching, another task-based approach but one that is not wedded to the theoretical framework and assumptions of TBLT. Many aspects of TBLT have yet to be justified, such as proposed schemes for task types, task sequencing, and evaluation of task performance. And the basic assumption of Task-Based Language Teaching – that it provides for a more effective basis for teaching than other language teaching approaches – remains in the domain of ideology rather than fact.

Bibliography and further reading

Bell, J., and B. Burnaby. 1984. *A Handbook for ESL Literacy.* Toronto: Ontario Institute for Studies in Education.

Beretta, A. 1990. Implementation of the Bangalore Project. *Applied Linguistics* 11(4): 321-337.

Beretta, A., and A. Davies. 1985. Evaluation of the Bangalore Project. *English Language Teaching Journal* 30(2) 121–127.

Breen, M. 1987. Learner contributions to task design. In C. Candlin and D. Murphy (eds.), *Language Learning Tasks.* Englewood Cliffs, N.J.: Prentice Hall. 23–46.

Brown, G., and G. Yule. 1983. *Teaching the Spoken Language.* Cambridge: Cambridge University Press.

Bygate, M. 1988. Units of oral expression and language learning in small group intereaction. *Applied Linguistics* 9: 59–82.

Bygate, M., P. Skehan, and M. Swain. (eds.) 2000. *Task-Based Learning: Language Teaching, Learning, and Assessment.* Harlow, Essex: Pearson.

Candlin, C. 1987. Towards task-based language learning. In C. Candlin and D. Murphy (eds.), *Language Learning Tasks.* Englewood Cliffs, N.J.: Prentice Hall. 5–21.

Candlin, C., and C. Edelhoff. 1982. *Challenges: A Multi-media Project for Learners of English.* Harlow, Essex: Longman.

Crookes, G. 1986. *Task Classification: A Cross-Disciplinary Review.* Technical Report No. 4. Honolulu: Center for Second Language Classroom Research.

Crookes, G., and S. Gass (eds.). 1993. *Tasks in a Pedagogical Context.* Clevedon, Philadelphia, and Adelaide: Multilingual Matters.

Day, R. (ed.). 1986. *Talking to Learn.* Rowley, Mass.: Newbury House.

Doyle, W. 1983. Academic work. *Review of Educational Research* 53(2): 159–199.

Ellis, R. 1992. *Second Language Acquisition and Language Pedagogy.* Clevedon: Multilingual Matters.

English Language Syllabus in Malaysian Schools, Tingkatan 4–5. 1975. Kuala Lumpur: Dewan Bahasa Dan Pustaka.

Feez, S. 1998. *Text-Based Syllabus Design.* Sydney: National Centre for English Teaching and Research.

Foley, Joseph 1991. A Psycholinguistic framework for task-based approaches to language teaching. *Applied Linguistics* 12(1): 62–75.

Foster P., and P. Skehan 1996. The influence of planning on performance in task-based learning. *Studies in Second Language Acquisition* 18: 299–324.

Green, J. M. 1993. Student attitudes towards communicative and non-communicative activities: Do enjoyment and effectiveness go together? *Modern Language Journal* 77(1): 1–9.

Honeyfield, J. 1993. Responding to task difficulty. In M. Tickoo (ed.), *Simplification: Theory and Practice.* Singapore: Regional Language Center. 127–138.

Hover, D. 1986. *Think Twice.* Cambridge: Cambridge University Press.

Johnson, K. 1996. *Language Teaching and Skill Learning.* Oxford: Blackwell.

Lantoff, J., and G. Appel (eds.). 1994. *Vygotskian Approaches to Second Language Research.* Norwood, N.J.: Ablex.

Legutke, M., and Thomas, H. 1991. *Process and Experience in the Language Classroom.* London and New York: Longman.

Long, M., and G. Crookes 1991. Three approaches to task-based syllabus design. *TESOL Quarterly* 26: 27–55.

Long, M., and G. Crookes. 1993. Units of analysis in course design – the case for task. In G. Crookes and S. Gass (eds.), *Tasks in a Pedagogical Context: Integrating Theory and Practice.* Clevedon: Multilingual Matters.

Munby, J. 1988. *Communicative Syllabus Design.* Cambridge: Cambridge University Press.

Nation, I. S. P. (1990). *Language Teaching Techniques.* Wellington: English Language Institute, Victoria University.

Norris, J., J. Brown, T. Hudson, and J. Yoshioka. 1998. *Designing Second Language Performance Assessments.* Honolulu: University of Hawaii Press.

Nunan, D. 1989. *Designing Tasks for the Communicative Classroom.* New York: Cambridge University Press.

Pica, T. 1994. Research on negotiation: What does it reveal about second language learning, conditions, processes, outcomes? *Language Learning* 44: 493–527.

Pica, T., R. Kanagy, and J. Falodun. 1993. Choosing and using communicative tasks for second language instruction. In G. Crookes and S. Gass (eds.), *Tasks and Language Learning: Integrating Theory and Practice.* Clevedon: Multilingual Matters. 9–34.

Plough, I., and S. Gass. 1993. Interlocutor and task familiarity: effect on interactional structure. In G. Crookes and S. Gass (eds.), *Tasks and Language Learning: Integrating Theory and Practice.* Clevedon: Multilingual Matters. 35–56.

Prabhu, N. S. 1987. *Second Language Pedagogy.* Oxford University Press.

Richards, J. C. 1985. Conversational competence through role-play activities. *RELC Journal* 16(1): 82–100.

Richards, J. C. 1999. Addressing the grammar-gap in task work. *Prospect* 14(1): 4–19.

Resource Kits: English for Upper Secondary Schools. 1979. Kuala Lumpur: Pusat Perbangunan Kurikulum, Kementarian Pelajaran Malaysia.

Robinson, P. 1995. Task complexity and second language narrative discourse. *Language Learning* 45(1): 99–140.

Sato, C. 1988. Origins of complex syntax in interlanguage development. *Studies in Second Language Acquisition* 10: 371–395.

Skehan, P. 1996a. A framework for the implementation of task-based instruction. *Applied Linguistics* 17(1): 38–61.

Skehan, P. 1996b. Second language acquisition research and task-based instruction. In J. Willis and D. Willis (eds.). *Challenge and Change in Language Teaching.* Oxford: Heinemann. 17–30.

Skehan, P. 1998. *A Cognitive Approach to Language Learning.* Oxford: Oxford University Press.

Smith, D. 1971. Task training. In *AMA Encyclopedia of Supervisory Training.* New York: American Management Association. 581–586.

Swain, M. 1985. Communicative competence: Some roles of comprehensible input and comprehensible output in development. In S. Gass and C. Madden (eds.), *Input in Second Language Acquisition.* Rowley, Mass.: Newbury House. 235–256.

Willis, J. 1996. A flexible framework for task-based learning. In J. Willis and D. Willis (eds.), 235–256 *Challenge and Change in Language Teaching.* Oxford: Heinemann. 52–62.

Willis, J., and D. Willis (eds.). 1996. *Challenge and Change in Language Teaching.* Oxford: Heinemann.

19 The post-methods era

From the survey of approaches and methods presented in this book we have seen that the history of language teaching in the last one hundred years has been characterized by a search for more effective ways of teaching second or foreign languages. The commonest solution to the "language teaching problem" was seen to lie in the adoption of a new teaching approach or method. One result of this trend was the era of so-called designer or brand-name methods, that is, packaged solutions that can be described and marketed for use anywhere in the world. Thus, the Direct Method was enthusiastically embraced in the early part of the twentieth century as an improvement over Grammar Translation. In the 1950s the Audiolingual Method was thought to provide a way forward, incorporating the latest insights from the sciences of linguistics and psychology. As the Audiolingual Method began to fade in the 1970s, particularly in the United States, a variety of guru-led methods emerged to fill the vacuum created by the discrediting of Audiolingualism, such as the Silent Way, Total Physical Response, and Suggestopedia. While these had declined substantially by the 1990s, new "breakthroughs" continue to be announced from time to time, such as Task-Based Instruction, Neurolinguistic Programming, and Multiple Intelligences, and these attract varying levels of support. Mainstream language teaching on both sides of the Atlantic, however, opted for Communicative Language Teaching (CLT) as the recommended basis for language teaching methodology in the 1980s and it continues to be considered the most plausible basis for language teaching today, although, as we saw in Chapter 14, CLT is today understood to mean little more than a set of very general principles that can be applied and interpreted in a variety of ways.

This book describes approaches and methods in language teaching. We have described an approach as a set of beliefs and principles that can be used as the basis for teaching a language. The following are examples of approaches that have been described in this book:

- Communicative Language Teaching
- Competency-Based Language Teaching
- Content-Based Instruction
- Cooperative Learning

- Lexical Approaches
- Multiple Intelligences
- The Natural Approach
- Neurolinguistic Programming
- Task-Based Language Teaching
- Whole Language

Each of these approaches (or at least those that have been more fully elaborated and adopted) has in common a core set of theories and beliefs about the nature of language, of language learning, and a derived set of principles for teaching a language. None of them, however, leads to a specific set of prescriptions and techniques to be used in teaching a language. They are characterized by a variety of interpretations as to how the principles can be applied. Because of this level of flexibility and the possibility of varying interpretations and application, approaches tend to have a long shelf life. They allow for individual interpretation and application. They can be revised and updated over time as new practices emerge.

A *method*, on the other hand, refers to a specific instructional design or system based on a particular theory of language and of language learning. It contains detailed specifications of content, roles of teachers and learners, and teaching procedures and techniques. It is relatively fixed in time and there is generally little scope for individual interpretation. Methods are learned through training. The teacher's role is to follow the method and apply it precisely according to the rules. The following are examples of methods in this sense:

- Audiolingualism
- Counseling-Learning
- Situational Language Teaching
- The Silent Way
- Suggestopedia
- Total Physical Response

Compared to approaches, methods tend to have a relatively short shelf life. Because they are often linked to very specific claims and to prescribed practices, they tend to fall out of favor as these practices become unfashionable or discredited. The heyday of methods can be considered to have lasted up till the late 1980s.

However, methods offer some advantages over approaches, and this doubtless explains their appeal. Because of the general nature of approaches, there is often no clear application of their assumptions and principles in the classroom, as we have seen with a number of the approaches described in this book. Much is left to the individual teacher's interpretation, skill, and expertise. Consequently, there is often no clear right or wrong way of teaching according to an approach and no prescribed body of practice waiting to be implemented. This lack of detail can be a source of frustration and irritation for teachers, particularly those with little training or experience. Methods, on the other hand, solve many of the problems beginning teachers have to struggle with because many of the basic decisions about what to teach and how to teach it have already been made for them. Moreover, method enthusiasts create together a professional community with a common purpose, ideology, and vernacular. This provides adherents with a cohort group of like-minded teachers with whom they can share ideas and experiences. Methods can also be seen as a rich resource of activities, some of which can be adapted or adopted regardless of one's own ideology. Like the "P-P-P" prescription of Present, Practice, and Produce, a method offers to the novice teacher the reassurance of a detailed set of sequential steps to follow in the classroom.

The extent to which new approaches and methods become widely accepted and have a lasting impact on teachers' practices also depends on the relative ease or difficulty of introducing the changes the approach or method requires. Curriculum changes are of many different kinds. They may affect teachers' pedagogical values and beliefs, their understanding of the nature of language or second language learning, or their classroom practices and uses of teaching materials. Some changes may be readily accepted, others resisted. The following questions will therefore affect the extent to which a new approach or method is adopted:

- What advantages does the new approach or method offer? Is it perceived to be more effective than current practices?
- How compatible is it with teachers' existing beliefs and attitudes and with the organization and practices within classrooms and schools?
- Is the new approach or method very complicated and difficult to understand and use?
- Has it been tested out in some schools and classrooms before teachers are expected to use it?
- Have the benefits of the new approach or method been clearly communicated to teachers and institutions?
- How clear and practical is the new approach or method? Are its expectations stated in ways that clearly show how it can be used in the classroom?

Practicality is a key issue. A methodology that can readily be turned into teaching materials and textbooks and whose use requires no special training will generally be more readily adopted than one lacking these features. The support networks available in promoting or explaining a new teaching approach or method are also crucial. Here a ministry or department of education, key educational administrators, leading academics, and professional bodies and organizations can play an important role in promoting a new approach or method.

From the descriptions given in this book it is clear that some approaches and methods are unlikely to be widely adopted because they are difficult to understand and use, lack clear practical application, require special training, and necessitate major changes in teachers' practices and beliefs. This is true of many of the alternative approaches and methods described in this book.

Yet the notion of methods came under criticism in the 1990s for other reasons, and a number of limitations implicit in the notion of all-purpose methods were raised. By the end of the twentieth century, mainstream language teaching no longer regarded methods as the key factor in accounting for success or failure in language teaching. Some spoke of the death of methods and approaches and the term "post-methods era" was sometimes used. What were the major criticisms made of approaches and methods?

The "top-down" criticism

While approaches tend to allow for varying interpretations in practice, methods typically prescribe for teachers what and how to teach. Teachers have to accept on faith the claims or theory underlying the method and apply them to their own practice. Good teaching is regarded as correct use of the method and its prescribed principles and techniques. Roles of teachers and learners, as well as the type of activities and teaching techniques to be used in the classroom, are generally prescribed. The role of the teacher is marginalized; his or her role is to understand the method and apply its principles correctly. Likewise, learners are sometimes viewed as the passive recipients of the method and must submit themselves to its regime of exercises and activities. Absent from the traditional view of methods is a concept of learner-centeredness and teacher creativity: an acknowledgment that learners bring different learning styles and preferences to the learning process, that they should be consulted in the process of developing a teaching program, and that teaching methods must be flexible and adaptive to learners' needs and interests. At the same time, there is often little room for the teacher's own personal initiative and teaching style. The teacher must submit herself or himself to the method.

Role of contextual factors

Both approaches and methods are often promoted as all-purpose solutions to teaching problems that can be applied in any part of the world and under any circumstance. In trying to apply approaches or methods, teachers sometimes ignore what is the starting point in language program design, namely, a careful consideration of the context in which teaching and learning occurs, including the cultural context, the political context, the local institutional context, and the context constituted by the teachers and learners in their classrooms.

For example, attempts to introduce Communicative Language Teaching in countries with very different educational traditions from those in which CLT was developed (Britain and the United States and other English-speaking countries) have sometimes been described as "cultural imperialism" because the assumptions and practices implicit in CLT are viewed as "correct" whereas those of the target culture are seen in need of replacement. Similarly, Counseling-Learning and Cooperative Learning both make assumptions about the roles of teachers and learners that are not necessarily culturally universal.

The need for curriculum development processes

Curriculum planners view debates over teaching method as part of a broader set of educational planning decisions. These traditionally involve:

a) The careful examination, drawing on all available sources of knowledge and informed judgement, of the teaching objectives, whether in particular subject courses or over the curriculum as a whole.
b) The development and trial use in schools of those methods and materials which are judged most likely to achieve the objectives which teachers agreed upon.
c) The assessment of the extent to which the development work has in fact achieved its objectives. This part of the process may be expected to provoke new thought about the objectives themselves.
d) The final element is therefore the feedback of all the experience gained, to provide a starting point for further study.

(Nicholls and Nicholls 1972: 4)

These elements are viewed as forming a network of interacting systems. Choice of teaching method cannot, therefore, be determined in isolation from other planning and implementation practices (Richards 2000).

Lack of research basis

Approaches and methods are often based on the assumption that the processes of second language learning are fully understood. Many of the books written by method gurus are full of claims and assertions about how people learn languages, few of which are based on second language acquisition research or have been empirically tested. With some exceptions, such as Krashen, researchers who study language learning are themselves usually reluctant to dispense prescriptions for teaching based on the results of their research, because they know that current knowledge is tentative, partial, and changing. Much of such research does not support the often simplistic theories and prescriptions found in some approaches and methods. Skehan, for example, commenting on the standard lesson sequence in Situational Language Teaching as well as other methods consisting of a Presentation phase, a Practice phase, and a Production phase (the P-P-P lesson model), points out that such a sequence does not reflect principles of second language acquisition:

The underlying theory for a P-P-P approach has now been discredited. The belief that a precise focus on a particular form leads to learning and automatization (that learners will learn what is taught in the order in which it is taught) no longer carries much credibility in linguistics or psychology. (Skehan 1996: 18)

Similarity of classroom practices

Another criticism is that it is very difficult for teachers to use approaches and methods in ways that precisely reflect the underlying principles of the method. Swaffar, Arens, and Morgan (1982: 25) commented:

One consistent problem is whether or not teachers involved in presenting materials created for a particular method are actually reflecting the underlying philosophies of these methods in their classroom practices.

Swaffar and her colleagues studied how teachers using different methods implemented them in the classroom and found that many of the distinctions used to contrast methods, particularly those based on classroom activities, did not exist in actual practice:

Methodological labels assigned to teaching activities are, in themselves, not informative, because they refer to a pool of classroom practices which are used uniformly. The differences among major methodologies are to be found in the ordered hierarchy, the priorities assigned to tasks. (1982: 31)

Brown (1997: 3) makes a similar point:

Generally, methods are quite distinctive at the early, beginning stages of a language course, and rather indistinguishable from each other at a later stage. In the first few days of a Community Language Learning class, for example, the students witness a unique set of experiences in their small circles of translated language whispered in their ears. But within a matter of weeks, such class-rooms can look like any other learner-centered curriculum.

It is perhaps for this reason that video samples of different approaches and methods typically demonstrate the first lesson (or an early lesson) of a foreign language class. There are no convincing video "demonstrations" with intermediate or advanced learners, perhaps because, as Brown points out, at that level there is nothing distinctive to demonstrate.

Beyond approaches and methods

What alternative approaches to the study of teaching are available out-side of the framework of brand-name approaches and methods? We believe that because approaches and methods have played a central role in the development of our profession, it will continue to be useful for teachers and student teachers to become familiar with the major teaching approaches and methods proposed for second and foreign language teaching. Mainstream approaches and methods draw on a large amount of collective experience and practice from which much can be learned. Approaches and methods can therefore be usefully studied and selectively mastered in order:

– to learn how to use different approaches and methods and understand when they might be useful
– to understand some of the issues and controversies that characterize the history of language teaching
– to participate in language learning experiences based on different ap-proaches and methods as a basis for reflection and comparison
– to be aware of the rich set of activity resources available to the imagina-tive teacher
– to appreciate how theory and practice can be linked from a variety of different perspectives

However, teachers and teachers in training need to be able to use ap-proaches and methods flexibly and creatively based on their own judg-ment and experience. In the process, they should be encouraged to trans-form and adapt the methods they use to make them their own. Training in the techniques and procedures of a specific method is probably essential for novice teachers entering teaching, because it provides them with the confidence they will need to face learners and it provides techniques and strategies for presenting lessons. In the early stages, teaching is largely a matter of applying procedures and techniques developed by others. An approach or a predetermined method, with its associated activities, prin-ciples, and techniques, may be an essential starting point for an inexperienced teacher, but it should be seen only as that. As the teacher gains experience and knowledge, he or she will begin to develop an individual approach or personal method of teaching, one that draws on an established approach or method but that also uniquely reflects the teacher's individual beliefs, values, principles, and experiences. This may not lead to abandonment of the approach or method the teacher started out using but will lead to a modification of it as the teacher adds, modifies, and adjusts the approach or method to the realities of the classroom.

In developing a personal approach to teaching, a primary reference point for the teacher is his or her personal beliefs and principles with regard to the following:

- his or her role in the classroom
- the nature of effective teaching and learning
- the difficulties learners face and how these can be addressed
- successful learning activities
- the structure of an effective lesson

Beliefs and theories about these aspects of teaching result in the development of core principles that provide the source for teacher's plans and instructional decisions (Richards 1998). An individual teacher may draw on different principles at different times, depending on the type of class he or she is teaching (e.g., children or adults, beginners, or advanced learners). The following are examples of such principles (Bailey 1996):

- Engage all learners in the lesson.
- Make learners, and not the teacher, the focus of the lesson.
- Provide maximum opportunities for student participation.
- Develop learner responsibility.
- Be tolerant of learners' mistakes.
- Develop learners' confidence.
- Teach learning strategies.
- Respond to learners' difficulties and build on them.
- Use a maximum amount of student-to-student activities.
- Promote cooperation among learners.
- Practice both accuracy and fluency.
- Address learners' needs and interests.

Only a few of these principles will be consciously referred to at a given time. Some may be derived from the approaches and methods teachers are familiar with. Others are personally constructed over time based on experience.

All classroom practices reflect teachers' principles and beliefs, and different belief systems among teachers can often explain why teachers conduct their classes in different ways. Clark and Peterson (1986) noted that:

251

- The most resilient or "core" teachers' beliefs are formed on the basis of teachers' own schooling as young students while observing teachers who taught them. Subsequent teacher education appears not to disturb these early beliefs, not least, perhaps, because it rarely addresses them.
- If teachers actually try out a particular innovation that does not initially conform to their prior beliefs or principles and the innovation proves helpful or successful, then accommodation of an alternative belief or principle is more plausible than in any other circumstance.
- For the novice teacher, classroom experience and day-to-day interaction with colleagues has the potential to influence particular relationships among beliefs and principles, and, over time, consolidate the individual's permutation of them. Nevertheless, it seems that greater experience does not lead to greater adaptability in our beliefs, and thereby, the abandonment of strongly held pedagogical principles. Quite the contrary, in fact. The more experience we have, the more reliant on our "core" principles we have become and the less conscious we are of doing so.
- Professional development that engages teachers in a direct explanation of their beliefs and principles may provide the opportunity for greater self-awareness through reflection and critical questioning as starting points of later adaptation.
- The teacher's conceptualizations of, for example, language, learning, and teaching are situated within that person's wider belief system concerning such issues as human nature, culture, society, education, and so on.

Therefore, there is much more to teacher development than learning how to use different approaches or methods of teaching. Experience with different approaches and methods, however, can provide teachers with an initial practical knowledge base in teaching and can also be used to explore and develop teachers' own beliefs, principles, and practices.

Looking forward

How do we feel the language teaching profession will move ahead in the near, or even more distant, future? The approaches and methods surveyed in this book have identified a number of issues that we expect to continue to shape the future of language teaching in different ways. Some of the responses to these issues may take the form of new approaches and methods; others may lead to a refining or reshaping of existing approaches and methods as the teaching profession responds to the findings of new research and to developments in educational theory and practice. The initiatives for changing programs and pedagogy may come from within the profession – from teachers, administrators, theoreticians, and researchers. Incentives or demands of a political, social, or even fiscal nature may also drive change, as they have in the past. Particular personalities and leaders in the field may also shape the future of language teaching. Change may also be motivated by completely unexpected sources. We close, therefore, by identifying some of the factors that have influenced language teaching trends in the past and that can be expected to continue to do so in the future.

Government policy directives. Increased demands for accountability on the part of funding agencies and governments have driven educational changes on a fairly regular basis for decades and are likely to continue to do so in the future.

Trends in the profession. The teaching profession is another source for change. Professional certification for teachers, as well as endorsement of particular trends or approaches by professional organizations and lobby groups promoting particular issues and causes, can have an important influence on teaching.

Guru-led innovations. teaching has sometimes been described as artistry rather than science and is often shaped by the influence of powerful individual practitioners with their own schools of thought and followers. Just as Gattegno, Lozanov, and Krashen inspired a number of teachers in the 1970s and 1980s, and as Gardner does today, so doubtless new gurus will attract disciples and shape teaching practices in the future.

Responses to technology. The potential of the Internet, the World Wide Web, and other computer interfaces and technological innovations is likely to capture the imagination of the teaching profession in the future as it has in the past and will influence both the content and the form of instructional delivery in language teaching.

Influences from academic disciplines. Disciplines such as linguistics, psycholinguistics, and psychology have an impact on the theories of language and language learning and support particular approaches to language teaching. As new theories emerge in disciplines such as these, they are likely to have an impact on future theories of teaching. Just as in the past Audiolingualism and Cognitive Code Learning reflected linguistic theories of their day, so new insights from functional linguistics, corpus linguistics, psycholinguistics, or sociolinguistics, or from sources now unknown, may play a dominant role in shaping language pedagogy.

Research influences. Second language teaching and learning is increasingly a field for intensive research and theorizing. Second language acquisition research provided impetus for the development of the Natural Approach and Task-Based Language Teaching, and it will doubtless continue to motivate new language teaching approaches.

Learner-based innovations. Learner-based focuses recur in language teaching and other fields in approximately 10-year cycles, as we have seen with individualized instruction, the learner-centered curriculum, learner

253

training, learner strategies, and Multiple Intelligences. We can anticipate continuation of this trend.

Crossover educational trends. Cooperative Learning, the Whole Language Approach, Neurolinguistic Programming, and Multiple Intelligences represent crossovers into second language teaching of movements from general education and elsewhere. Such crossovers will doubtless continue because the field of language teaching has no monopoly over theories of teaching and learning.

Crossovers from other disciplines. Encounters with cognitive psychology, psychotherapy, communication science, ethnography, and human engineering have left their imprint on language pedagogy and exemplify the way that such diverse disciplines can influence a field that is always looking for inspiration.

Despite changes in the status of approaches and methods, we can therefore expect the field of second and foreign language teaching in the twenty-first century to be no less a ferment of theories, ideas, and practices than it has been in the past.

Bibliography and further reading

Bailey, K. 1996. The best-laid plans: Teachers' in-class decisions to depart from their lesson plans. In K. Bailey and D. Nunan (eds.), *Voices from the Language Classroom*. New York: Cambridge University Press. 15–40.

Brown, H. D. 1994. *Teaching by Principles*. Englewood Cliffs, N.J.: Prentice Hall/Regents.

Brown, H. D. 1997. English language teaching in the "post-method" era: Toward better diagnosis, treatment, and assessment. *PASAA* (Bangkok) 27: 1–10.

Clark, C. M., and P. Peterson. 1986. Teachers' thought processes. In M. Wittrock (ed.), *Handbook of Research on Teaching*. 3rd ed. New York: Macmillan. 255–296.

Holliday, A. 1994. *Appropriate Methodology*. Cambridge: Cambridge University Press.

Kumaravadivelu, B. 1994. The post-method condition: Emerging strategies for second/foreign language teaching. *TESOL Quarterly* 28, 27–48.

Nicholls, A. H., and H. Nicholls. 1972. *Developing Curriculum: A Practical Guide*. London: George Allen and Unwin.

Nunan, D. 1989. *Understanding Language Classrooms: A Guide for Teacher Initiated Action*. New York: Prentice Hall.

Pennycook, A. 1989. The concept of method, interested knowledge, and the politics of language teaching. *TESOL Quarterly* 23: 589–618.

Pennycook, A. 1994. *The Cultural Politics of English as an International Language*. London: Longman.

Phillipson, R. 1992. *Linguistic Imperialism*. Oxford: Oxford University Press.

Prabhu, N. S. 1990. There is no best method – why? *TESOL Quarterly* 24: 161–176.

Richards, J. C. 1998. Teachers' maxims. In J. C. Richards, *Beyond Training*. New York: Cambridge University Press. 45–62.

Richards, J. C. 2000. *Curriculum Development in Language Teaching*. New York: Cambridge University Press.

Skehan, P. 1996. Second language acquisition research and task-based instruction. In J. Willis and D. Willis (eds.), *Challenge and Change in Language Teaching*. Oxford: Heinemann. 17–30.

Swaffar, J., K. Arens, and M. Morgan. 1982. Teacher classroom practices: Redefining method as task hierarchy. *Modern Language Journal* 66(1): 24–33.

Author index

Subject index